The Book of Latina Women

150 Vidas of Passion, Strength, and Success

Sylvia Mendoza

Adams Media
Avon, Massachusetts

Published by
Adams Media, an F+W Publications Company
57 Littlefield Street, Avon, MA 02322. U.S.A.
www.adamsmedia.com

ISBN: 1-59337-212-4

Printed in Canada.

J I H G F E D C B A

Library of Congress Cataloging-in-Publication Data
Mendoza, Sylvia.
The book of Latina women / Sylvia Mendoza.
p.   cm.
ISBN 1-59337-212-4
1. Women–Biography. 2. Hispanic American women–Biography. 3. Women–Spain–Biography.
4. Women–Latin America–Biography. I. Title.

CT3203.M46 2004
920.72'089'68--dc22

2004009160

This publication is designed to provide accurate and authoritative information with regard to the subject matter covered. It is sold with the understanding that the publisher is not engaged in rendering legal, accounting, or other professional advice. If legal advice or other expert assistance is required, the services of a competent professional person should be sought.

—From a *Declaration of Principles* jointly adopted by a Committee of the American Bar Association and a Committee of Publishers and Associations

Many of the designations used by manufacturers and sellers to distinguish their products are claimed as trademarks. Where those designations appear in this book and Adams Media was aware of a trademark claim, the designations have been printed with initial capital letters.

This book is available at quantity discounts for bulk purchases.
For information, call 1-800-872-5627.

Table of Contents

"All we have to decide is what to do with the time that is given us."
—J.R.R. Tolkien

Kayla, Cassy, and Bryan:
I believe in you and in what you have to share with the world.

Acknowledgments

This project was one of the most humbling and inspiring I have ever worked on. We all know that behind every dream book there are many who help breathe it to life. Here are just a few of the angels, cheerleaders, and lifesavers who helped this book take flight:

The backbone: Marcela Landres, for believing in me enough to hand me this project. Your influence on Latinos in the publishing field has made many of us venture into exciting new realms. June Clark, my patient agent, who hustled to get this out there. My editor, Danielle Chiotti, whose excitement and passion equaled my own and made the project very real. Adams Media—copyeditors, layout geniuses, cover artists, marketing, and publicity—I appreciate every single thing you have done to produce this book.

The sources: I appreciate those whose biographical works preceded this project. Now I know what a true labor of love it is to research this intensely and to bring to light those who should have been in the spotlight all along. Vicki Ruiz, a true historian, your works so deeply resonated with me. Thank you for your contributions to American history. The Arizona Historical Society, San Diego Historical Society, the National Women's History Project, among others, your rich archives and purpose blow me away.

The sounding board: the Encantadoras—wonderful writers, the lot of them. Tracy Montoya, Lara Rios, Caridad Pineiro, Lynda Sandoval, Berta Platas, Reyna Rios, Erica Fuentes—you're good sports for putting up with my repeated requests for names. I value your input and as always, you came through—with enough suggestions for a sequel.

The writers: Janet Wellington and Mary Leo, who so believed in this book when I explained it, they got goosebumps, which gave me goosebumps. Judy Duarte, Crystal Green, and Sheri Whitefeather for believing in my writing. Ann Collins, your words of wisdom keep me plugging along. Patricia Santana, your beautiful writing voice and outlook on life make you my hero. *San Diego Union-Tribune* editors, Lee Schoenbart and Julie Pendray, whose editing savvy over the years has helped me grow as a writer.

The core: Cloe McKay, Diane McSweeny, Patti Cook for sticking around all these years through thick and thin. I love you. Michelle Ancira, my true sister, for making me laugh and appreciate the moments. Debbie Wilson, Peggy Harger, Chris Fink, Diana Saenger, and Antoinette Kuritz, for sharing your love of books. Dale Fetherling, for being a brilliant teacher of nonfiction proposals. It takes a village to raise those kids . . . for stepping in to help when I was glued to my seat for days at a time: Linda Rauch, Marie Concha, Cheri Mitchell, Christy Guerin, Marcia Corke, and Lei Wai. Thanks for being there.

The heart: my mom and dad, Guadalupe and Jesus Mendoza, I couldn't have done this without you. Bro Jesse, Sharon, Neil, and Carly, you blaze your own trails and I'm in awe. Mike, who lives with the chaos every day, walks through the maze of my office and still supports me unconditionally. Bryan, Kayla, and Cassy, you drive me to be a better person. You bring balance, hope, and utter joy to my life. We can only hope to learn from the women within these pages. They are vibrantly alive. Now go out and do *your* thing.

Introduction: The Spirit of Latinas

*T*he *Book of Latina Women* celebrates stories of the spirit and the resiliency of Latinas whose contributions have shaped history. Though the term *Latina* is relatively new, the spirit that goes with it carries an important legacy. For centuries, Latina women have inspired us beyond words. Their actions have inspired great change, and their spirit has made its mark on our contemporary world.

Throughout history, Latinas have broken down barriers and stereotypes, blazing their own trails as entertainers, artists, scientists, educators, writers, activists, athletes, and in every field in between. They have followed their passions, stirred up controversy, stood up against the majority, and died for their beliefs.

Today's Latinas do it all, in every field, without a second thought. Their paths are easier to navigate because of the Latinas who went before them—whether from decades or centuries ago.

Within these pages, we celebrate Latinas' achievements, contributions, and sacrifices. We give Latinas their rightful place in history. This book will help you witness this amazing handful of Latinas from all over the world. They have touched individuals, communities, and nations—now their stories will touch your life as well.

1

Trailblazers: Opening the Door

Queen Isabella I de Castile (Spain, 1451–1504)

Patron to Christopher Columbus and advocate of the education of women.

Queen Isabella I lived by her extreme motto: One king, one law, one faith. Conquering lands and religions helped her restore autonomic, royal power to her Spanish kingdom. Embracing and promoting education and the arts balanced out her reign.

Born in Madrigal de las Altas Torres, in the castle of La Mota, Isabella was the daughter of John II, king of Castile, and his second wife, Isabella of Portugal. Isabella was destined for the crown, despite discord with her sister, Joan, and half brother, Enrique (Henry IV).

She balked at Enrique's attempts at arranging her marriage. She had her eye on Ferdinand of Aragon, a second cousin, knowing that their marriage would bring great political power by uniting several of their kingdoms. They married in 1469.

When Enrique died as the reigning king in 1474, Isabella inherited the throne. After a family feud between her and Joan for the position, she declared herself queen. She was devoted to her country and restored power, religion, education, and law.

Isabella was viewed in two extreme ways: as a dignified, gracious, pious, and feminine force much like the Virgin Mary, a symbol of the country's unity and purpose; or as an unbending, self-serving, and tyrannical powerhouse.

> 🔖 Queen Isabella de Castile was viewed in two extreme ways: as a dignified, gracious, pious, and feminine force much like the Virgin Mary, a symbol of the country's unity and purpose; or as an unbending, self-serving, and tyrannical powerhouse.

One of her nicknames was "The Queen of Law and Order." No longer were noblemen allowed to call themselves "kings" of their own estates. She curtailed their privileges, burned old castles, and forbade the building of new ones. To help control the nobility, she resurrected the Brotherhood, an order of peacekeepers who worked with the throne under Queen Isabella's directives. She also named Ferdinand the grand master of the religious armies in order to gain control over their assets.

Backing Italian explorer Christopher Columbus when no one else would made Isabella a visionary. Sympathetic to the man's pleas and belief, she saw his ventures as an opportunity to gain more power for Spain and the chance to spread Christianity to other lands beyond her borders.

Finding "the New World" went beyond her expectations. When Columbus returned with Native Americans as slaves, however, she ordered him to return and free them, and to treat them with justice and fairness.

Her strong beliefs made her view Catholicism as the end-all religion. When she and Ferdinand were blessed by the pope as Los Reyes Católicos, (the Catholic Monarchs), she took the title to heart. She was determined to make Catholicism the religion of the land.

In her blind devotion, there was no room for other religions. The Spanish Inquisition, which began in 1483, tore through her country, persecuting non-Christians, Jews, and Muslims with great economic and cultural influence. For them, Isabella's reign turned into one of terror. Thousands died, burned at the stake, their lands and funds seized. Those who survived the tortures were expelled from Spain in 1492. Her defense for these acts was that she acted out of "love for Christ and the Holy Mother."

Isabella's devotion to her children and to education rivaled her religious fervor. Her five children were tutored by monks in poetry, philosophy, music, sewing, and horseback riding. In time, she had a school constructed in the palace. She also had other learning institutions built that were open to women, for Queen Isabella believed they had the right to education.

Although her children were a great disappointment, her daughter Catherine became the first wife of Henry VIII of England. Her will was the only writing she left to her legacy, but it was filled with an account of her reign's achievements and what she hoped for her country's future.

Benvenida Abravanel (Spain, 1473–1554)
Successful businesswoman and philanthropist who saved thousands of Jewish people during the Spanish Inquisition.

Being Jewish and living in Renaissance Spain could most certainly have meant death for Benvenida Abravanel. Abravanel became a wealthy businesswoman and philanthropist, saving thousands of persecuted Jews along the way of her financial success.

Although it was rare to find educated and financially independent women in this era, there were always exceptions like Benvenida Abravanel. Jewish women sometimes practiced medicine, served as midwives to royalty and Christians, or became merchants and moneylenders. Still others took their faith seriously and if prosperous, donated generously to their synagogues. Abravanel fell into many of these categories.

Her father-in-law was the chief financier for Queen Isabella I and King Ferdinand, backing Christopher Columbus's voyages, for example. Abravanel, who was married to her first cousin, was a welcome asset in the palace as well. Educated and well versed in cultural niceties, Abravanel earned her place in Spanish society and was sought after for her teaching capabilities.

Because of the Abravanel family's relationship with the Catholic monarchs, their positions were secure and they could have stayed in Spain under their protection. Nevertheless, they elected to flee with the rest of the Jewish community as the Spanish Inquisition took root in 1492. They escaped to Naples, Italy, where they started again, mostly in banking.

> Although it was rare to find educated and financially independent women in this era, there were always exceptions like Benvenida Abravanel.

The family proved competitive and fair, and once again, the royalty embraced them. They had education, noble station, and wealth—a great combination. They assisted the royal family, especially Tuscany leader Viceroy Pedro de Toledo. His daughter, Leonora, looked up to Abravanel as a mentor and even called her "mother." As Abravanel taught her, they became fast friends. Abravanel also helped with the family business and ran a finishing school for women that would help ensure the women good marriages and hefty dowries.

The Abravanels lived there for nine years before they again had to flee. This time they headed to Ferrara, Italy. Leonora became duchess of Tuscany when she married, and she remained in touch with Abravanel, which proved to be another lifesaver.

Abravanel set up her own court in Ferrara, where the family finally settled. Their home became a cultural oasis, drawing scholars and artisans as well as political and business figures, who were drawn there for the entertainment.

In 1547, the first Jewish bank was established in Pisa, owned by financier Ishmael da Rieti. His biggest competition was the rival firm led by Benvenida, who had inherited the financial empire based in Naples. Widowed that same year, she took over the family's import-export business, exhibiting great business savvy. She negotiated with the government to set up bank branches throughout the region and formed business alliances that strengthened her position. When necessary, she united forces with her rivals to secure their positions against lesser competition.

Her connections helped save her time and again. When it was time for Jews to take flight yet again, Abravanel appealed to Leonora, who managed to delay the Jewish exile.

Abravanel died in 1560, but her legacy and generosity left a lasting impression on the Jewish community. Having provided dowries to orphans, and donated large sums to synagogues and individual charities, she also promoted education and cultural awareness.

Most telling about Abravanel's personality was that she ultimately helped free thousands of Jews who had been held hostage in hostile anti-Semitic cities by paying their ransoms.

La Malinche (Mexico, c. 1500 – 1527)

Negotiated peace between the Aztec people and the invading Spanish conquistadors through her skills as a translator and advisor.

To many of her Aztec people, La Malinche was a traitor and a harlot—a sellout. Others believed La Malinche was a visionary and a peacemaker—a savior.

She saved thousands of her people's lives when she became an interpreter for the Spanish conquistadors as they infiltrated the beautiful, bountiful country in the heart of Mexico. Aztecs, Mayans, and many other Indian tribes had prospered there until foreign intruders came on behalf of their countries' honor and financial gain.

La Malinche believed she could serve the Spaniards and the indigenous people as a go-between and as a voice for both simultaneously. So began her contradictory reign.

Born Malintzin Tenepal, an Aztec noblewoman, La Malinche was allowed an education and other benefits because of her title. She was stripped of her status and shunned when her father, a chief, died.

She learned the meaning of betrayal firsthand. Her mother remarried, had a son, and felt he would be more deserving of a title than her

5

daughter. La Malinche was sold as a slave to the Cacique of Tabasco. It was there that she learned the Mayan dialects of the Yucatán and became proficient in Nahuatl, the language spoken by Aztecs and non-Mayans.

Spanish explorer Hernando Cortés landed at Veracruz in 1512 with his own vision. He wanted to bring gold back to his queen, claim land for her as the New Spain, and convert the pagan Indians to Christianity.

Thinking he and his crew were gods who would save them from eternal suffering, the Indians offered up twenty young women to join Cortés as he traveled throughout the country. Malintzin was one of the twenty. She attracted the attention of the Spanish conquistadors because she was a fast learner with a good ear for languages.

Jeronimo Aguilar, a priest, had been translating for Cortés but did not know Nahuatl. Malintzin joined their efforts in negotiations with the various Indian tribes they encountered. Cortés would speak to Aguilar in Spanish, who would speak to Malintzin, who would translate the needed dialect depending on the tribe they were dealing with.

Her influence spared many of her people. She convinced many leaders to surrender rather than allow their people to be killed and their villages to be pillaged. Many converted to Christianity.

The name *malinche* today can refer to a person who turns his back on his own culture, a traitor. It is a harsh perception of the woman who was born an Indian, lived a mestizo life, and died a Spaniard's mistress and strategic advisor.

Montezuma II, one of the most powerful leaders, hesitated in joining Cortés. The Spaniards attacked Tenochtitlan, where much of their wealth was amassed, until the city was completely destroyed. Montezuma later died from injuries sustained in the conflict. This started the true downfall of the Aztec civilization at the hands of the Spanish conquistadors. In one subsequent account, Cortés wrote, "After God, we owe this conquest of New Spain to Doña Marina."

La Malinche fell in love with Cortés, and she bore him a son who became the first official offspring of mixed blood. As such, she is considered the mother, or "Mexican Eve," of the mestizo race, the blend of Spanish and Indian bloodlines.

Today, the name *malinche* can refer to a person who turns his back on his own culture, a traitor. It is a harsh perception of the woman who was born an Indian, lived a mestizo life, and died a Spaniard's mistress and strategic advisor.

A myth about La Malinche still lingers. When Cortés was heading back for Spain, he intended to take their son but leave La Malinche behind. It is said she drowned the child and that she is the ghost, La Llorona (the weeper), crying over her tragic loss. Her cries can still be heard all across Mexico and the American Southwest.

Saint Teresa de Avila (Spain, 1515-1582)

A primary figure in the Counter Reformation and the founder of numerous convents, Saint Teresa de Avila was among the first women to be named a Doctor of the Church and is considered one of the most important mystics for her seminal religious writings.

Teresa Sanchez Cepeda Davila y Ahumada spelled controversy. Better known as Saint Teresa of Avila, she reformed the Carmelite order of sisterhood against popular opinion. She took to heart a vow of poverty, which was a direct contrast to the luxurious convent living of the day.

She believed she had a different kind of connection to God. As a child, Teresa knew the ways of the world, the riches of life, and material abundance. Even so, she wanted to become a martyr, and tempted one of her ten siblings to run away with her so they could have their heads cut off in the glory of God. Their plans were thwarted and they were returned to their parents.

Her religious zeal subsided for a while, and she returned to her material and social life, spending her time reading books on chivalry that her mother hid from her worried and strict father. Eventually, he sent Teresa off to a convent to keep her from falling into temptation.

As her love for God grew, she noticed hypocrisy in the convent. The nuns and women there lived well, wore jewelry, and entertained visitors, including men. Teresa thought she was destined to be an almost unredeemable sinner as long as she lived in that environment, but she believed prayer was the answer.

Searching for truth and inner peace, Teresa moved to several convents. When she turned forty, she began praying in earnest. She started having visions of hell, which propelled her into action to start the reform of the Carmelite order. They would live on alms and meager meals, turning to a life of austere poverty, service, and prayer.

At the height of her fight for reform, she contracted malaria and became gravely ill. At one point she had a seizure and fell into a coma for days. Everyone was so convinced she would die, they dug a grave for her. She survived but was paralyzed for three years and would experience great physical pain for the rest of her life.

🖎 In the twentieth century, Pope Paul VI touted Saint Teresa de Avila as a Doctor of the Church.

Still, the pain from her illness did not slow her down in her mission. She was charismatic and social, but it was difficult to gather a following when people were also afraid of her. Mystical, inexplicable things happened to her when she prayed. She fell into trances or levitated. God came to her in apparitions and spoke to her. She suffered the Transverberation (crosses through her heart). This behavior frightened religious brethren and laypeople alike. They did not believe she was experiencing a new level of consciousness with God; rather, they thought she was possessed by the devil. Despite this, she withstood scrutiny from Church officials and sometimes violent opposition to her attempts at reform. She was spared the rod of the Inquisition.

In 1562 she started the convent of Discalced Carmelite Nuns of the Primitive Rule of Saint Joseph at Avila. In 1566 the general of the Carmelites, John-Baptist Rubeo (Rossi), granted her permission to continue her mission. Even as her health deteriorated, she set up convents throughout Spain, in cities such as Malagon, Toledo, Salamanca, Caravaca, Segovia, Veas, and Seville. By 1568, she also established reform among friars.

Her book, *The Interior Castle*, was revolutionary in its view of prayer and was embraced for its excellence by John of the Cross. In the twentieth century, Pope Paul VI touted Saint Teresa of Avila as a Doctor of the Church.

Beatified in 1614, Teresa Cepeda was proclaimed the Patroness of Spain in 1617 and canonized Saint Teresa of Avila in 1622. She is the patron saint of headaches.

Sor Juana Inés de la Cruz (Mexico, 1651–1695)
One of the greatest scholars, feminists, and poets of her time, Sor Juana dedicated her life as a Carmelite nun to learning, steadfastly defending women's right to an education.

> "Silly, you men—so very adept
> at wrongly faulting womankind,
> not seeing you're alone to blame
> for faults you plant in woman's mind . . .
> —*"You Men," by Sor Juana Inés de la Cruz*

Considered "the first feminist of the New World," Sor (Sister) Juana Inés de la Cruz was one of the foremost intellectual scholars of her time. When women were supposed to be seen and not heard, she refused to remain silent or be suppressed.

As a Mexican nun, a mystic poet, and prolific writer, Juana did not speak or write as an act of rebellion, but rather as a way to express all she had learned. She pursued her scholarly rights and fought to bring recognition to women and their works and contributions.

Born Juana Inés Ramirez de Asbaje in San Miguel Nepantla near Mexico City, she was the illegitimate child of a Spanish Captain and Isabe

Ramirez. She lived with her mother, two sisters, and grandfather in the quiet village. By the time she was three, she followed her older sister to school and asked the teacher to teach her to read. She immersed herself in her grandfather's extensive library.

> 🔖 When women were supposed to be seen and not heard, Sor Juana refused to remain silent or be suppressed.

Juana read voraciously and became well versed in literature, the arts, and social opinions and influences. When she learned that there was a university in Mexico City, she begged her mother to let her dress like a boy so that she could attend. Her mother refused. Her family did, however, send her to live with an aunt and uncle where she was to learn Latin. Away from home restrictions, she also learned mathematics, logic, history, classical literature, and Aztec languages.

She took her studies seriously. While learning Latin, if she did not learn a certain point according to her own timetable and expectations, she cut off chunks of her hair as a punishment for her head's ignorance.

A viceroy of Mexico and his wife, Leonor Carreto, learned of Juana, the child prodigy. They invited her to stay with them at their palace. She was a maid-in-waiting and Carreto was twice her age, but they became friends, sharing their mutual interests in art, literature, and music.

Sor Juana wrote plays, songs, poetry, and essays. By the time she turned seventeen, forty university professors from every branch of learning including math, philosophy, science, and poetry gave her a comprehensive oral examination. She answered their questions without error. She finally received validation for her intellectual brilliance, but she was considered a threat to intellectual men.

Her family urged her to marry, but she refused and headed for the Convent of the Discalced Carmelites of Saint Joseph in 1669, where she became Sor Juana Inés de la Cruz (Sister Juana Inés of the Cross). Even though the nuns could not leave the convent, Sor Juana was able to pursue

10

her education and engage in stimulating intellectual interchanges with countless visitors.

She amassed 4,000 volumes in her library, the largest collection in Mexico at the time. By the time she was thirty, she was a celebrated poet with three published volumes of poetry.

In 1690, Juana wrote a criticism of a sermon. Her view was attacked by Archbishop Francisco Aguiar y Seijas. Sor Juana responded with "Reply to Sor Philothea," which defended her intellectual history and a woman's right to education. She claimed her drive to learn was beyond her control, a gift from God.

The bishop ordered her to stop writing and devote herself to religious literature and studies only. In 1694, she renounced her love of books and learning by selling her library, scientific and musical instruments, and art supplies. The ultimate penance was cutting herself off from her intellectual friends.

Sor Juana's spirit died long before she died physically, a result of caring for her sick sisters afflicted by the plague. Physical death, at the very least, released her from the oppressive world in 1695.

Maria de las Mercedes Barbudo (Puerto Rico, 1800s)
A leader in the revolt against Spanish tyranny, Barbudo gave her life fighting for Puerto Rico's independence.

Tired of Spanish rule and their oppression of women and ill treatment of slaves, Maria de las Mercedes Barbudo took up the cry for Puerto Rico's independence in the 1800s. She was a rebel who fought for emancipation and abolition, a revolutionary who sought to restore Puerto Rican autonomy.

An uprising of peasants, laborers, slaves, and landowners who wanted to break away from Spanish rule followed her lead. With the help of Venezuelans, they launched an all-out revolt against Spanish authorities.

Barbudo's spirit and cry for freedom lived on.

The Spanish easily crushed their heroic effort, and Barbudo was captured and jailed. She was eventually exiled and later put to death for her participation in the revolt, but her spirit and cry for freedom lived on.

Juana Briones (Mexico/California, 1802–1889)
A businesswoman, jack-of-all-trades, and gifted healer, Juana Briones's legacy as a humanitarian lives on today.

Juana Briones was a businesswoman like no other. She owned thousands of acres of land at a time when women were rarely deeded property. She was a seamstress and innkeeper, raised cattle, sold milk and produce, kept a tavern, practiced midwifery, and was a mother of eight.

Yet, she shared her wealth with a good dose of compassion. As a gifted and renowned curandera who healed with the herbs she grew, she was a friend to all, regardless of nationality, race, or circumstance.

She was lauded for her achievements and loved for her charity. A 1919 San Francisco, California, newspaper knighted her "the ministering angel and California's Clara Barton."

In the times when California was a Spanish colony, Briones was a "Californio" woman, the daughter of Spanish colonists. She spent her early years in the Santa Cruz, California, area, one of eight children. Her father was stationed at the San Francisco Presidio. She may have learned her extensive knowledge of herbal medicine from Native Americans who took her under their wing, teaching her to recognize and harvest plants for medicinal purposes.

She married Apolinario Miranda, a cavalryman stationed at the Presidio. Her husband turned abusive, and she was eventually granted a legal separation by a local bishop. It was the only way she could acquire land in her own name. She moved her children to Yerba Buena (San Francisco today). It was a land of grizzly bears and smallpox, runaway sailors and lynching.

She saw the flags of three nations hoisted over her home during her lifetime: Spain, Mexico, and the United States. When Mexico won its independence from Spain, California became a Mexican province. The influx of foreigners brought trade opportunities.

🖎 A San Francisco, California, newspaper knighted Briones "the ministering angel and California's Clara Barton."

Briones kept her ranch afloat by supplying incoming ships with produce and meat. Her hospitality made her ranch a famous guesthouse for visitors from Europe and Mexico. More than once she gave sanctuary to sailors jumping ship when she could have received a bounty for turning them in. The beach where the ships she supplied anchored later became known as "La Playa de Juana Briones."

As a healer, she tended to people of all nationalities—Native American, Mexican, Spanish, and English. She delivered babies and set bones. Once while helping during a smallpox epidemic, she took along her nephew, Pablo. He was so inspired by her, he became the town's doctor and practiced medicine there for over fifty years.

In the mid-1840s, she bought a 4,400-acre ranch named La Purisíma Concepción near the Palo Alto area for $300. She built a house and continued to farm. She also adopted five more children who were orphaned shortly after emigrating from New Zealand.

By the time California became the thirty-first state in 1850, Briones owned a considerable amount of property. Landowners were required to prove their title to the United States Land Commission or lose property. Without a deed, Briones fought the U.S. government for twelve years through extensive legal actions. Though she could neither read nor write, she won her case and retained complete control of her land.

Area schools, parks, and buildings have been named in her honor. In 1997, the first ever San Francisco landmark plaque to a woman was presented in her honor. Set into an elegant bench, it symbolized the hospitality Briones extended to visitors. Today, the Juana Briones Heritage Foundation works to preserve her heritage.

Loreta Janeta Velázquez (Cuba, 1842–?)

A soldier in the American Civil War who wrote a controversial book about her exploits as a woman disguised as a man fighting in the Confederate Army.

Loreta Janeta Velázquez disguised herself as a man and slipped into the frontlines for the Confederate Army to fight in the American Civil War. Following in the footsteps of her hero, Joan of Arc, her lifelong dream had been to earn glory from fighting in battle for a great cause.

Taking on the identity of Lieutenant Harry T. Buford, she supposedly fought in such battles as Bull Run, Shiloh, Ball's Bluff, and Blackburn's Ford. She documented her war experiences in a book she wrote, entitled *The Woman in Battle: A Narrative of the Exploits, Adventures, and Travels of Madame Loreta Janeta Velázquez, Otherwise Known as Lieutenant Harry T. Buford, Confederate States Army.*

Historians today still dispute the validity of the book, citing inconsistencies in Velázquez's accounts. Proud of her Castilian roots and her family's contributions to Spanish history, she stood by her accounts as true, mainly concerned with harming her family's reputation.

She was originally from Cuba, and wanted to emulate Joan of Arc's courage, intelligence, and determination in battle.

Velázquez attributed her sense of adventure, stubbornness, and duty to her roots. Her grandfather, Don Diego Velázquez, she said, was the conqueror and first governor of Cuba. Her father was a scholar and diplomat for the Spanish Embassy in Paris. Her mother was the wife of a French naval officer and an American lady.

When her father's commission was up, he was assigned to Cuba, where Velázquez was born. When she was just six, she was sent to New Orleans to live and study with an aunt. Her love was books.

When she turned of age, an arranged marriage awaited her, but she met an American Army officer and they eloped. Her family disinherited her until she had children.

Over the course of a few years, her three children died from fever. When her husband died in battle, she decided to follow her lifelong secret dream. She prepared an elaborate disguise and started her military adventure.

🖎 Velázquez wanted to emulate Joan of Arc's courage, intelligence, and determination in battle.

Velázquez sneaked into camps as an independent recruiter. Although she loved the battles, she grew bored waiting between them and took to spying and relaying information back to her officers.

When she was shot in the foot and her cover was blown, she headed back to New Orleans. She was arrested for disguising herself as a man, fined ten dollars, and spent ten days in jail. As soon as she was released, she donned a new disguise and re-enlisted. When she was wounded again and her disguise was discovered for the second time, she gave up on soldiering. She took up spying and worked for the secret service as a woman.

Velázquez's alleged adventures after the war included traveling throughout Europe and once back in the United States, heading west to find gold. Intrigued by the Mormons in Utah, she remained awhile. In her accounts, she left there with another baby of an unknown father. She supposedly wrote the book to help her and her son financially. Her book remains controversial today, with no proof of its validity.

Lola Rodríguez de Tío (Puerto Rico, 1843–1924)
Revolutionary, poet, and highly regarded intellectual, Lola Rodríquez de Tío wrote what became the national anthem of Puerto Rico's rebellion against Spanish rule.

The revolt was known as "El Grito de Lares," and Lola Rodríguez de Tío was caught up in the passion it incited in her country. De Tío was one of the greatest intellectuals of her time. She would be exiled from Puerto Rico time and again, which would only inflame her activism and inspire her writing.

Her fame went beyond the island's limits, yet revolved around her devotion to home, intellectual work, and political activities. She was passionate about learning, about her country, and about her involvement in her country's future. The tumultuous, trying times of Spanish rule inspired de Tío's poetry. Injustices against her people persisted and had to be stopped.

In the Grito de Lares revolt more than 400 Puerto Ricans armed with knives, machetes, and a few guns overtook Lares. They fought to overcome the oppression of the Spanish military and government. They freed slaves. They arrested government officials. It was a short-lived victory because the Spanish then came in numbers. But the revolt gave Puerto Ricans a taste of true independence.

In 1868, inspired by the fight for Puerto Rican independence and more specifically, with the Grito de Lares, de Tío wrote "La Borinquena," a patriotic song that was to become the national anthem of the revolution. It reflected the belief that freedom could be won only through armed struggle, and signaled the end of surrendering to Spanish colonialism.

In 1868, inspired by the fight for Puerto Rican independence and more specifically, with the Grito de Lares, de Tío wrote "La Borinquena," a patriotic song that was to become the national anthem of the revolution.

She received her primary education in Puerto Rico, but her real education came from the various intellectuals and politicians she met at her home. Her father, Sebastian Rodríguez de Astudillo, was a lawyer and one of the founders of the Puerto Rican College of Lawyers. Her mother, Carmen Ponce de Leon, hailed from a noble family. Dona Carmen graced her with spirituality and an appreciation for the arts. De Tío was an avid reader and her father hired a tutor to expand her knowledge in history, Spanish literature classics, morality, religion, and travel. She began writing her first poems, influenced by Fray Luis de Leon, and would read her poetry and play classical music on the piano for her father's distinguished guests.

In 1863, she married Bonocio Tío Segarra, a liberal writer who was anti-Spanish. In 1876 they moved to Mayageuz, Puerto Rico, where she published her first book of poetry, *Mis Cantares*. In 1877, the family chose to flee to Venezuela for that country's political activism.

When they returned to Puerto Rico, she and Segarra founded the magazine *La Almojabana*. They were exiled yet again in 1887 and ended up in Cuba. Once they settled there, their home became a gathering point for politicians and intellectuals as well as other exiled Puerto Ricans.

When *Mi Libro de Cuba* was published she was once again seen as revolutionary in voicing her opinion for Cuban independence. In 1895 she was exiled once more for helping Cuban revolutionaries and for voicing her concerns over Puerto Rican patriots jailed at El Morro. This time she and her husband moved to New York City.

The pattern continued for a few years. In 1899 however, de Tío was allowed to return to Cuba, her adopted homeland. She established the Cuban Academy of Arts and Letters in 1910 and continued writing.

Dolores Jiménez y Muro (Mexico, 1848–1925)

A colonel in the Mexican revolutionary army who spent her life fighting for the civil rights of all her people, not only as a soldier but also through her work as an editor, writer, and educator.

> "It is better to die on your feet
> than live on your knees!"
>
> —*Emiliano Zapata*

Dolores Jiménez y Muro lived by Zapata's freedom cry during the Mexican Revolution. Fearless, outspoken, and willing to die for her country, she was a freedom fighter—a *soldadera*—and quickly became public enemy number one. Even at age seventy, Jiménez was considered a threat and there was a price on her head.

As in many wars, when most men were on the frontlines, women stepped up to the plate. Jiménez was one such woman. She joined other women intellectuals, activists, and journalists to fight against the dictatorial ruler, Porfirio Diaz. With the power of her pen as well as her guns, she stirred up people in the battle for the rights of the poor, indigenous peoples of Mexico and for civil rights over all.

> Even at age seventy, Jiménez was considered a threat and there was a price on her head.

Born in Aguascalientes, Jiménez became a firm believer and follower of Emiliano Zapata in the Mexican Revolution. Impressed with her expression, passion, ideals, and suggested reforms, Zapata invited her to join his forces in 1913. She rose in rank and became a colonel in the revolutionary army, a true *soldadera* and Zapatista.

Jiménez was on the editorial staff of the feminist journal *La Mujer Mexicana*, and she wrote for many publications under pseudonyms such as "Espartaco" for her political diatribes and "Anima" for literary works. As editor of *Diario del Hogar, El Libertario,* and *Tierra y Justicia,* her opinions and pieces were read by people throughout the country.

As president of Las Hijas de Cuauhtemoc, her written works and activism put her in the spotlight regularly. In 1910, the Hijas were arrested during a large but peaceful demonstration march in Mexico City, protesting Diaz's policies. She refused to stop in her mission despite her arrest.

From her jail cell Jiménez founded a feminist group called Regeneración y Concordia, which would work to improve the lives of the indigenous, the poor, and the working class and elevate women economically, morally, and intellectually. Her plan was to start a rebellion to put Madero in power, which she thought would be the catalyst in providing better working conditions, wages, and work hours and provide sufficient and affordable housing and return lands to the poor.

She believed locally funded and controlled schools could start community reform. Before Jiménez took up the revolutionary cry, she had been a schoolteacher, an advocate for women's rights and for educational reform. She knew that education was the key to meeting the needs of many classes of people.

Her political career and influence skyrocketed and she was able to bring about some change for her people as a result of her time and efforts in Zapata's army and with her journalistic endeavors. She led a rich political life until Zapata's assassination in 1919. For all her courageous efforts, Jiménez died near poverty and anonymity until the undersecretary of education, Gilberto Valenzuela, granted her a small pension just months before her death.

Sophia Hayden (Chile, 1868–1953)

The first woman admitted to MIT's architecture program, Sophia Hayden opened the door for women architects of the future. She designed the Woman's Building for the World's Columbian Exposition in 1893.

Sophia Hayden was the first woman admitted into the architecture program at the Massachusetts Institute of Technology (MIT), graduating with honors in 1890. MIT had the first school of architecture in the United States, which opened in 1865.

At the institute, she shared a drafting room with Lois Lilley Howe, another female architect. She won the respect of her professors as a brilliant and dedicated student. Yet, her first commission, an exposition building to symbolize nineteenth-century women's advancement, would also be her last. She was the victim of gender discrimination at its worst.

Hayden was sent to live with her paternal grandparents in Boston, Massachusetts, when she was just six years old. Architecture intrigued her while she was in high school and she decided to pursue her education in that field. After graduation, she could not find employment in the field because she was a woman. Instead, she began teaching mechanical drawing in Boston high schools.

In 1891 there was a competition inviting women architects to submit designs for a Woman's Building for the World's Columbian Exposition. The exposition was to take place in Chicago, Illinois, in 1893. The building would feature women in the art world.

> ⁀⅃ The Women's Building was the only design to Hayden's credit. Without a structural record of her brief career, she left no legacy, yet was a trailblazer in the architectural field.

Twenty-three-year-old Hayden won the competition with a three-story, white building design. There was a striking resemblance between her thesis project for a "Fine Arts Museum" and the Woman's Building. Both seem influenced by Eugene Letang, with Italian Renaissance-style detailing, arches, and columned terraces, pavilions, and skylights. Hayden was paid approximately $1,500 for her design, while men were earning three times that much for their works.

The Woman's Building, which was under the control of an all-female board, featured architectural details by women artists, inside and out. There were sculptures, crafts of all kinds, paintings, home design, and a library in the exhibition spaces. Mary Cassatt's large mural "Modern Woman" hung in the Great Hall of the Woman's Building. Its center section, "Women Picking the Fruits of Knowledge," featured robust female figures. It was not well received in the United States, and disappeared after the exposition.

The board awarded Hayden a gold medal "for delicacy of style, artistic taste and geniality and elegance of the interior hall." Male critics, however, focused on the fact that she was a woman and cited her work as inferior, insisting it looked "too feminine." The Women's Building was torn down without a second thought after the exposition ended. Frustrated with the biased treatment she had received, she retired from architecture.

Hayden married artist William Blackstone Bennett around 1900, lived in Massachusetts, and was active in local women's societies.

The Women's Building was the only design to Hayden's credit. Without a structural record of her brief career, she left no legacy, yet was a trailblazer in the architectural field. At the time of her death in 1953, there were just over 300 women architects in the United States. By the mid-1990s, there were more than 10,000.

Mercedes Cubría (Cuba, 1903–1980)

The first Cuban-American woman to earn the rank of lieutenant colonel in the United States Army and the first Latina to be elected into the United States Army Intelligence Hall of Fame. Mercedes Cubría earned the Bronze Star and the Legion of Merit Award (twice) for her professional and personal work throughout her thirty-year career.

Born in Guantánamo, Cuba, Mercedes Cubría emigrated to the United States when she was thirteen. She joined the women's army corps in 1943. She earned a commission and was sent to England for cryptography training. During the war she worked in various capacities of security.

Cubría was the first woman assigned to the Panama Canal Zone. She was the first Cuban-American woman to become a lieutenant colonel in the United States Army, which she was recognized for in 1973.

In 1953, she received a medical discharge and was awarded the Bronze Star for meritorious achievement in ground operations. She was called out of retirement in 1962, during the Cuban missile crisis. Cubría's job was to debrief Cuban refugees and defectors. She also helped them find jobs and places to live on her own time, and she was awarded the Legion of Merit for her efforts. She retired a second time in 1973, and won another Legion of Merit Award.

Her efforts helped add to the intelligence base collected by the army and the Central Intelligence Agency. Cubría became the first Latina to be elected into the United States Army Intelligence Hall of Fame.

Sandra Ortiz del Valle (United States, 1951–)

The first woman and Latina to referee professional men's basketball, Sandra Ortiz del Valle won a gender discrimination lawsuit against the NBA and opened the door for other female referees.

Sandra Ortiz del Valle had one goal: to be the first female referee to officiate in the National Basketball Association (NBA). She had already been the first woman to officiate a men's pro game, with the United States Basketball League (USBL) in 1991, as well as a few preseason scrimmages. The NBA's own scouts recommended her.

She had risen to number two on the NBA list to officiate, but despite her credentials and experience, she was repeatedly passed over for the position. For eight years, Ortiz del Valle tried to get into the league's referee training program but was consistently rejected.

Reasons varied, but none of them were valid. She was shut out for not filling out applications correctly or not being in good physical shape or not having enough experience.

> For eight years, Ortiz del Valle tried to get into the league's referee training program but was consistently rejected.

Instead of being the first female NBA referee, Ortiz del Valle was the first woman to bring a lawsuit against the NBA for gender discrimination in violation of Title VII. She was awarded $100,000 for lost wages, $750,000 for emotional distress, and $7 million in punitive damages. It was the first time the NBA had ever lost a discrimination case.

The NBA moved for a new trial. A federal judge reduced the $8 million jury award to $350,000. The judge acknowledged that the league had been liable for its discrimination against her, but the award was reduced because it was fifty-eight times the amount awarded in similar discrimination cases.

Later it was found that the NBA had hired ten men with less experience than Ortiz del Valle had. Ironically, the league hired two women just before the case went to trial, and in a public statement, the NBA noted that it was the only one out of the four major sports to have female officials.

Born and raised in New York, Ortiz del Valle developed a lifelong love of basketball in high school. Supported by her electrician father and mother who served on a school board, Ortiz del Valle went on to play center and forward in college. She earned a bachelor's degree in education in 1974 and a master's degree in administration and supervision in 1983.

She immediately began refereeing youth basketball, followed by the Biddies League and the men's Pro-Am League. In 1989 she was offered a job by the USBL, making her the first woman and first Latina to referee men's professional basketball games.

Despite the court ruling against the NBA and monetary compensation, del Valle did not get to enjoy the victory herself. She was in a car accident and suffered severe back injuries. After some time, she made it back onto the courts, coaching a boys' high school basketball team.

She was, however, seen as a pioneer. Because of the case, women were officially allowed into men's professional basketball when the NBA hired two other female referees.

Ortiz del Valle was listed among the 100 Most Powerful People in Sports by the *Sporting News*, one of only six women on the list.

Athletes: Tearing Up the Playing Field

Conchita Cintron (Peru, 1922–)
The most famous female bullfighter of all time and a pioneer in the sport.

With flourish and flair, Conchita Cintron entered the bullring, confident that she belonged there. Known as La Diosa de Oro—the Golden Goddess—Cintron would become one of the most famous, trailblazing female bullfighters of all time.

In her autobiography, she acknowledges that she was not the first, nor the only female bullfighter, but that she did fight for equality in the ring. Not wanting to limit herself to fighting bulls on horseback—the only way women were allowed to take part in the sport—Cintron often broke rules to get in the ring on foot.

In 1908, women were forbidden from fighting bulls while on foot and this tradition continued while Conchita tried to make a name for herself in the sport. Other women took up her cause but the rules did not change. Still, bullfighting on horseback was better than not bullfighting at all.

Born in Peru, she was raised by supportive parents of Portuguese and Irish descent. At the age of twelve, she found her calling. She found obstacles all along the way, fighting for recognition and respect as well as facing the hefty bulls.

Bullfighting took her into South America and Mexico, France, Spain, and Portugal. She fought in the great arenas in Europe and was once arrested in France for even appearing in a ring.

Her reputation preceded her. By the time Cintron was twenty-one, she had killed more than 400 bulls on foot. In her lifetime, she slew more than 1,000.

> By the time Cintron was twenty-one, she had killed more than 400 bulls on foot. In her lifetime, she slew more than 1,000.

She paved the path for other female bullfighters. When she married into Portuguese nobility, she ended her bullfighting career with a flourish. It was 1949. Hopping off her horse, she gored the bull with three short barbs in the neck and shoulder area with textbook precision. But then in an act of defiance, she threw her sword on the ground, refusing to kill the bull. She was arrested for her actions but was quickly released when the audience roared its disapproval and instead showed its enthusiastic support of her.

Cintron started second careers exporting paso fino horses—pure-blooded Portuguese horses—and as a dog breeder. She bred Portuguese water dogs that were close to extinction, sending them to a United States kennel to ensure their continued breeding according to AKC sanctions. They are still bred there today. She fled Portugal when the revolution hit in 1974 and settled in the United States with her six children. Later she became a diplomatic attaché.

Donna de Varona (United States, 1947–)

A gold medalist and world record holder in swimming, Donna de Varona was the first female sportscaster on network television and the first woman to do television commentary on the Olympics. A hall of famer, Emmy Award winner, and Gracie Award winner, she is cofounder of the Women's Sport Foundation.

> "I will always be an activist. That is a lifetime commitment."
>
> —Donna de Varona in *Great Women in Sports*

The water had a magical appeal for Donna de Varona and the 1960s were a good time for awakening female athletes. As a thirteen-year-old, de Varona was the youngest member of the United States swim team at the Rome Olympics.

In the 1964 games in Tokyo, she broke eighteen world records and captured two gold medals, in the 400 individual medley and 400 freestyle relay—her relay team set a world record (4:03.8 minutes). She had thirty-seven wins in the backstroke, butterfly, and individual medley events.

She appeared on the October 1964 cover of *Life* magazine as a swimming sensation but retired after the 1964 Olympics. She became the first woman sportscaster on network television at the age of seventeen and was the first woman to do television commentary on the Olympics (1988).

Raised in Southern California, de Varona's first coach was her father, a champion rower. Her first love was baseball. She wanted to play with her older brother in Little League but was barred because she was a girl. Not willing to settle for the only position she could get—a bat girl—she took up swimming.

It became her passion. In high school she trained up to six hours a day and still remained a good student. When she went on to college, however, there was no athletic program for women and so she retired from swimming before her prime. After earning her political science degree from the University of California Los Angeles (UCLA), she decided to pursue a career in television broadcasting.

Since leaving competitive swimming, de Varona has worked for various television and radio networks. She received an Emmy Award for her report on a 1991 Special Olympics athlete.

She served on the President's Commission on Olympic Sports, spent five terms on the President's Council on Physical Fitness and Sports, and served as the chair of the U.S. Olympic Committee's Public Relations and Information Committee.

Raising money and awareness for women athletes, de Varona cofounded the Women's Sports Foundation with Billie Jean King in 1974. She served as president and chairperson.

She worked tirelessly into the 1970s to pass Title IX of 1972's Equal Education Amendment Act, which ensured that girls and women receive the same opportunities and federal funding in sports education as boys and men.

Working with a federal antipoverty program, she helps ensure that inner-city youths learn to swim. She educates on health, authored *Hydro-Aerobics—Swim Your Way to Total Fitness,* and narrated a video called *Swimming for Fitness.*

De Varona received the Susan B. Anthony Trailblazer Award (2001) and the 2003 Theodore Roosevelt Award, the highest honor the NCAA bestows on an individual. Known as the "Teddy," the annual award is presented to a "distinguished citizen who is a former college student-athlete and who has exemplified the ideals and purpose of college athletics by demonstrating a continuing interest and concern for physical fitness and sport."

The AP and United Press International voted her Most Outstanding Female Athlete in 1965. In 2000 she received the Gracie Award, presented by the American Women in Radio and Television for "outstanding radio commentaries profiling women and women's issues in sports." *Sports Illustrated Women* magazine listed her as one of the Top 100 Greatest Female Athletes.

Rosemary "Rosie" Casals (United States, 1948–)
Seven-time Wimbledon champion and hall of famer who fought for women's equality in tennis and made her mark on the tennis world with her unique style and flair.

Fighting for equality was a sign of the times in the 1960s. Tennis star Rosie Casals was considered a rebel who believed women had a destiny in professional tennis and deserved equal rights on the courts.

A tireless advocate on behalf of women and women athletes, Casals was instrumental in helping women gain prestige, money, and recognition at the professional level. She was a major force behind many of the controversial changes that shook the tennis world, leading to the women's tennis boom of the 1960s and 1970s.

The seven-time Wimbledon women's and mixed doubles champion came from an immigrant family from El Salvador, a family so poor, she and her sister had to be raised by their aunt and uncle, Maria and Manuel Casals. Manuel saw their need for an outlet and took them to the public tennis courts of San Francisco, California.

The seven-time Wimbledon women's and mixed doubles champion came from an immigrant family from El Salvador, a family so poor she and her sister had to be raised by their aunt and uncle, Maria and Manuel Casals.

He would be the only tennis coach Casals would ever have. She was a natural on the courts and by the time she was a teen, she was bored competing in junior tournaments. She counted the days when she could play on the women's circuit.

But what Casals learned once she got there began another uphill battle. She not only had to face being a woman in a man's arena but also being poor and Latina in a sport that had a tradition of being exclusive.

Despite the obstacles, by age seventeen Casals ranked number five in the world and was in the U.S. women's top five. She would remain there for the next eleven years. Her career skyrocketed, especially when paired with the outspoken Billie Jean King. They became the most winning female doubles combo.

Casals challenged the controlled environment of the country club set. She wanted to get the recognition and praise she deserved for her all-out, aggressive efforts by hearing real clapping. She turned heads when she showed up to play in clothes that were not completely white. When she appeared at Wimbledon in a dress lined with purple squiggles, spangles, and sequins, the referee evicted her from the courts, sending her off to change her clothes. She complied but continued to push the envelope to change the white-dress restrictions.

Since only the wealthy could afford to remain amateurs, Casals fought to get tennis recognized as a professional sport so that athletes could earn a living from what they did best.

Casals was one of the first women to claim professional status but became disillusioned when she saw the vast difference in prize monies between male and female players. She and other women players threatened to boycott USTA tournaments if changes weren't made. The USTA ignored their threats. The women found support from the media and from Gladys Heldman, editor of *World Tennis* magazine.

Casals became a pioneer of the Women's Tennis Association, seeking sponsors who saw the value of promoting professional women's sports. She and Billie Jean King were among the original nine founders who laid the groundwork for the association.

In 1970, Casals became the first winner of the Virginia Slims Invitational, a professional women's tennis tournament, and took home the top prize of $1,600. The seven players who participated in this tournament were suspended by USTA.

Still they continued. They played twice as many tournaments to earn a few thousand dollars in minimal award money, while paying their expenses out of pocket, but their pioneering efforts opened doors for future female players.

Casals pushed through those doors. Playing a record 685 tournaments in her lifetime, in 1973 Casals won the largest purse ever awarded to any female at that time—$30,000—for a women's single event in the Family Circle Cup. In a tournament in 1988, she won over $1 million.

Casals served as the color commentator alongside Howard Cosell in the infamous "Battle of the Sexes" between Billie Jean King and Bobby Riggs.

She continues to promote women and their athletic careers. Her marketing company established a "Tennis Classics Tour," a circuit tour for women and men over the age of thirty who have won a Grand Slam title or earned $1 million in prize money.

Working with Billie Jean King, she supports tennis opportunities for disadvantaged young girls. In her San Francisco community, she serves as an athletic ambassador working to bring the 2012 Olympics to her hometown. She sponsors a Rosie Casals Celebrity Tennis Invitational and still plays on the senior Invitational at Wimbledon and the U.S. Open. In 1996 Casals was inducted into the International Tennis Hall of Fame.

Nancy Marie Lopez (United States, 1957–)

The youngest woman to be inducted into the LPGA Hall of Fame, Nancy Lopez won a record-breaking number of tournaments during her career and helped put women's golf on the map.

Women's golf in the 1970s was synonymous with Nancy Lopez. Regarded as the best woman golfer of all time, her record-breaking first year in the pros stunned crowds and set new standards for women's golf.

She took the golf course by storm, turned people on to women's golf as a spectator sport, and fostered an appreciation for the Ladies Professional Golf Association (LPGA). She accumulated such a fan base that it became known as "Nancy's Navy."

> ☙ Lopez's loyal fans were known as "Nancy's Navy."

Lopez was born in California but raised in New Mexico. The entire family took up golf to help improve her mother's health. When she was only eight years old, Lopez's father, Domingo, cut down a four wood to her size. She started swinging the club every chance she could. By the time she turned eleven, she beat both her mother and father on the course.

When Lopez quickly became championship material, her parents sought ways to supplement her learning experience and made many sacrifices to get her onto challenging courses. They could not afford and were not allowed country club membership. They took detours in stride, and Domingo remained her coach.

Making her amateur debut at the age of twelve, Lopez won the New Mexico State Women's Amateur Championship and placed second in the Women's Open. By the time she was sixteen, she was among the top-ranked amateurs in the world.

Lopez became the first female student to join her high school golf club and won the USGA Junior Girls Championship, the Western Junior, and the Mexican Amateur in 1975. On scholarship, she entered the University of Tulsa, Oklahoma. In 1976 she turned All-American and was named the Tulsa University Female Athlete of the Year. She went on to win the intercollegiate title.

While a college sophomore in 1975, she turned professional. Her debut year was phenomenal. She was named Rookie of the Year and Female Athlete of the Year.

Lopez joined the LPGA in 1977 and in 1978 won nine tournaments, including a record five in a row. This included the prestigious LPGA title. She set other LPGA records, including her 275-stroke total for the 72-hole LPGA Championship.

In 1979, she was named Pro Golfer of the Year, winning eight tournaments and accumulating more than $1 million that year.

Her best year was in 1985 when she earned more money than any other player on the circuit. This was followed by her induction into the LPGA Hall of Fame in 1987. She was the youngest woman ever to be elected, which requires thirty-five official tournament wins. In 1989, she was inducted into the Professional Golf Association's World Golf Hall of Fame and won her third LPGA Championship that year.

By 1998, she had forty-eight career victories with over $3 million in earnings. The grueling schedule of balancing more than twenty tournaments a year along with raising a family and dealing with physical ailments took its toll.

It took Nancy another two years to regain her strength after knee surgery repercussions and get back onto the course. She announced that her twenty-fifth LPGA season in 2002 would be her last.

Lopez now serves as a goodwill ambassador of golf. She devotes the rest of her time to her husband, ex–New York Mets third baseman Ray Knight, their three children, and to the American Heart Association and Aid for the Handicapped.

Rachel Elizondo McLish (United States, 1958–)

The first Latina to win the Ms. Olympia title, Rachel McLish helped put women's bodybuilding on the map and is a legend in the sport.

Women's bodybuilding was just taking off. It was the days before steroids, and tough women did not sell. Beauty and brawn proved a winning combination for Rachel Elizondo McLish. She was the first Latina to win the title of Ms. Olympia in the Women's World Championship Bodybuilding Competition in 1980.

In the spotlight, her body was oiled up, the muscles in her biceps bulged, her calves were perfectly sculpted. She had just won the U.S. Women's Bodybuilding Championship in 1980. Known as the "Queen of Women's Bodybuilding," she helped put the sport on the map.

The win boosted her into stardom. She changed the image of a healthy woman. A fit and strong physique could still be sexy and feminine.

In 1982, she again won both the Ms. Olympia and the Women's World Professional Championship title.

McLish became a regular fixture in fitness magazines like *Muscle & Fitness, Flex,* and *Muscular,* not only through photo spreads but also in the columns and articles she has written. Her fitness video, *In Shape with Rachel McLish,* did well on the stands and complemented her books, *Flex Appeal* and *Perfect Parts.* She has appeared in several movies including *Pumping Iron II: The Women, Aces: Iron Eagle III,* and *Raven Hawk.*

McLish remains a pioneer in women's bodybuilding and a legend in fitness culture.

Pam Fernandes (United States, 1960–)

Gold medalist and world record holder in tandem cycling, Pam Fernandes received the prestigious Olympic Spirit Award and is a tireless activist for the disabled.

> "Being blind doesn't define who I am. On the back of a bike I don't have a disability."
>
> —Pam Fernandes, Paralympic tandem cycling gold medalist

Pam Fernandes did not let the fact that she is blind slow her down when she climbed onto her first tandem bike. The faster she could go, the better she felt. Her passion and determination to master tandem bicycle racing led to her qualifying for the United States Paralympic team.

In the 2000 Paralympic Games in Sydney, Fernandes and her tandem partner, Al Whaley, were the first tandem team from the United States to win a gold medal in Paralympic history. They set new world and Paralympic records.

Fernandes is a world-class athlete who happens to be blind. Only four years old when she was diagnosed with type 1 insulin-dependent diabetes, she lost her brother to the disease when he was in his early thirties. She was the youngest of seven but managed the disease so that she was able to play softball and basketball in high school.

When she turned eighteen, however, she started losing her eyesight—one of the most common complications of the disease. Still, she earned her degree in education while undergoing dialysis treatments three days a week for kidney disease, the second major diabetic complication. She received her diploma to a standing ovation.

She underwent thirty surgeries due to complications of the disease and five years of dialysis. A kidney transplant when she was twenty-seven (1987) gave her a second chance at life and really living.

Her life began to change when she was allowed to exercise again. She climbed on a bike and never stopped pedaling. She loved the freedom and speed it offered after years of having been physically restricted.

33

Training five to six days weekly and logging more than 500 miles a month, Fernandes competes in numerous cycling events annually. It keeps her in shape and her diabetes under control.

She has earned three Paralympic and one World Championship medal, numerous national titles, and international awards. She was selected to be on the United States Disabled Elite Cycling Team formed in 2002, a national program that offers coaching to exceptional cyclists.

In the 2000 Sydney Paralympics she broke her foot just ten days before her event. Fernandes still competed with Whaley, the pilot on their tandem team, and won the gold medal in the one-kilometer time trial, setting a world record.

For exhibiting courage and determination in the competition, she was the first woman Paralympian to receive the prestigious Olympic Spirit Award—given to only two Olympic and two Paralympic athletes. She was selected the 1994 Athlete of the Year by the U.S. Olympic Team, and in 1995 she was named Female Athlete of the Year by the United States Association of Blind Athletes.

Fernandes founded Team with a Vision, a group of blind, partially sighted, and sighted runners who compete in the Boston Marathon to raise money for the Massachusetts Association for the Blind. She has been a spokesperson for the American Diabetes Association, an advocate for health and fitness, and has worked to educate the public about the capabilities of people with disabilities.

She is a member of the Women's Sports Foundation, the Diabetes Exercise and Sports Association, the United States Association of Blind Athletes, and the Council of Public Representatives for the National Institute of Health.

As she has throughout her life, Fernandes continues to face new challenges with optimism. Recently she became the first blind cyclist to reach the summit of Mount Washington in New Hampshire.

Wendy Lucero-Schayes (United States, 1963–)

Two-time U.S. Female Diving Athlete of the year and winner of numerous other awards and medals throughout her diving career, Wendy Lucero-Schayes placed sixth in the 1988 Olympics.

Wendy Lucero-Schayes wanted to be in the Olympics. She just did not know which sport she was going to pursue to get there. She tried a variety of sports throughout her teens and finally found her niche in springboard diving. She became a member of the U.S. National Diving Team and made it all the way to the 1988 Olympics in Seoul.

The roundabout approach was unique, but Lucero-Schayes was a natural athlete, and had built-in competition with her older sister. When she was nine years old, she decided she wanted to become an Olympic contestant.

First, she tried her hand at gymnastics, but realized that as a preteen she was too old since many of the young gymnasts had started training years before. The same went for ice-skating. Once she found diving, she knew that was her sport and poured all her energy into it. Her gymnastics training helped her agility as she ventured into springboard diving. She started placing in state competitions in her sophomore year in high school, and by the time she was a senior, she competed in the Junior Olympics on the one-meter springboard.

Her competitive performances grew more polished. In 1981 Lucero-Schayes was named the Hispanic Athlete of the Year. It was the same year she earned a full athletic scholarship to the University of Nebraska. She was an Academic All-American.

> In 1981 Lucero-Schayes was named the Hispanic Athlete of the Year. It was the same year she earned a full athletic scholarship to the University of Nebraska. She was an Academic All-American.

Once she began winning awards, the Olympics did not seem like such a far-fetched idea after all. She transferred to the University of Illinois and practiced diligently to learn the three-meter springboard, an entirely new event for her since it was not offered at the high school level.

She won the one-meter event in the 1985 NCAA Championships and earned her first national titles. She also earned a spot on the United States National Diving Team. It started one of the best athletic times of her life. In the midst of training, she graduated with a degree in television sales and management and worked as a sports event production assistant, a sportscaster, and talk show host in Denver, her hometown. In 1987 she won her first three-meter titles at the U. S. Olympic Festival and the American Cup II.

During training for the Olympic trials, Lucero-Schayes had to deal with the news that her mother, whom she saw as her greatest role model, was diagnosed with breast cancer. When she was able to complete chemotherapy and attend the trials, everything fell into place for Lucero-Schayes.

She placed second and her dream of making the Olympic team came true. She represented her country at the 1988 Olympic Games in Seoul, Korea. Lucero-Schayes placed sixth in her event. When she returned stateside, she won nine national titles—three U.S. Olympic Festival medals, and several international medals, including a silver in the 1991 World Championships. She was the U.S. Female Diving Athlete of the Year in 1990 and 1991. It was also a pivotal year personally. She wed professional basketball player Dan Schayes.

Severe illness kept her from making the U.S. team that would travel to the Olympics in Barcelona, Spain, in 1992. But the entire diving experience made her that much richer—in knowledge, travel, camaraderie. Lucero-Schayes had achieved what she set out to do.

Mia "the Knockout" Rosales-St. John (United States, 1967–)

Professional boxer who went ten rounds with the legendary Christy Martin, Mia Rosales-St. John holds a black belt in tae kwon do, with a 27-1 record.

K nocking people unconscious is part of her job, but tough cookie Mia Rosales-St. John is a picture of contradiction.

Her home is filled with collectible dolls. She is a model and has appeared in magazines and calendars to put herself through college. She graduated with a degree in psychology from California State University, Northridge. She posed in *Playboy* in boxing attire in a twelve-page spread.

And she is a featherweight/junior lightweight boxer who fights in her trademark pink tights. Inspired by the *Rocky* movies, Rosales-St. John began competitive amateur tae kwon do when she turned eighteen.

Born in California to Mexican parents, she is one of three siblings. Fighting has been in her blood since she was a kid. When she was six years old, she competed in tae kwon do and earned a black belt with a 27-1 record.

Boxing aficionados have criticized her style of boxing. She is an aggressive fighter and uses a head-down, windmill style. The criticism does not affect her passion for the sport.

Mia Rosales-St. John made her debut on Valentine's Day in 1997 and knocked out her opponent fifty-four seconds into the first round. She decided to pursue boxing full time.

Her record at one point was twenty-nine wins, three losses, and thirteen knockouts. She was earning $20,000 per game, ten times what other boxers were making in four rounds against unranked opponents. Boxing diehards picked another bone: Her opponents had not been good competition and going four rounds was not indicative of a good fight.

Rosales-St. John worked her way up in the ranks and changed divisions so that she could box against the legendary Christy Martin. Rosales-St. John gave her a run for her money in the welterweight (140-plus pounds) division. She went the entire ten rounds. Rosales-St. John lost by a decision.

> Mia Rosales-St. John made her debut on Valentine's Day in 1997 and knocked out her opponent fifty-four seconds into the first round. She decided to pursue boxing full time.

Her strength and inspiration is her mother, Maria Rosales, who coaches her daughter during her fights, along with trainer Robert Garcia.

She is the mother of two. Upon retiring, Rosales-St. John plans to take up an offer to host a television sports show.

Lisa Fernandez (United States, 1971–)

Two-time Olympic gold medalist for the United States softball team who broke numerous softball records during her career as a pitcher before becoming a prominent pitching and hitting coach.

In the very first softball game Lisa Fernandez pitched, she walked twenty players. Her team lost 28 to 0. She was only seven at the time, but the softball bug had bit. With her mother's support, she decided to dedicate herself to learning all she could about the sport. She practiced every chance she could. Everytime she stepped on the mound, she was determined to show improvement. If she walked twenty batters one day, the next game she would walk no more than eighteen.

Practice made perfect. Fernandez became a two-time Olympic gold medalist as a pitcher for the United States softball team.

As one of the world's most recognized softball players, Fernandez's not-so-secret weapon is the windmill, a style of fast-pitch. When she is on the pitcher's mound, her arms whip around, her foot pushes off the rubber mat, and she lets loose pitches that have been clocked at an average speed of 68 miles per hour. In baseball, that is comparable to 101 miles per hour.

Despite setbacks along the way, she persevered. One coach had told Fernandez when she was twelve that she would never be a champion pitcher because her arms were too short. She took that as a challenge.

She might be a natural, but the love of softball and her talent might just be hereditary. Her father, Antonio, was a semiprofessional baseball player in Cuba. Her mother, Emilia, played slow-pitch and coached Fernandez's first softball team. Both parents thought it fun to play softball with the young Fernandez and whet her appetite for the sport.

Emilia could only go so far. While Fernandez improved steadily, Emilia had to use bigger and better gloves to warm her up. Before long she added a mask, chest pad, and shin guards, protecting herself in full catcher's gear. It was not enough. Emilia feared Lisa's pitches, which had become too fast for her to handle. Antonio took up the position behind the plate, but he eventually gave it over to a private pitching coach. The training opened new doors.

> One coach had told Fernandez when she was twelve that she would never be a champion pitcher because her arms were too short. She took that as a challenge.

In high school, Fernandez had seventy shut-outs in a row. As a University of California, Los Angeles (UCLA), student and player, she was a four-time NCAA All-American and pitched her school to two NCAA Women's College World Series Championships.

Her batting average by her senior year led the nation, along with her ninety-three wins and seven losses as a pitcher. Her career records at UCLA covered the gamut, with record singles, hits, walks, runs scored, pitching wins, and no-hitters.

Fernandez played for the United States softball team and earned two Olympic gold medals, one in 1996 and the other in 2000. She has also earned medals in the Pan American games, the ISF Women's World Championship, and South Pacific Classic, among others. On the United States national softball team, she earned three more gold medals, and the United States Olympic Committee (USOC) named her a Top 10 Athlete of the Year.

Playing in the Amateur Softball Association, Fernandez was Female Athlete of the Year in 1999. She helped her team make it into seven ASA Women's Major Fast-Pitch National Championships. Two-time ASA Sports Woman of the Year, nine-time ASA All-American, and six-time MVP (most valuable player), Lisa broke records in all areas of softball.

Currently a coach for her alma mater, Fernandez is a hitting and pitching expert. Honored by MANA, a national Latina organization that mentors young Latinas, Fernandez was recognized for her contribution in the field of sports.

Milka Duno (Venezuela, 1972–)

The first Latina to ever be considered "expert" in the racing world, Milka Duno was named the Venezuelan Auto Racing Driver of the Year, and became the first woman to win a Ferrari Challenge in the United States.

"You must never let them intimidate you. I'm just another driver in the field."

—Milka Duno, "And She Drives!"
by Neevy Hadar, *Men's Fitness* magazine

Checkered flags, speed, and the best sports cars. Give Milka Duno a Ferrari, a Porsche, a Sebring—or just about any other power machine where she can put the pedal to the metal—and she is one happy woman. She loves cars and loves to drive them fast. She has driven a Porsche Supercup, Ferrari Challenge 355, Formula 2000 Dodge, Dodge Viper GTS, and the Panoz GT-RA, among many others. This love launched her career.

Duno turned professional race car driver after joining club racing in Venezuela in 1996. Since then, she has broken many "firsts" as a woman and as a Latina in professional race car driving.

In 2004, she and her partner Andy Wallace placed first in the Rolex Sports Car Series, which is considered the Grand Prix of Miami. This bumped her up the ladder of racing as the first woman in the history of the Grand American Road Racing Series to earn an overall win. She drove a Pontiac Crawford Daytona Prototype for this race.

She is the first Latina to ever be considered "expert" in the racing world. In 2002, she was the first woman and only Venezuelan to compete on three continents and the first woman to ever drive the Le Mans Prototype 900, a lightning-fast, technologically advanced sports car.

The year 2000 was a banner year for Duno—she was selected the Venezuelan Auto Racing Driver of the Year. She also won her first title in the Panoz GT Winter Series Champion. That year also saw her become the first woman to ever win a Ferrari Challenge in the United States.

In 2001, she hit a double jackpot. Duno was the American Le Mans Series 2001 Vice Champion Driver and the first woman to ever score points in the Open Telefonica Formula Nissan, the most prestigious European series after the Formula One. She was invited to participate in the Telefonica after her performance in the most famous sports car race in the world—the 24 Hour Le Mans.

Duno races individually, with another racer, or on teams and has attended various driving schools including the Derek Daly Academy Advanced Formula course. Sponsored by CITGO, which markets and transports industrial products like lubricants and waxes and fuels, Duno is able to compete internationally, full time. CITGO is owned by Venezuela-based Petróleos de Venezuela, S.A., a national oil company.

Speed is not the only thing that drives Duno. She has brains to go with her brawn and unconventional career choice. Education is a priority. A naval engineer, she has earned five master's degrees in subjects such as marine biology, naval architecture, and economic development.

Rebecca Lobo (United States, 1973–)

The youngest member of the 1996 United States Olympic women's basketball team that captured the gold, Rebecca Lobo had a prolific college basketball career, went on to be one of the original players for the WNBA, and was named to the 1999 All-Star Team.

When she was just a girl in the 1970s and 1980s, Rebecca Lobo dreamed about playing professional basketball. She was in third grade when she wrote a letter to the general manager of the Boston Celtics and informed him that she wanted to be the first woman to play for the team. He didn't reply, but then, girls and basketball didn't mix. The idea was as far-fetched as having a girl play basketball in the Olympics.

> ❧ Rebecca was in third grade when she wrote a letter to the general man-ager of the Boston Celtics and informed him that she wanted to be the first woman to play for the team.

As Lobo grew to her full height of six feet four, she was rarely seen without a basketball in her hand, and her parents encouraged her to hold fast to her dream. Lo and behold, the tides changed.

One of her biggest dreams came true when she was named—as the youngest player on the team—to the 1996 United States Women's Olympic "Dream Team." The team went on to win a gold medal at the Olympic games held in Atlanta.

Her joy didn't stop there. Lobo went on to become one of the original players for the Women's National Basketball Association (WNBA).

Lobo was only five years old when she started playing basketball, mostly with her siblings. In addition to being an athlete, she remained true to her studies. In high school, she graduated as the class salutatorian. She played the saxophone and was in the school band. Lobo also enjoyed playing softball, soccer, track, and field hockey.

Her grandfather, who was from Cuba, helped her take pride in her Hispanic heritage. Her family has remained her constant source of support. When a teacher confronted her when she was a teenager and told her to stop playing with the boys and to try to start acting more feminine, they were there. It was a defining moment for her, because they supported her and her vision.

She was recruited by more than 100 different colleges. Lobo chose the University of Connecticut. She led the Huskies to an undefeated (35-0) season and went on to the 1995 National Championship. She also earned the college Player of the Year title. She was named the NCAA Women's Basketball Player of the Year, the Associated Press Female Athlete of the Year, and received two ESPY awards, including Outstanding Female

Athlete of the Year, and Woman of the Year by the Women's Sports Foundation.

She missed her college graduation because she was at the Olympic trials, but earned a bachelor's degree in political science.

Lobo played for the New York Liberty from 1997 to 2002, when she was traded to the Houston Comets. In 1997, Rebecca was named to the All-WNBA Second Team and played on the 1999 All-Star Team in Madison Square Garden.

The entire experience was groundbreaking. There were professional female basketball players where once there had been none. A major television network like ESPN was covering the games, providing national exposure to the WNBA. Coverage showed there was a true audience interest in women's basketball.

Her sense of commitment followed her off the courts. When her mother was diagnosed with breast cancer, Lobo refocused her energies. Together they wrote *The Home Team,* which tells about their special relationship and their battle with breast cancer. The experience prompted her activism with several different organizations that support breast cancer awareness.

Retirement from her dream sport in 2003 came much too early, due to serious knee injuries.

Ana Gabriela Guevara (Mexico, 1977–)

A gold medal winner, Ana Guevara is among the best female distance runners in history and holds the world record in the 400 meter.

She runs like the wind. Faster, in fact. Ana Guevara has been called the "Fastest Woman in Mexico's Athletic History." Guevara holds the women's world record in the 400 meter in international track and field competitions. She broke the world record in 2003 when she came in at 48.89 seconds in the Paris Athletic World Championship. She became the eighth woman to break the 49-second time.

Guevara has won gold medals in the Pan-Am Games. She had twenty-five consecutive victories, starting in 2001 in Germany, and had two major victories in the 4x4 relays in the Madrid World Cup and the San Salvador Central American Games in 2002. Her victories place her among the best in the history of distance running.

⚝ Ana Guevara has been called the "Fastest Woman in Mexico's Athletic History."

Living by her adopted theme song, "My Way" as sung by Frank Sinatra, keeps her on her own victory path and inspires her to think of the future. Another inspiration is Michael Jordan. She was a basketball player herself before taking to the track. Guevara admires his way of thinking and his demeanor, and hopes she exudes the same confidence and compassion.

Despite ankle injuries, Guevara intends to break her own record in 2004.

Vanessa Torres (United States, 1986–)

Among the top female street skateboarders in the world, Torres won the first gold medal in women's skateboarding at the X Games.

S he can whip a skateboard into tricks that defy gravity. Her favorite is the "nollie kickflip," though she continually works to perfect more challenging tricks like the "switch heelflip varial."

Vanessa Torres is an X-treme skateboarder. Terms like noseslides, kickflips, and grinding are music to her ears. At sixteen she put girls on the map and in the skateboarding parks.

She is a pioneer in a new sport for women—professional skateboarding. Torres first skated as a pro in 2001 at the All-Girl Skate Jam. She was fourteen and won the first two events she entered. She took first place. The X-treme sport athlete is making a name for herself.

In the summer of 2002, she was invited as one of seven female skateboarders to a women's skate demo at the Summer X Games in Philadelphia, Pennsylvania. It was an honor and a breakthrough because the prestigious games had never had a women's skateboarding division. She has traveled throughout Europe, Australia, Mexico, and the United States in competitions and for promotions.

In 2002, she placed first at the Vans Triple Crown, first in the All-Girl Skate Jam in California, and second at the Slam City Jam in Canada. She won the female Skateboarder of the Year title in 2002.

Torres has secured major sponsors like Hurley International, Gallaz Footwear, and Element Skateboards. She was featured in a documentary video called *AKA: Girl Skater,* which focused on Torres and three other girls as rising stars in the relatively new sport. It covers the struggles, challenges, and rewards related to a professional skateboarding career.

3

The Arts: Stunning Creations

Luisa Roldán—La Roldana (Spain, 1656–1704)
First "official" woman sculptor and the only woman ever appointed as a royal sculptor in Spain.

I nheriting her father's artistic skills, Luisa Roldán had a propensity for getting her hands dirty. Known as La Roldana, she was recorded as the first woman sculptor in Spain. It was the seventeenth century.

Her father, Pedro Roldán, created religious sculptures in his workshop in Sevilla. His other children helped in the shop, but Luisa dug into clay and experimented with little-known substances like terra cotta, creating a different look in her works.

The sculpture business was steady since the Church was very active in acquiring art, displaying saints in statue form in processions, religious events, and in chapels and churches.

La Roldana became the primary source of income for her family when she began receiving more and more requests for her work. She married another sculptor, Luis Antonio de Los Arcos, when she was just fifteen and they made their living working side by side on their statues.

They received a commission as a team to make statues of angels and saints for a cathedral in Cadiz. This impressed an envious King Charles II in 1692, and he asked them to Madrid to be the official "Sculptor of the Chamber." Luisa made one of her greatest works, *Saint Michael and Christ Bearing the Cross*, for the king.

‣ Luisa Roldán had a propensity for getting her hands dirty. Known as La Roldana, she was recorded as the first woman sculptor in Spain. It was the seventeenth century.

Perhaps she got the break because of her family's longstanding business and artistic contributions to the court. At any rate, if she had not found her way to the king's court, her work might not have been included in any records of the official sculptor's guild—because she was a woman.

As it was, La Roldana and Luis were prolific and were able to turn out hundreds of works, both life-sized and smaller compositions. La Roldana's figures are characterized by clearly delineated profiles, thick locks of hair, flowing robes, and mystical faces with delicate eyes, furrowed brows, and rosy cheeks.

When the famine struck, La Roldana and her family no longer received payment for their work. They resorted to begging for a time until a new king came into power. He paid her and she was allowed a little more creative expression. She tried her hand at different mediums besides relief sculptures and wooden figures.

La Roldana became best known for her terra cotta creations of smaller groups of figures that she called "jewels." Up until then, these groups had only existed as architectural adornments. They would prefigure the Rococo porcelain groups with their "bits of still life, flowers, and animals."

Her son, Tomás, continued in his parents' footsteps, carrying on their name in the art world of Spain. Many of their works are still on worldwide display today.

Frida Kahlo (Mexico, 1907–1954)

The most famous Mexican female artist of all time, Frida Kahlo's self-portraits are unsurpassed and her work continues to gain in popularity as time passes.

Often described as disturbing and fantastical, the paintings of Frida Kahlo have mesmerized, terrorized, and revolutionized in vivid detail. The raw emotion that her art evokes makes it clear why she is the most famous female Mexican artist.

With a third of her work said to be self-portraits, the bloody, graphic, curious, and unforgiving interpretations and creations read like an autobiography, a window into her soul and psyche. Her paintings might also have been a form of therapy for her, to help her deal with the pain and frustration of her physical limitations.

> Frida Kahlo's interpretations and creations read like an autobiography, a window into her soul and psyche.

Born Magdalena Carmen Frida Kahlo y Calderon, Frida was just a teenager when she was in a horrific, life-altering bus accident. A metal rod had pierced her body. Her pelvis and spine were crushed, her right leg and foot were shattered. Doctors thought she would die.

She remained in a body cast for a year. Undergoing more than thirty-five operations, her fiery spirit pulled her through the ordeal just as it had when she was afflicted with polio. She would always walk with a limp, have chronic back problems, and never be able to have children, a thought that wracked her young body and filled her mind with anguish.

As she lay on her back recuperating, her mother gave her an easel and that is when she began painting. She depicted her physical pains and frustrations in each piece she painted.

Her art has often been described as surreal, but near the end of her lifetime she said, "I never painted dreams. I painted my own reality."

The third daughter of Guillermo and Matilada Kahlo, her father was a Hungarian-Jewish photographer who adored Frida's spunk. He saw a fire in her eyes and enrolled her in the Preparatoria (the National Preparatory School), the most prestigious educational institution in Mexico. There were only thirty-five girls out of 2,000 students.

When she met famed artist Diego Rivera, she was only fifteen, yet swore she would someday marry him. Not intimidated by his loud opinionated diatribes, she built up her courage to ask for a truthful critique of her work. Her art and her flippant fearlessness impressed him.

They married and through fiery tempers and creative outbursts complemented each other artistically and politically—both were communist militants. The difference in their artwork was as vast as the difference in their statures. Rivera's works were huge murals, public treasures with political overtones. Kahlo's works were disturbingly personal and revealing.

They traveled extensively throughout the world in artistic and social avant-garde circles, Frida wearing her traditional, flowing colorful Mexican attire and braided hair. It was Diego's work the public wanted to see, however.

During a trip to Detroit, Kahlo miscarried. Her anguish is visible in her most graphic and heartwrenching self-portrait, which she created shortly after she lost the baby. They still headed for New York so that Rivera could work on another commission—an ill-fated and scandalous mural for the Rockefeller Center. He wanted to remain in the United States. She wanted to return to the land and family she loved and missed.

Their marriage ripped apart. Rivera's betrayal with her younger sister devastated Kahlo further. They divorced in 1939. She cut off her hair, dressed in men's clothes, and in her despair and anguish, she hardly painted in two years—her self-imposed time of mourning.

In 1941, they remarried. Her work was also finally exhibited in New York. In France her work was praised by Kandinsky and Picasso, had good reviews, and resulted in a sale to the Louvre.

In 1953, her debut exhibit in her homeland at the Galeria de Arte Contemporaneo in Mexico City was her crowning glory. Her health was already in severe decline and she had to be carried in on a stretcher and four-poster bed for her grand entrance.

After her death, her popularity soared. Her home, the Blue House, was eventually turned into the Frida Kahlo Museum and her works were declared national treasures. In 2003, a five-by-seven drawing entitled "Self Portrait with Curly Hair" went on the auction block at Christie's for a reported $2 million. The painting was a rare work created during Kahlo's dry spell.

Amalia Hernández (Mexico, 1917–2000)
A pioneer of folk revival and founder of one of the world's pre-eminent ethnic dance companies, the Ballet Folklórico de México.

When Amalia Hernández asked her father for dance lessons at an early age, he hired the best instructors he could afford. A primary dancer with the Pavlova Dance Company and Madame Dambré from the Paris Opera Two came to their home to teach Hernández the magic of ballet.

Before long, she felt limited by the rigorous routines. She tried Spanish flamenco and modern dance. She learned the basic steps, the formality, and the techniques, but not one type of dance was emotionally fulfilling despite her reputable teachers. She felt no connection to the foreign dances and music.

She began teaching modern dance at the Fine Arts National Institute but her search continued. Hernández traveled throughout Mexico, to the mountainsides, the valleys, the little towns, the rural country, the coastline. She talked to people and explored each community's culture. She heard her own native music and saw her own native dance in every corner she visited. And she felt a connection.

In 1952 she left the institute to start her own company, her vision finally in place. She founded the Ballet Folklórico de México de Amalia Hernández.

This was her passion, to share the beauty and the richness of her culture through folkloric dances that had survived generations. The dances

celebrated life and Mexico's diverse culture and folklore through movement, music, and color.

An opportunity arose to air her uniquely choreographed ballets on
a weekly television program. It caught the attention of the Tourism
Department, which asked if she would travel to other countries to represent
Mexico in the arts. What began as a company of eight dancers that produced dances based on Mexican folklore for television and concert performance grew to be one of the world's pre-eminent ethnic ballet companies.

In 1959, their touring proved successful, starting with the Chicago,
Illinois, Pan-American Games. Based on that tour, the Mexican government offered to sponsor and support the ballet in any way necessary to
make her company one of the best ballets in the world.

Headquartered at the National Institute of Fine Arts in Mexico
City, the ballet toured worldwide. Ballet Folklórico was selected as an
official representative of the Mexican government at the Paris Festival of
Nations in 1961. Her troupe earned what would be its first award of more
than 200.

 Amalia Hernández's dances celebrated life and Mexico's diverse culture
and folklore through movement, music, and color.

The Ballet Folklórico continued to grow. Based at the Palacio de
Bellas Artes (Palace of Fine Arts) in Mexico City, the company has approximately seventy-five performers at one time but more than 20,000 students
and dancers have passed through the company and school.

Hernández continued to choreograph as well as dance in her productions until close to her retirement. The Ballet Folklórico won the
National Prize for Culture, Mexico's highest award in the arts. The
Hispanic Women's Council named Hernández International Woman of
the Year.

Her daughters Norma Lopez and Viviana Hernández continue
their mother's vision and tradition as the Ballet Folklórico's directors
and choreographers.

Alicia Alonso (Cuba, 1921–)

Prima ballerina and founder of the Cuban National Ballet, Alicia Alonso is also a world-renowned choreographer who has devoted her life to the ballet through her own career as a ballerina and as a teacher.

Every time Alicia Ernestina de la Caridad dei Cobre Martinez Hoyo heard music as a child, she wanted to move. She wore towels on her head so that she could imagine her hair long, streaming behind her as she floated through the room. When she was ten years old she joined a private ballet school. Her life changed the moment she put her hand on the barre.

Alonso has been on stage for more than sixty years. Known as one of the prima ballerinas of the last century, ballet and movement are her life. She brought that passion to other dancers when she founded the Cuban National Ballet, which started out as the Ballet Alicia Alonso in Havana in 1948.

She moved to New York with her husband, fellow dancer Fernando Alonso, in 1935. It was a dream dancing with the American Ballet Caravan, the predecessor of the New York City Ballet, and under the direction of George Balanchine, Leonide Massine, and Mikhail Fokine.

In 1940, she became a founding member of the American Ballet Theater (ABT) and made a name for herself as a prima ballerina. She starred in ballets like *Fall River Legend* by Agnes de Mille. In the back of her mind, she always had the desire to open a ballet school in her own country.

Tragedy struck just as her career was taking off when she suffered a detached retina, which blinded her. She had to remain in bed for a year or risk losing her eyesight permanently. During the traumatic year, she replayed in her mind the movements of every character in the ballet *Giselle*. Listening to the music repeatedly, tracing the choreography with her hands, and keeping it all in her mind's eye, she imagined herself learning the movements. When most of her sight returned, Alonso returned to the stage. *Giselle* became her signature ballet.

That inner sight helped Alonso create movement in her head as she choreographed for her own ballet company and school throughout the years. She wanted her dancers to dance with emotion, to respect the purity of original works, and to know they had a message to give and a story to tell. Technique was secondary.

The international spotlight shone on the brilliant careers of the expressive, award-winning dancers and artists of Ballet Alicia Alonso. Over the years, despite her failing eyesight, Alonso worked tirelessly behind the scenes, restaging classics so they were more in tune with contemporary audiences. She brought in high-profile friends to teach at her school and perform in her productions.

> Alicia Alonso is known as one of the prima ballerinas of the last century.

The success of Alonso's ballet company impressed Fidel Castro and he offered annual funding. Because of this connection, however, the company was not allowed to perform in the United States until 1975. Nonetheless, they traveled the world over and became internationally known for their classic performances.

Alonso was awarded the 1999 UNESCO award and the Pablo Picasso Medal for her outstanding contribution to dance. As the UNESCO Goodwill Ambassador, she developed and preserved classical dance through education and heritage.

At ABT's fiftieth anniversary in 1990 Alonso was seventy years old. Despite her failing eyesight she performed an excerpt from *Swan Lake*. Her performance ended to a standing ovation and thunderous applause.

Carmen Zapata (United States, 1927–)

Actress, producer, teacher, translator, and lecturer, Carmen Zapata is an Oscar nominee, cofounder of the first minority faction of the Screen Actors Guild, and founder of the Bilingual Foundation of the Arts. She earned a star on the Hollywood Walk of Fame in 2003.

$f$or Carmen Zapata, Broadway was home. She appeared in such musicals as *Oklahoma!*, *Bells Are Ringing*, and *Guys and Dolls*, starting in 1945. In order not to be typecast, she changed her name to Marge Cameron. Her effort backfired. She ventured into clubs with singing and comedy acts and received many roles in television and movies, but directors and producers who offered her the parts said she did not look all-American.

She reclaimed her real name, but in so doing was stereotyped in menial roles. Even though she continued to make a good living as an actress with high visibility, her dissatisfaction grew. She vowed to someday make a difference for Latinos in the business. Zapata held true to her vow, helping to form the first minority faction of the Screen Actors Guild. Eventually, she also founded the Bilingual Foundation for the Arts.

Raised in Spanish Harlem, New York, Zapata drew on the strength she inherited from her parents' strict upbringing. All she wanted to do, all she could ever see herself do, was act.

She held her head high when she came across racism as an ethnic actress and that dignity opened other doors. Approached by Cuban director Margarita Galban to lead in the Spanish-language play, *Seis Actores*, Zapata desperately wanted to return to the stage but was frightened to take a lead role in Spanish, something she had never done before. Galban persuaded her, and Zapata not only performed the role, but also fell in love with the beauty of Spanish literature and portraying it on the stage.

Although she was born in New York, her parents, who were from Argentina and Mexico, had spoken only Spanish at home. When Carmen had to go to school and learn English, it traumatized her. What made her transition easier was that she acted, sang, and played the piano and violin at school functions. Appreciation for the arts was universal. Her parents sacrificed much to provide her with dancing and music lessons.

Dubbed the "The First Lady of Hispanic Theater," she founded the Bilingual Foundation of the Arts in 1973. As the only full-time professional bilingual theater on the West Coast, it offers Latino actors, directors, and producers a venue to showcase the versatility of their talents while promoting Hispanic culture, literature, and tradition.

Zapata also founded the Teatro Para los Jovenes (Teen Theater Project), which works with middle and high school teens identified as "at risk." She has helped reach more than 2 million children and teens with the touring theater-in-education programs, which she hopes decreases the number of school dropouts.

Her acting career continued on stage, in television, and in films, yet she also worked as a producer, translator, lecturer, teacher, and narrator. Films include *Sol Madrid*, *Sister Act 2*, and *Boulevard Nights*. A few of the television shows among her 300 performances include *The Dick Van Dyke Show*, *Mod Squad*, *The Streets of San Francisco*, and the soap opera, *Santa Barbara*. For nine seasons she was featured in the PBS bilingual children's series, *Villa Alegre*.

She received a star on the Hollywood Walk of Fame in 2003 and a Hispanic Heritage Lifetime Achievement Award. She earned an Emmy Award for the documentary *Cinco Vidas* and an Oscar nomination for the documentary *Las Madres de la Plaza de Mayo*. An award likened to knighthood came from His Majesty Juan Carlos I, king of Spain, the Civil Order of Merit. It recognized Zapata's "commitment to Hispanic concerns within the arts and in the realm of community service."

Zapata continues to promote a better understanding and appreciation of Spanish literature and traditions in a bilingual format as commissioner of Los Angeles's Cultural Affairs Department.

Marisol Escobar—"Marisol" (France, 1930–)

A successful and highly sought-after artist of the pop art era, Marisol incorporated elements from her Latin-American roots using various mediums to create her unique expressive art.

*I*n the 1960s "pop art" reigned for a new generation of artists. Using objects and images from everyday life and popular culture, artists like Andy Warhol, Willem de Kooning, Jasper Johns, and Robert Rauschenberg led the movement.

Marisol reigned as the only woman pop art icon among her friends and colleagues.

Her work stood out from the other abstract expressionists because she incorporated elements of folk culture, primitive art, and mythology from her Latin-American roots. Some of her famous works were life-size sculptures and unique pieces such as *Baby Boy, Baby Girl, The Kennedys, The Party,* and *The Last Supper.*

Born in Paris, Marisol's parents, Gustavo Escobar and Josefina Hernandez, were wealthy and their social lifestyle allowed them to travel and live in Europe, Venezuela, and the United States. They settled in Los Angeles, California, when Marisol's mother died. The death had a profound effect on eleven-year-old Marisol.

She inflicted acts of penance upon herself as a teen and would walk on her knees until they bled. She kept a vow of silence for long periods, and tied ropes tightly around her midsection to emulate saints and martyrs. She escaped into her art, surrounded by spiritual and supernatural elements.

President Lyndon B. Johnson commissioned her to create a piece for the vice-presidential mansion in Washington, D.C., and her work filled the homes of Hollywood stars.

When Marisol was sixteen, she moved to Paris to study more than traditional painting at the prestigious Ecole des Beaux-Arts. When she returned to New York in 1950, she studied at the Art Students' League under her most influential mentor, the "dean of abstract expressionism," Hans Hofmann.

By 1954, she delved into terra cotta, wood, metal, and fabricated sculpture. Influenced by her studies of pre-Columbian and South American folk artifacts, she took classes in clay, plastering, and wood-carving, which would become the trademark of her unique sculptures.

She injected humor into her work through self-portraitures, using bits of clothing to adorn them. On the other end of the spectrum, her works depicting the Dust Bowl migrants, Father Damien with his leprosy marks, poor Cuban families, and Native Americans illuminate tragic human conditions.

After her first one-woman exhibition at the Leo Castelli Gallery in 1958, Marisol moved to Italy for a year to reassess her artistic direction. When she returned to New York, she had a renewed sense of purpose.

Her work became easily identifiable simply by "Marisol." Her renditions of famous paintings like Leonardo da Vinci's *Last Supper* caused a stir. Her works were photographed by *Life* magazine. Even though she was not comfortable in the spotlight, she appeared in two Andy Warhol movies, *The Kiss* and *13 Most Beautiful Women.*

President Lyndon B. Johnson commissioned her to create a piece for the vice-presidential mansion in Washington, D.C., and her work filled the homes of Hollywood stars. Her piece the *American Merchant Mariner's Memorial* stands at Battery Park in New York City. She designed stage sets for Martha Graham's *The Eyes of the Goddess* in 1992. One of her Native American creations became the United States' contribution to the Seville Fair in Spain.

The Vietnam War affected her deeply. She abandoned her studio for five years, exploring the Caribbean, South America, and the Far East. She took up scuba diving, and when she returned to her studio, her work featured underwater influences.

Her art changed focus or mediums every few years, but the bottom line was that "Marisol" was synonymous with expressive art.

Her works have been featured at the Museum of Modern Art in New York, the National Portrait Gallery in Washington, D.C., the Art Institute of Chicago, the Galeria de Arte Nacional and the Museo de Arte Contemporaneo in Venezuela, the Wallraf-Richartz Museum in Germany, the Tokushima Modern Art Museum in Japan, and the Hanover Gallery in London.

Graciela Daniele (Argentina, 1939–)

Choreographer, director, writer, and lyricist, Graciela Daniele started her career on Broadway as a dancer. A recipient of multiple Tony Award nominations for her work behind the scenes, her enduring talent keeps her in the spotlight.

Classical and creative versus controversial and criminal. Graciela Daniele choreographed stage works that pushed the envelope. Her creative streak challenged audiences just as often as it entertained them. Whether passionately good or bad, choreographer Daniele evoked emotion in whatever Broadway stage production she undertook.

Daniele began her stage career as a dancer. She was perfectly content as a ballet soloist for the Opera Ballet of Nice in France—until she saw the Paris production of *West Side Story.* The production moved her to such an extent that she knew she had to move to New York to pursue her career at a different level. Unable to speak English at the time, she did not let that stop her from trying out and earning spots on Broadway in a variety of musicals.

With a background in dance—she graduated from the Theatre Colón in Buenos Aires with a fine arts degree—Daniele made an impression on choreographer Matt Mattox, with whom she studied. She performed in his *What Makes Sammy Run.* The breakthrough gave her roles in other productions including *Coco, Follies, Chicago,* and *Promises, Promises.*

Before long, Daniele started designing her own musical numbers, and choreography seemed like an inviting detour on her career path. She got a break and served as choreographer at a Milliken industrial show at the Waldorf Astoria Hotel in New York. She choreographed works such as *The Most Happy Fella, A History of the American Film, Joseph and the Amazing Technicolor Dreamcoat,* and the New York Opera's *Naughty Marietta.*

Her star shot straight to the top, especially once she choreographed *The Pirates of Penzance,* which brought rave reviews, a Tony (Antoinette Perry) Award nomination, and the Los Angeles Critics Award. She earned another Tony nomination for her next effort, *The Rink,* in 1983, and more favorable reviews for *The Mystery of Edwin Drood.*

Her popularity and credibility plummeted with her next two works—*Tango Apasionado* and *Dangerous Games*, which she created and directed. She might have pushed the envelope a bit too far when these controversial and violent works backfired. They offended audiences and critics did not "get it"—"it" being the show's brutality, punctuated by violence in its treatment of women and approach to sex.

> ✥ Whether passionately good or bad, choreographer Daniele evoked emotion in whatever Broadway stage production she undertook.

Daniele's climb back to a level plateau was difficult but she never gave up. Although her next few works were generally reviewed as passable, they couldn't shake the shadowy repercussions from her previous works. Mostly she received mixed reviews. In the production *Chronicle of a Death Foretold*, an adaptation of the Gabriel García Márquez novella, a review said that the dancing fit every Latino musical cliché rather than letting the audience focus on the story.

Still, with all her determination, talent, and passion she made a comeback, starting with *Once on This Island*. Numerous directors, playwrights, and actors continued to work with her in a variety of theaters and professional companies. As choreographer and director, Daniele's creative spirit never faltered. Recovering from the setbacks, she came back even stronger on the stage and in the spotlight to earn ten Tony nominations, the Elán Award for choreography, six Drama Desk nominations, and the Fosse and Ovation awards.

Carolina Herrera (Venezuela, 1939–)

A top international fashion designer and wildly successful businesswoman, Carolina Herrera is an icon of class, elegance, and sophistication in the fashion world. In 1987 she became the third recipient of the MODA Award for Top Hispanic Designer.

*I*n the 1980s Carolina Herrera made the International Best Dressed List many times and was recognized as one of the Ten Most Elegant Women in the World by *Elle* magazine.

Herrera loved couture and decided to design her own fashionable creations. Today she oversees an international design firm that encompasses her signature fashion collection, a bridal collection, fragrances, color cosmetics, and accessories. The House of Herrera is her castle and she is one of the world's top fashion designers.

Herrera's designs have been worn by celebrities the world over, as well as by royalty such as Princess Elizabeth of Yugoslavia, the duchess of Feria (Spain), Countess Consuelo Crespi, U.S. First Ladies Nancy Reagan and Jacqueline Kennedy Onassis, and Britain's Princess Margaret. She designed the wedding dress for Caroline Kennedy, daughter of President John F. Kennedy.

Using the best fabrics, her lines are sleek and simple, graceful and tasteful. She still believes that taste is universal and that certain elements like sophistication, elegance, luxury, and simplicity are always constant indicators of fine fashion and couture. Her impeccable suits, dresses, and gowns are indicative of her line of thinking.

> Carolina Herrera believes that sophistication, elegance, luxury, and simplicity are constant indicators of fine fashion and couture. Her impeccable suits, dresses, and gowns are indicative of her line of thinking.

Born María Carolina Josefina Pacanins y Niño, Herrera's wealthy family came from prominent landowners and statesmen. Her dashing father, Guillermo Pacanins Acevedo, was an important figure in Venezuelan military aviation. He was governor of Caracas and a pioneer of commercial aviation. Her mother, María Cristina Niño de Pacanins, was a fashionable society woman. She taught the young Herrera to look and behave with a certain grace and noble sensibility, drawing strength from discipline and structure.

Herrera attended her first couture fashion show in Paris with her grandmother when she was thirteen. The experience definitely influenced how she looked at clothes from that moment on. For her first social ball, she wore a white gown from the House of Lavin.

Herrera's first marriage ended in divorce, but in 1969 she married Reinaldo Herrera, the editor of *Vanity Fair* and another native Venezuelan from noble blood. She designed her own open collar, just-above-the-knee length wedding dress. They settled at Reinaldo's Venezuelan mansion, La Vega, which was built in 1590.

Their jet-set lifestyle suited Herrera. She spoke three languages—English, Spanish, and French—traveled extensively, and was elegantly dressed as she raised her four daughters. She continued choosing her wardrobe from world-famous designers but found herself making her own adjustments to them. Eventually she started working with seamstresses—directing her ideas since she did not know how to make patterns or cut fabric. She also started designing outfits for friends.

Her friends Diana Vreeland, *Vogue* magazine editor, and Count Crespi urged Herrera to design a test line in 1981. Her first show was such a success, that Herrera moved her entire family to New York, where she started Carolina Herrera, Ltd.

She was creative. Dubbed "Our Lady of the Sleeves" early in her career by *Women's World* magazine, her trademark was plunging necklines, big fairy-tale sleeves, and broad-shouldered creations. She designed these outfits for women who were often at dinner banquets and seen only from the waist up.

Stores started buying her designs immediately. Her business has expanded to include collections of knitwear, handbags, leather goods, accessories, and fragrances. Her daughters have collaborated with her on various lines.

Herrera won the 1987 MODA Award for Top Hispanic Designer, the third such recipient, alongside Oscar de la Renta and Adolfo.

Tania León (Cuba, 1943–)

One of the first Latina orchestral conductors and a founding member of the Dance Theatre of Harlem, Tania León is the recipient of numerous awards as a world-renowned conductor, composer, and educator.

oleros, bossa nova, popular—all of it is music to Tania León's ears. As a composer, conductor, and music director, contemporary music is Tania's inspiration—and she in turn has inspired contemporary music.

In the 1970s, León never imagined that she could be a conductor until her colleagues urged her to pick up a baton. She became one of the first Latina orchestral conductors in the world when she conducted the Juilliard Orchestra performance, which was accompanying the Dance Theater in Italy. It brought a new twist to her musical repertoire.

With a background in violin, piano, and music theory, Tania graduated from the National Conservatory of Music in Havana, earning a degree in music education in 1965. She immediately went to work performing piano solos and served as music director of a Havana-based television station.

When she moved to the United States in 1968, she became one of the founding members of the New York Dance Theatre of Harlem. Within a year, she became the first music director and a composer for the theater—a position she held for ten years. She established the theater's music department and orchestra.

After earning a master's in music composition at New York University in 1975, she formally studied conducting with Lazlo Halasz, one of the founders of the New York City Opera. León went on to found the Brooklyn Philharmonic Community Concert Series in 1977, where she was a conductor for more than ten years.

León presents her interpretations of many classical and modern scores, and composes her own works. Incorporating her love of different types of music, she blends gospel and jazz as well as Latin-American and African elements into her pieces to create a highly rhythmic signature beat.

She has served as conductor and musical director of *The Wiz* on Broadway and *Maggie Magalita* at the Kennedy Center for the Performing Arts. Other venues include the Whitney Museum, the New York Philharmonic, the Beethovenhalle Orchestra in Bonn, the Leipzig, the Santa Cecilia Orchestra in Rome, and the National Symphony Orchestra of South America.

The scores she has written include *Paisanos Semos* for solo guitar, *Momentum* and *Rituál* for solo piano, and *Indígena*, which is a collection of her chamber music. Her orchestral work *Desde* was premiered by the American Composers Orchestra in 2001 in Carnegie Hall. *Drummin*, a full-length cross-cultural work for indigenous percussionists and orchestra, was commissioned and performed by Miami Light Project and the New World Symphony in 1997. Her works have been performed at the Festival Centro Historico in Mexico City, the Munich Biennale, the Grand Théâtre de Genève in Switzerland, the Opéra de Nancy et de Lorraine in France, and the St. Pölten Festspielhaus in Austria.

Believing that music is a universal language, León offers master classes to youths to keep classical music alive well into future generations. She has been guest lecturer at universities such as Yale, Harvard, and the Musikschule in Hamburg.

> Incorporating her love of different types of music, Tania León blends gospel and jazz as well as Latin-American and African elements into her pieces to create a highly rhythmic signature beat.

She received the CINTAS Award in composition, the National Council of Women in the United States Achievement Award, the ASCAP Composer's Award, and the New York Governor's Lifetime Achievement Award. She served as Latin-American Music Advisor to the American Composers Orchestra until 2001.

Miriam Colón (Puerto Rico, 1945–)

Actress and founder of the Puerto Rican Traveling Theater and the Nuevo Círculo Dramático, the first Spanish-language theater in New York. Miriam Colón is the recipient of an Obie Award for lifetime achievement in theater.

Wanting to be remembered as the artist who never forgot her people, Miriam Colón dedicated her life to the performing arts. Her goal was simple: to promote the Hispanic community's artistic development and to increase recognition and opportunities for Hispanics in the performing arts.

Colón founded the Puerto Rican Traveling Theater in 1966 and still serves as its artistic director. The bilingual company stages plays by Latinos, as well as the classics. She also founded the Nuevo Círculo Dramático (the New Dramatic Circle), the first Spanish-language theater in New York.

Born in Puerto Rico in 1945, Colón found her greatest source of encouragement in her mother, who urged her to go into acting if that was her heart's passion. Colón attended the University of Puerto Rico and then earned a scholarship to the Erwin Piscator Dramatic Workshop and Technical Institute in New York City. She was the first Puerto Rican student admitted into the New York Actors Studio.

She was right where she was meant to be. The experience opened her eyes to the endless possibilities within the field of acting. She made contributions to the entertainment field by writing plays, working behind the scenes, and performing on stage, television, and in film before starting her own theater group.

Her Broadway debut was in 1953 in *In the Summer House*. In film, Colón got her break when she was selected by Marlon Brando to be among the cast of *One-Eyed Jacks*. Brando directed and produced the film.

She appeared in many other films, including *Possession of Joe Delaney* with Shirley MacLaine, *Back Roads* with Sally Field, *Scarface* with Al Pacino, and *All the Pretty Horses* with Matt Damon in 2001. She has also appeared in more than 250 television shows and commercials.

Appointed to the New York Council on the Arts by then-governor Nelson Rockefeller, Colón held the position for more than ten years.

Her influence expanded. The Puerto Rican Traveling Theater nurtured Hispanic playwrights, acting talent, and education in the dramatic arts. It offered a forum for numerous plays by dramatists from Chile, Spain, Venezuela, Colombia, Brazil, and Mexico, as well as her native Puerto Rico. Performances were alternately in English and Spanish in the heart of communities, whether as street performances in one of New York's boroughs or on tour in Spain, Mexico, Colombia, or Puerto Rico.

> Miriam Colón was appointed to the New York Council on the Arts. She held the position for more than ten years.

Colón earned the Obie Award for lifetime achievement in theater and the Dramalogue Award for outstanding achievement in theater. She also earned the White House Hispanic Heritage Award in 1990 and an Athena Award from the New York Commission on the Status of Women.

Zarela Martínez (Mexico, 1945–)

Award-winning chef, author, restaurateur, and humanitarian, Zarela Martínez is highly celebrated for the unique cuisine that she creates through combining authentic culinary elements from various regions of Mexico.

For Chef Zarela Martínez, cooking means sharing and a way of "speaking" to people. It is universal in the way it celebrates and honors those who eat the meals she creates. It embraces nearly every aspect of culture and human relationships.

If the image of Mexican food is tacos and enchiladas, Chef Zarela Martínez dispels those notions every time she unveils a new culinary creation true to her native Sonora, Mexico. Dubbed "The True Goddess of Mexican Cuisine," she adds creative flair to the exquisite, the tasty, and the beautifully presented dishes she invents.

65

Zarela started cooking to supplement her social worker income in her hometown. She was married to a widower with three children and was pregnant with twins. She sold Christmas cookies, catered parties, and became more creative with each job she undertook.

Martínez traveled throughout Mexico, tasting and learning, and she applied what she learned to her own way of thinking. She layered flavors and combined elements from different culinary regions. Her signature dishes included Sweet Corn Fritters, Stuffed Chilies and Authentic Guacamole, Poblanos Rellenos, Camarónes al Ajillo, and Salpicón de Huachinango (Red Snapper Hash), which she adapted from a dish she sampled in a Tampico-based bar.

> Dubbed "The True Goddess of Mexican Cuisine," Zarela Martínez adds creative flair to the exquisite, the tasty, and the beautifully presented dishes she invents.

She moved to El Paso, Texas, where she learned the ropes of catering and earned her way to becoming a full-time chef. When Paul Prudhomme noticed her work and took her under his wing, new opportunities opened to her. Martínez found herself in the national spotlight when in 1983 she designed the menu for a meal at the California ranch of former United States President Ronald Reagan, in honor of the visiting Queen Elizabeth II.

She took her work on the road and headed for New York where she eventually served as executive chef for Cafe Marimba. Then she made the leap to open her own restaurant.

In 1987 she opened Zarela's, a restaurant in the heart of New York City, to bring to the city a vivacious alternative and an eye-opener to stereotypical Mexican food.

An award-winning chef, Zarela has received loads of accolades. She developed a catering service, served as master chef on several television shows, including *Julia Child: Cooking with Master Chefs,* and *Martha Stewart Living.* She offers cooking classes, makes other television appearances, and has led culinary demonstrations at huge food and cooking conferences, such as Expo Comida.

In an effort to help cooks and diners everywhere discover the unique Mediterranean and African accents of the regional cooking of Veracruz, she produced a thirteen-part public television series called *Zarela! La Cocina Veracruzana*. With a companion cookbook, *Zarela's Veracruz*, she offers the best smorgasbord of dishes in several mediums.

She serves as a marketing consultant for big-name clients such as Best Foods, Nestlé, Marriott, and Taco Bell. Her books include *Food from My Heart*, which weaves her autobiography together with the exotic recipes, and *The Food and Life of Oaxaca*.

That passion for cooking might just be in the genes. Zarela's son, Aaron Sanchez, opened his own restaurant, Paladar, and is cohost of the Food Network show *Melting Pot*. Zarela helped her daughter, Marissa Sanchez, open the restaurant Danzon.

A believer in giving back to the community, Zarela works with City Meals on Wheels, the New York Public Library, the Women's Venture Fund, and the Hispanic Children's Fund. Her restaurant is now a New York landmark for lovers of authentic regional Mexican food.

Judith Baca (United States, 1946–)

Artist Judith Baca has devoted her life to bringing together different cultures and inspiring appreciation of diversity through community mural projects like the highly acclaimed Great Wall of Los Angeles.

"If we cannot imagine peace as an active concept, how can we ever hope for it to happen?"

—Judith Baca in *Latino Biographies*

The neighborhood was already covered with graffiti. Tough students had driven prospective community center directors out of town. The teens   67 were heading for dead-end lives. Judith Baca took them off the streets, out of her classrooms, and away from their gangs and brought them together to express themselves through art on a grand scale.

Baca's answer was painting murals. Painting together made turf wars, racial differences, sexism, and segregation fade away. They worked together peacefully. Their murals covered entire walls on buildings and told stories about their communities, preserved their history, gave them a voice, and promoted acceptance of differences between cultural groups.

> Judith Baca realized that having her art exhibited in galleries was not as important as having artwork that was accessible and stirred reaction.

Baca saw the bigger picture—bringing peace and harmony to a troubled world through a mural movement would also preserve the generations-old, rich tradition of Mexican muralists.

Born to immigrant parents, Baca never knew her musician father, but she thrived in her matriarchal household and had a deep connection to her grandmother. She had a strong sense of both American history and her Latino roots. She did not speak English when she started school but a teacher allowed her to work on art during lessons.

When she attended California State University at Northridge, she felt isolated from any sense of her own culture. She missed her family, there were only a handful of Latinos and African Americans, and the art she studied was of European influence.

When her grandmother asked her to explain her abstract work, Baca looked deep within herself to analyze what she was doing and why. She realized that having her art exhibited in galleries was not as important as having artwork that was accessible and stirred reaction. She wanted her art to be real and speak to people like her grandmother.

After earning her bachelor's and master's degrees in art, she went to Mexico to study the great muralists Diego Rivera, José Clemente Orozco, and David Siqueiros. Their work moved Baca, and she realized that was the type of artwork she was meant to do.

She returned to the United States ready to teach mural painting at her old high school, but she was fired for taking part in peace marches protesting the United States' participation in the Vietnam War.

In 1974, Baca was appointed director of the City of Los Angeles Citywide Mural Project. She worked as a roving teacher, going from schools to parks to get kids to paint. She started her own group, Las Vistas Nuevas, made up of twenty teens from four different gangs and neighborhood groups and expanded the mural project to the entire city of Los Angeles. After securing financial backing, more than 1,000 people created more than 250 murals.

Among her best-known works are *La Memoria de Nuestra Tierra*, located in the Denver Airport, and *Female Dragon* in the Interior Library of the California Institute for Women.

The half-mile-long Great Wall of Los Angeles is the most acclaimed. Created over five summers, more than 400 youths, artists, and historians produced a historical timeline mural with information on ethnic groups and women not normally taught in public schools. It chronicles the history of California with images of Chumash Indian life and culture, farm union organizers, black activists fighting for equal housing, and the plight of Japanese Americans during World War II and on through the 1950s.

In 1976 Baca founded the Social and Public Art Resource Center (SPARC), a nonprofit public art program. She also developed the Great Walls Unlimited: Neighborhood Pride Program, to create murals in nearly every ethnic neighborhood in Los Angeles.

In 1987 she began her largest mural project, the *World Wall: A Vision of the Future Without Fear* to promote the theme of peace and cooperation among cultural groups from around the world. The portable mural, painted on moveable panels for easier transportation, traveled to seven countries where artists painted their own visions of peace.

Lourdes Lopez (Cuba, 1958–)

A long-time principal dancer with the New York City Ballet, Lourdes Lopez is founder of the Cuban Artists Fund and now serves as executive director of the renowned George Balanchine Foundation.

Corrective orthopedic shoes looked nothing like the delicate ballet pointe shoes sitting next to them. The young Lourdes Lopez wanted so desperately to slip on the pointe shoes, but she had to wait until her orthopedic problems were corrected.

When she grew up, she wore the ballet shoes for a living, rising above her earlier setback to become a principal dancer with the New York City Ballet.

Born in Havana, Cuba, Lopez lived there only a year and was raised in Miami, Florida. When she no longer needed to wear the special orthopedic shoes, her doctor suggested that dance exercises could help strengthen her legs further.

Lopez and her older sister took ballet lessons after school, learning the names of steps, the music, the story ballets, and exercises she could perform daily to improve. When a class assignment had Lourdes focus on a career, she opened the encyclopedia and found six ballet companies in the United States alone. She knew what she wanted to be.

Her dedication in practicing six days a week sacrificed her social life but something inside her drove her to continue. When she turned ten, she auditioned for the Joffrey School and the School of American Ballet, and Lopez was offered scholarships by both. She chose the School of American Ballet so that she could continue her studies in Miami. When her friends had an opportunity to see her perform, they finally saw what she spent her time on. Their reaction validated her passion.

She moved to New York City when she turned fourteen to attend the School of American Ballet. Lopez met with George Balanchine, a founder and choreographer of the New York City Ballet. Since she was still in school, he invited her to join the New York City Ballet as an apprentice. Right after her sixteenth birthday, and after stepping up her classes to finish her schooling, she was accepted into the company as a member of the corps.

Her career skyrocketed as she led the corps in the company's repertory including *The Nutcracker*, as Coquette in *La Sonnambula*, and in a principal role in Divertimento No. 15. She was promoted to soloist in 1981. In 1984, she became a principal dancer.

Lopez underwent foot surgery in 1989 and had to come to grips with the possibility that it could be the end of her dance career. She remained optimistic and spent time with her husband and daughter, continued her education in child psychology, worked with the New York City Ballet Education Department, and did some dance numbers on *Sesame Street*, a public television children's series. She received a Gold Medal of Honor for her volunteer work with underprivileged children, which included teaching an integrated arts program she created.

When a class assignment had her focus on a career, Lourdes opened the encyclopedia and found six ballet companies in the United States alone. She knew what she wanted to be.

After her recuperation, she performed on world tours, appeared with the New York City Ballet on the PBS series *Dance in America*, and in the film version of *The Nutcracker* in 1993.

When she retired in 1995, she began a second career as a freelance cultural arts reporter. Lopez returned to Cuba for the first time in 1997 to cover the National Ballet of Cuba. She felt a connection to the dancers and artists there and was moved to do something for them. Lopez founded the Cuban Artists Fund, a not-for-profit organization that provides supplies and nurtures Cuban and Cuban-American artistic vitality and spirit. The fund helps build cross-cultural understanding through the arts in all mediums while celebrating and bridging differences.

In September 2002, Lopez was appointed executive director of the George Balanchine Foundation, which promotes the highest standards of excellence in dance and the arts throughout the world.

Maria Martinez-Cañas (Cuba, 1960–)

Maria Martinez-Cañas's provoking works are widely exhibited throughout the United States.

The simplicity in the photographic art by Maria Martinez-Cañas is striking. Whether she is spotlighting the beauty of nature, depicting feelings of isolation, embracing the cycle of life and death, or lifting spirituality, the simplicity touches a chord.

Born in Cuba but raised in Puerto Rico and the United States, her work has expressed her own feelings of connection and division between the cultures. She has worked with issues of isolation and belonging, and addressed the feelings of displacement faced by Cubans leaving their homeland. At times, she incorporates the plants and flowers indigenous to Cuba and Puerto Rico in such a way that shows chaos and symmetry of life under the soil, yet represents life experiences.

Her fascination with flowers grew when she came across the seventeenth-century book *Hortus Eystettensis*, a catalogued presentation of a variety of flowers. She was struck by the power projected by each specimen's austerity on the printed page.

In one of her art forms, Martinez-Cañas creates her own negatives "by drawing, cutting, and collaging information onto Rubylith, a film-covered acetate." She has layered flower petals, snail forms, bulb roots, fossils, and broken tree limbs in the photographs. Her work shows the duality of nature in its potential to nourish as well as its power to destroy.

Martinez-Cañas's most prominent work is on display at Miami International Airport. Other works have been featured in major collections at the Museum of Modern Art, the national Museum of American Art in Washington, D.C., the San Francisco Museum of Modern Art, the Los Angeles County Museum of Art, the Museum of Contemporary Art in Chicago, and many corporate collections as well.

Her works were among those on display in "Photography's Multiple Roles," a traveling exhibit organized by the Museum of Contemporary Photography in Chicago. The artists' works were cited as the most ambitious exhibitions of twentieth-century photography. A coffee-table book of the same name resulted.

Her works have also appeared in other books such as *Encounters, Photography by Cintas Fellows*, and *Black Totems: Photography by Maria Martinez-Cañas*. She is also listed in *Women in Photography International*, a bibliography of books by and about women photographers.

Martinez-Cañas earned her bachelor's of fine arts degree from the Philadelphia College of Art and a master's of fine arts from the School of the Art Institute of Chicago. She lives in Little Havana in Florida, renowned as a cultural mecca for bohemian lifestyles.

Christy Turlington (United States, 1969–)
Successful supermodel and businesswoman who is the face of Calvin Klein and Maybelline.

The Metropolitan Museum of Art commissioned 120 castings of Christy Turlington's face to replace the heads of its mannequins, immortalizing her beauty in a nontraditional way.

As an international supermodel, Turlington has that type of unforgettable face that leaves a lasting impression. Her olive-skinned good looks speak to everywoman. Her success in the fashion world confirmed the advertising truth of the 1990s: ethnic sells.

By the time she was in her mid-twenties, she was a campaign girl for Calvin Klein and Maybelline, she had already appeared on the cover of *Cosmopolitan* four times, and was earning over $1 million a year from modeling alone. She is a supermodel to the nth degree.

Although she was born and raised just outside of San Francisco, California, she traveled extensively because her Texas-born father was a pilot for Pan-Am Airlines. He met Christy's mother, a stewardess from El Salvador, when they worked together on a flight to Hawaii.

They moved to Coral Gables, Florida, and when she was only eleven,

Christy was discovered by photographer Dennie Cody while out riding in a competitive horse show. She started modeling after school, became a requested model, and earned a decent living locally.

When her father suffered a heart attack, they moved back to the San Francisco area. When she turned fifteen, she and her mother traveled to Paris to see if she actually had a chance to succeed at the modeling business as a high-end professional. She did not receive the reaction she had hoped for.

> With her mother by her side, Christy Turlington returned to New York, determined to break into the field of professional modeling. They pounded the pavement. On the day before she was to return to California, she received "the call" from *Vogue*.

Still, with her mother by her side, she returned to New York, determined to break into the field of professional modeling. They pounded the pavement and on the day before she was to return to California, she received "the call" from *Vogue*.

The rest was a whirlwind. Photo shoots took her throughout New York and Paris, and though she returned in time to attend school in the fall, her career was launched. The following summer she moved to New York permanently and modeled for Eileen Ford.

A change in the fashion tide brought brunettes to the forefront. Turlington found herself requested for countless fashion and modeling jobs, alongside Linda Evangelista, Cindy Crawford, and Naomi Campbell. She worked with top photographers such as Herb Ritts, Irving Penn, and Steven Meisel. Designers such as Chanel, Versace, Christian Lacroix, and Azzedine Alaia requested her for their fashion shows.

In 1987 she was selected for the cover of Italian *Vogue*. In 1988, after already working on an ad campaign for Calvin Klein's Obsession perfume, she was hired to be the face of Klein's Eternity fragrance line. She earned almost $3 million for three months' worth of work.

In 1992, she signed a five-year, nonexclusive contract deal with

Maybelline, the cosmetics giant, which allowed her to continue working with noncompetitive ad campaigns or runway jobs.

Turlington keeps herself grounded despite her high-profile career by promoting breast cancer research, animal rights, and community needs. Her entire proceeds from a bathing suit calendar, for example, went to a relief fund aiding the poor in El Salvador.

With a degree in literature and philosophy, she hopes to try her hand at writing books someday. For now, she tries different business ventures. She and three other supermodel partners developed the Fashion Cafe in 1995, a theme restaurant for New York tourists. She is also a partner in the Up & Down Club, an acid blues club in California.

Yasmin Hernandez (United States, 1975–)

A Cornell University graduate in fine arts, Yasmin Hernandez's culturally, politically, and spiritually inspired art incites passion by addressing significant and often controversial contemporary and historical issues.

Thirteen-year-old Yasmin Hernandez watched Bob Ross's *Joy of Painting* series on PBS television and did her own renditions of his lessons. She kept a portfolio of those works and used it to apply to the LaGuardia High School of Music and Art and the Performing Arts, where she was accepted as an art major. She went on to earn her fine arts degree at Cornell University.

Hernandez's culture now inspires her art. The recurring themes of culture, politics, and spirituality in her work reflect her indigenous, African, and Spanish ancestries.

Many historical events inspire Hernandez's creativity. She finds value in negative aspects and dark periods in history. She tries to unveil what has resulted from racism, slavery, and colonialism. Through her creative process she uncovers historical fragments of her culture. When she pieces them together, she reveals perspectives she is compelled to share through her art. Her intellectual interpretations incite passion, pride, and anger. They may offend as well as educate.

⌘ The recurring themes of culture, politics, and spirituality in Yasmin Hernandez's art reflect her indigenous, African, and Spanish ancestries.

In one exhibit in the late 1990s, "A Sense of Self: Contemporary Ethnic Women Artists," she dedicated her painting *U.S. Colonial Penitentiary* to the Puerto Rican women she considers political prisoners in the United States, arrested and imprisoned for seditious conspiracy.

Superimposed on a Puerto Rican flag is a woman in chains, a United States flag draped around her. Around the woman there are words written in ink, with actual accounts of sexual abuse the women have been subjected to while in prison. It spoke of injustice.

Love, sacrifice, and struggle also inspire Hernandez. She covers stereotypes, objectification of women, and issues of ethnic and gender identity. Her works also express the beauty of cultural traditions passed down through generations.

Hernandez was born in Brooklyn, New York, to an artistic family with strong Puerto Rican roots. Her mother was into fashion design and arts and crafts, and her brother kept sketchbooks of his works. Hernandez was initially a dancer when she applied to the creative arts high school but felt that a greater force kept her from auditioning for a dance spot and urged her onto a new path as a visual artist.

She often uses transparent glazes and collaging of text and images in her paintings. The multilayering also represents the multiple layers of influence of the Caribbean and urban experience. She never paints without music, inspired by musicians like Eddie Palmieri and Ray Barretto. She would like to someday re-create their music on canvas.

Hernandez considers women the main educators in the world. Through her art, Hernandez is a storyteller, offering a different recording of history.

Tina Ramirez (Venezuela)

Founder of the pre-eminent Ballet Hispanico, Tina Ramirez is the recipient of numerous awards for her work as a dancer and educator, and for her devotion to fostering cultural awareness and enriching the lives of disadvantaged youths through programs in the arts.

Ballerina Tina Ramirez honored her dance and her promises. It was one such promise that brought her to New York City with a vision to start a dance program for inner-city youth.

She founded the Ballet Hispanico, pouring all her dance knowledge, expertise, and passion into it. Described as a visionary, Ramirez created Ballet Hispanico to blend ballet, modern, and ethnic dance forms with elements of salsa, flamenco, meringue, mambo, and other dances from places such as Spain, Mexico, the Caribbean, and Central and South America. Ballet Hispanico was soon known as a leading interpreter of Latino culture through dance.

The school's students have performed for almost 2 million people on three continents. The organization has given an outlet and hope to inner-city children, fostering an appreciation of the arts. Former students have gone on to bigger horizons including Jennifer Lopez, Leelee Sobieski, Rachel Ticotin, and Michael DeLorenzo.

Ramirez's passion for dance started when she was a young girl. She convinced her father, a Mexican bullfighter, and her mother, a Puerto Rican educator, to let her have a go at ballet. She traveled the world over, studying under respected names such as Lola Bravo, Alexandra Danilova, and Anna Sokolow. Her professional career began with the Federico Rey Dance Company and she toured extensively throughout Spain. On Broadway, she performed in *Kismet* and *Lute Song*; on television, she appeared in an adaptation of *Man of La Mancha*.

A back injury when she reached her thirties forced her to give up dancing. Instead of seeing it as a traumatic devastation, she saw it as a turning point in her life. Through all her touring and appearances, she had still felt a void in her life.

About the same time, Ramirez's former dance instructor, Lola Bravo retired. She contacted Ramirez to take over her studio, wanting someone who would continue her tradition of teaching children. Ramirez returned to New York to keep her promise, and set out on a path toward her divine destiny.

She would end up teaching dance for forty years, becoming a pioneer in the field of art education. She was a catalyst in changing and improving the lives of inner-city children.

In 1967 Ramirez started Operation High Hopes at Bravo's studio. The professional dance training program for minority and economically disadvantaged inner-city children gave them a chance to be expressive through movement while educating audiences about Hispanic culture. As students progressed, self-esteem and self-awareness bloomed. They became empowered with their newfound confidence.

The school evolved to encompass a variety of techniques and professional training in ballet, Spanish, and modern dance, and a much more intense and diversified program for advanced students and teachers. However, Hispanic influences remained at the core of the program.

Described as a visionary, Ramirez created Ballet Hispanico to blend ballet, modern, and ethnic dance forms with elements of salsa, flamenco, meringue, mambo, and other dances.

As she received more and more requests to have the students perform, Ramirez established the Ballet Hispanico in 1970. She added the award-winning Primeros Pasos, a nationwide public school program that brings dance to more than 25,000 children and teachers across the country.

Ramirez serves on the advisory commission for Cultural Affairs and the National Endowment for the Arts. She won the *Dance Magazine* Award, one of the highest honors in the dance field, the Hispanic Heritage Award for her outstanding achievement in education, and the GEMS (television network) Woman of the Year Award. The New York Governor's Arts Award recognized Ballet Hispanico's outstanding contribution to the quality of New York cultural life.

Suzanna Guzmán (United States)

World-renowned opera singer of stage, film, and television, and recipient of the Placido Domingo Award for contributions to the Latino community.

Suzanna Guzmán wanted to break stereotypes about opera singers. She learned that many Latino children had preconceived notions of what a female opera singer looked like. She was big, wore blond braids, sang really loud, and was intimidating.

When they met Guzmán, the only thing that fit the image was that "she sang really loud."

A world-renowned mezzo-soprano, Guzmán performs in operas around the world, but she has also made it her mission to enlighten others about opera, especially Latino children, through her one-woman show, *Don't Be Afraid, It's Just Opera.*

She herself never knew opera until she was practically immersed in it. Growing up in East Los Angeles, Guzmán was the daughter of a fireman father and a stay-at-home mother. In school, she loved to sing and act and be the class clown. Her biggest musical influence was her grandmother Avilia, who belted out Texas *rancheras* at the top of her voice at the drop of a hat. It gave Guzmán goosebumps, and she wanted to have that same effect on others with her own voice. Even though she never had piano or voice lessons, there was always music around the house, and she joined a rock band when she was eighteen. She played weddings, small gigs, and a short stint of small towns in a northwest circuit tour.

A friend urged her to take voice lessons to make sure she did not damage her voice completely. Shortly thereafter, she auditioned for *Carmen* and got the title role. She had always loved languages, theater, and passion, and *Carmen* had it all.

Even without the extensive operatic background, she played the part for one year, but the experience made her want to learn to read music, develop her repertoire, and learn other languages. Once she did, the opera world opened up to her in all its glory.

Guzmán has appeared with many international opera companies

including the Metropolitan Opera, Kennedy Center's Washington Opera, Geneva's Grand Théâtre, l'Opéra de Nice, and Dresden Musikfestspiele. She has brought hundreds of classical characters to life in *Carmen*, *Rigoletto*, *Madama Butterfly*, *La Traviata*, *Goya*, and many other performances.

As an associate artist with the Los Angeles Opera and an alumni of Ezio Pinza Council for American Singers of Opera, Guzmán also enjoys taking risks to perform in new works, such as Gabriel García Márquez's *Florencia en el Amazonas*. *Florencia* was the first Spanish-language opera written for a United States opera company and used Spanish magic realism.

> A friend urged her to take voice lessons. Shortly thereafter Suzanna Guzmán auditioned for *Carmen* and got the title role.

Guzmán has appeared in film, television, and in musical theater productions such as *The King and I*, opposite Yul Brynner, *Showboat*, *Carousel*, and *West Side Story*. She works with inner-city schools with the Bilingual Foundation of the Arts and the University of California, Los Angeles (UCLA), outreach group, Design for Sharing. As host of a weekly radio show, *Los Angeles Opera: LIVE!* she promotes a better understanding of opera for the public.

Guzmán received the Placido Domingo Award for her community work and was honored as one of the nation's Outstanding Latinos in Music, a Triumfadora (success) in the Silver Millennium 2000 magazine edition of *People en Español*. She received the El Angel Award from the Bilingual Foundation of the Arts and was honored by NBC in 1995 for her contributions as a role model to the Latino community in a profile, "Suzanna Guzmán, Outstanding Latina."

Viviana Guzmán (Chile, 1970–)

A graduate of the Juilliard School and the recipient of numerous awards, Viviana Guzmán maintains a prolific orchestral and solo recording career as a virtuoso flutist. She also shares her talent through teaching and is a published poet.

ivana Guzmán's hips were broken and completely displaced when she was born. She underwent numerous surgeries over the years. During the times when she was completely immobile after an operation, she found if she was propped up on her bed just so, she could play the piano with her right hand. Music was her relief from constant physical pain and rehabilitation that left her in wheelchairs, on crutches, or bedridden.

She developed an ear for and an appreciation of music.

When Guzmán was four years old, she heard a beautiful melody on the radio. Her heart turned in that moment and her life changed forever. She was determined to find the instrument that had impacted her so deeply.

She now has more than 100 flutes in her collection and she plays magically for audiences around the world.

Called a "musical virtuoso," she has performed as an orchestral musician in more than eighty concerts a year throughout the world, in fifty-six countries, with legendary greats like Mikhail Baryshnikov and Placido Domingo.

She has performed at Carnegie Hall in New York, the New World Symphony in Florida, Avery Fisher Hall in Lincoln Center, and as principal flutist with the Texas Opera Theater Orchestra. She worked on the Broadway musical *Sunset Boulevard* with Glenn Close, appeared on a John Denver national television music special, and was featured on National Public Radio and PBS television specials. Her music video aired on Univision television in thirty countries.

The whirlwind began early in her life. When she was just fifteen, Guzmán was a soloist with the Houston Youth Symphony. Her debut recital at New York's Carnegie Recital Hall came after winning the 1991 Young Artist Auditions of Artists International.

Initially she attended Rice University to study medicine, but her passion for music dictated her destiny. She transferred to the Juilliard School on scholarship, where she earned her master's degree. She studied with Jean-Pierre Rampal and James Galway.

She has since recorded with various record labels including Polygram, Well-Tempered World, and Sugo. She performs with ensembles like Festival of Four and Performers of the World. As one of the Divas Latinas, she performs "The Music of Passion" to critical acclaim with Argentine tango dancer Tianne Frias and flamenco dancer and singer Kristelle Monterrosa.

In her world travels, Guzmán makes up for lost time. She got married in a Budapest castle and married the same man again in the middle of the Atlantic Ocean. She has ridden a camel in Luxor, danced all night in Rio during Carnival, and snorkeled with stingrays near the Devil's Island Coast. She finds inspiration for her writing from areas like California's Big Sur, sitting on a ridge overlooking the Pacific Ocean.

She is living testimony in her belief that music can transform any situation for the better.

> When Viviana Guzmán was four years old, she heard a beautiful melody on the radio. Her heart turned in that moment and her life changed forever. She was determined to find the instrument that had impacted her so deeply.

Guzmán received the Lincoln Center Scholarship, Institute of Hispanic Culture Award, Shepherd Society Award, and the General Maurice Hirsch Award. She teaches workshops and master classes at Juilliard, the San Francisco Conservatory, and Stanford University.

She has recently translated the beauty of her music into poetry in her book *Love Soliloquies*, published by Simon and Schuster.

The Sciences:
Soaring to New Frontiers

Antonia Maury (United States, 1866–1952)
Astronomer whose pioneering work at the Harvard Observatory improved the classification system for stars.

The stars held the greatest fascination for Antonia Maury. She became an astronomer who developed a classification system for stars. It started when she took a good look at the Big Dipper. Upon closer inspection of its handle, Mizar, she saw that it was made of two stars, not one. Maury proved that binary stars—two stars grouped so close together they look like one—existed.

Maury came from a scientific family. Her father was a naturalist and editor of a geographic magazine. Her grandfather was William Draper, a doctor and astronomer. He was the first person to make a photograph of the moon (a daguerreotype).

Draper's son, Henry, was the first person to photograph a star's spectrum to reveal the lines it produced. Spectra are the bands of color that form when light passes through a prism. Each star produces a unique spectrum, so a spectrum can identify a star.

Maury would later use the method of gathering spectra developed by her uncle for her own research. She developed a method of photographing starlight as it passed through a prism placed in front of her telescope. From this, she was able to acquire more than 4,000 photographs. By analyzing them, she was able to improve the star classification system.

She was able to classify the bright northern stars according to their spectra. This is when she discovered that Mizar was a binary star with two distinct spectra.

Maury studied astronomy at Vassar College under Maria Mitchell, the first woman astronomer in the United States. Maury's degree was in astronomy, physics, and philosophy. She immediately went to work at the Harvard Observatory. Part of the observatory was named after her uncle— the Draper Observatory.

She worked for Edward C. Pickering but their styles of research clashed. After improving Pickering's classification system, she left and worked as a teacher and lecturer at Cornell University and other colleges.

When Pickering retired, Maury returned to the observatory. She continued her work on spectral analysis of binary stars. She also discovered the orbits of several binary stars. She later served as curator of the Draper Park Observatory Museum.

She was a member of the American Astronomical Society, the Royal Astronomical Society, and the National Audubon Society. As a conservationist and naturalist, Maury also helped preserve the giant redwood forests in the western United States.

As a conservationist and naturalist, Maury also helped preserve the giant redwood forests in the western United States.

Maury was awarded the Annie J. Cannon Prize from the American Astronomical Society for her work in star classification systems.

Ynez Mexia (United States, 1870–1938)

A leading botanist of her time, Ynez Mexia uncovered thousands of previously unknown specimens through her vast field research, greatly contributing to the field.

Ynez Mexia overcame age, race, and gender discriminations and headed for the wilderness—alone. At age fifty-seven she started on a trek on horseback and by mule that took her to remote jungles, vast dry lands, rain forests, and high mountaintops. In her expeditions, Mexia discovered thousands of new species of plants. She became one of the leading botanists of the times.

Her fascination with plants started with flowers when she moved to California. Until then, she had lived in Washington, D.C., with her family. Her father worked for the Mexican government.

She joined the local Sierra Club and learned more through field trips. Before long, that was not enough. At the age of fifty-one, she went back to school at the University of California, Berkeley, and took a shine to the natural sciences. After taking a course on flowering plants, Mexia narrowed down her field to botany.

She embarked on her first major expedition that she self-financed when she was fifty-six years old. She headed for Mexico where she met a civil engineer, J. Gonzalez Ortega, who was also interested in plants. He knew the terrain and was an invaluable tour guide to the area just outside Mazatlan. Captivated with the luscious vegetation, they ate the rich fruit of the guava trees that grew wild. She collected a variety of ferns, shrubs, and trees.

Hundreds of the plant specimens she collected were new findings. *Mimosa mexiae* was named after her by botanist Joseph Nelson Rose.

On a second trip to Mexico in 1926, she collected and preserved more than 33,000 plant specimens. In Cordillera, Mexia found mountain plants and wild hibiscus. In Tuxpan, near the Rio San Pedro, she found the oil-nut palm. She traveled by canoe to Mexcaltitlan, where she found a plant from the pepper family and named it after seven families that lived in the nearby cove, the families she stayed with while researching the area.

At one point she found a new genus (type) of plant and sent it to Harvard University for analysis. A Dr. B. L. Robinson named it *Mexianthus mexicanus* in her honor. Many of her findings would be used to develop different types of medicines.

Her Mexican research trip ended in April 1927. She had collected about 1,600 plants—lichens, mosses, ferns, grasses, herbs, shrubs, and trees on her first expedition, discovering one new genus and fifty new species.

Her subsequent trips took her to the Alaskan region around Mount McKinley in 1928, where she collected more than 6,000 specimens in one summer. Her South American trip was long—from 1929 to 1932—and she traveled the rainforests of Peru, Ecuador, Chile, and Argentina to collect specimens like the cinchona tree, which produces quinine in its bark.

Mexia became the only female administrator of the Materials Research Center of Excellence, a program that ensures superior science facilities around the country. As a botanist, she contributed greatly to our contemporary knowledge of botany.

For over twelve years she financed and led horseback expeditions to collect more than 100,000 plant specimens, thousands of which had never before been seen.

Mexia died in 1938 from lung cancer, but left an invaluable collection. Photographs of her expeditions were just as invaluable. Many of her specimens and photos are preserved in permanent collections, museums, and universities in the United States and Latin America.

Angeles Alvarino de Leira (Spain, 1916–)

Renowned biologist, oceanographer, and writer who was the first female scientist to serve on a British research vessel. Angeles Alvarino de Leira was awarded a Fulbright Scholarship and the Great Silver Medal of Spain for her contributions to science.

The ocean beckoned to Angeles Alvarino de Leira. She studied the ocean's microorganisms and became a renowned scientist for discovering twenty-two new marine species.

As a biologist, oceanographer, and writer, she studied animals and organisms in the fields of oceanography, biology, and histology, the study of living tissues. Her contributions to science have spanned decades.

🐟 Angeles Alvarino de Leira's contributions to science have spanned decades.

She traveled and taught throughout the world, studying oceanographic areas such as Antarctica. She wrote a book about the organisms found there, titled *Antarctic Chaetognatha: U.S. Antarctic Research Program Biology of the Antarctic Seas.*

Her love of the ocean started in her father's library. She perused his books on natural history and pursued her studies, earning a master's degree in 1941. Alvarino de Leira taught for seven years until she was offered a position with the Spanish Department of Sea Fisheries in Madrid.

Historically, the Spanish Institute of Oceanography banned women, but not Alvarino de Leira. She studied and researched oceanography until she was finally—offically—admitted in 1950. She received her doctorate the following year.

In 1956 she was awarded a Fulbright Scholarship for research in the United States, at the Woods Hole Oceanographic Institute in Massachusetts. She was soon after recommended for a position at the world-famous Scripps Institute of Oceanography in La Jolla, California.

Her research expertise was in the study of zooplankton. She served in several of the institute's expeditions, including the Downwind Expedition, which took vessels through the central Pacific and along the South American coast. The team learned a lot about plate tectonics on this expedition and de Leira's research findings were published as *Bathymetric Distribution of Chaetognathas, Pacific Science.* Several other of her works were published that focused on the biology of the Antarctic Seas and the Pacific.

She became a fisheries biologist with the Southwest Fisheries Science Center in 1970, a division of the newly formed National Marine Fisheries Service. De Leira was the first woman to serve as a scientist on a British research vessel. She officially retired in 1987 but continues to add to the body of knowledge on zooplankton. For her contributions to science, Alvarino de Leira was awarded the Great Silver Medal of Galicia King Juan Carlos I and Queen Sophia of Spain.

Ana Sol Gutierrez (El Salvador, 1942–)

Aeronautical engineer and politician Ana Sol Gutierrez is the first Salvadorian-American to hold a public office in the United States.

> "Education is the instrument not just for an individual to succeed but for us as a community to succeed."
>
> —Ana Sol Gutierrez

Aeronautical engineer Ana Sol Gutierrez has always believed in the power of education. She entered the scientific field of computer sciences and technical information services at a time when women were scarce in the field and recognition was hard to come by.

The field would be her launching pad to effect changes in technological services, communications, activism, education, and United States politics.

She earned her bachelor's degree in chemistry from Pennsylvania State University and received a master's degree in scientific and technical information from American University. She did her postgraduate studies in engineering at George Washington University.

Early in her career, she taught computer sciences and engineering courses at national universities in Bolivia and Venezuela. At the same time, she worked as a management consultant in contracted work around the world in such countries as Peru and Switzerland. Ana Sol Gutierrez speaks three languages—English, Spanish, and French. Her knowledge of language has helped her grow her expertise in the engineering field.

With more than thirty years of expertise in computer systems engineering and technology, she is the director and principal consultant with Computer Sciences Corporation's Strategic Information Technology Services.

She has worked for a number of federal government agencies, including NASA, the IRS, the Department of Justice, Department of Education, Department of Transportation, Ford Aerospace, the Goddard Space Flight Center, the Federal Aviation Administration (FAA), and the General Services Administration (GSA).

In 1994, President William Clinton appointed Gutierrez as the deputy administrator of the United States Department of Transportation's Research and Special Programs Administration. She represented the department on task forces dealing with information technology, directed public policy formulation, and managed all federal transportation research and a number of safety regulatory programs.

> Ana Sol Gutierrez speaks three languages—English, Spanish, and French. Her knowledge of language has helped her grow her expertise in the engineering field.

A mother of three sons, her focus on education was understandable. With a shift in her career, she was the first Latina elected to a school board in Maryland and served there from 1990 to 1998, including several years as president. Twice elected as regional vice president of the Hispanic Caucus of the National School Board Association, she has pushed for better representation on standardized state testing as well as educational rights for minorities.

She wanted to focus on basic civil and human rights, especially for Latinos and minorities.

When Gutierrez was elected in 2003 as a member of the Maryland House of Delegates, she became the first Salvadorian American to ever hold any public office in the history of the United States. As an elected official, she works for better health care, access to jobs, adult education, and more affordable housing, as well as immigration laws and viable alternatives for kids involved with gangs.

She has worked with nonprofit organizations such as United Way, the Center for the Advancement of Hispanics in Science and Engineering   89

Education, the Hispanic Council on International Relations, and has served as co-chair of the Latino Oversight Committee of the Smithsonian Institution in the mid-1990s.

Named one of the 100 Most Influential Hispanics in the USA by *Hispanic Business* magazine in 1996, Gutierrez was also featured in the book, *Latino Women of Science* and was listed in Outstanding Women in Nontraditional Careers by *VISTA* magazine. She is one of twelve Latinas profiled in the documentary film *Women of Hope: Latinas Abriendo Camino* (Bread and Roses Project, Inc.) for their contributions to the American quality of life.

France Anne Cordova (France, 1947–)

First woman and the youngest person to hold the position of chief scientist for NASA, astrophysicist and author France Anne Cordova is the recipient of the Distinguished Service Medal, NASA's highest honor.

Unlocking the secrets of the universe is no small feat, but astrophysicist France Anne Cordova decided to attempt it just the same. Her fascination with science and the mysteries of astronomy started when she watched television footage of *Apollo 11* and the world-famous first walk on the moon.

The experience had such an impact on her that she started a second career in science. Cordova became chief scientist at the National Aeronautics and Space Administration (NASA), the youngest person—male or female—and the first woman to ever hold that position

Her contributions in the field of space research have been so vast that NASA put her name inside a spacecraft that landed on Mars in 1997. The *Pathfinder* carried a CD-ROM with a dedication to Cordova for all her contributions to the Mars Pathfinder Space Program.

Cited as one of "America's Brightest Scientists Under 40" by *Science Digest* magazine in 1994, it is sometimes hard to believe that astrophysics was a second career for Cordova.

Her undergraduate degree from Stanford University was in English. A successful novelist, cookbook author, and guest editor for *Mademoiselle* magazine, she decided to go back to school and earn her Ph.D. in physics from the California Institute of Technology after watching the *Apollo 11* coverage.

But she had learned about survival, dedication, and reaching for goals from her family. She always had their support. Cordova was born in Paris while her Mexican-American, West Point graduate father, Frederick Cordova, oversaw a nonprofit organization that distributed food and clothing after World War II. The eldest of twelve children, Cordova was responsible for countless chores in her home while growing up, but loved school. She was selected as one of California's "Ten Outstanding Youths" when she was a senior in high school.

> France Ann Cordova's fascination with science and the mysteries of astronomy started when she watched television footage of *Apollo 11* and the world-famous first walk on the moon.

In college, a new world opened up to her when she went on an archeological dig in Oaxaca, Mexico. She immediately connected with the Zapotec Indian pueblo they explored, as well as her Mexican heritage. From the experience, she wrote a short novel called *The Women of Santo Domingo* and a companion cookbook. She entered her work in a contest held by *Mademoiselle* magazine, and it was declared one of the ten best entries.

She was working as a staff member for the *Los Angeles Times* news service when she decided to enroll in the California Institute of Technology to earn her Ph.D. In 1979, she was one of two women in her graduating class.

At Los Alamos National Laboratory she served in two capacities—as a staff scientist in the earth and space sciences division, and as deputy group leader of the space astronomy and astrophysics group. Described as a visionary, she pioneered a new approach to studying the stars.

She was the first astrophysicist to measure the x-ray radiation emanating from white dwarfs—old stars with intense gravitational fields and pulsars. Pulsars are the dense, superhot cores of exploded stars.

91

To get away from the intensity of her research, France's favorite past-time was rock climbing. On one of these expeditions in 1983 she met her husband, high school science teacher Christian Foster. In her late thirties, she began a family.

Cordova continued her work with the Hubble Space Telescope and on various satellite projects, including Europe's X-Ray Multi-Mirror Mission, and NASA's Constellation X Mission. Her expertise settled on multiwavelength observational astronomy and space instrumentation. She collected more than 100 scientific papers and produced another book, *Multiwavelength Astrophysics*, a collection of review papers in all aspects of the field.

Cordova headed the Department of Astronomy and Astrophysics at Pennsylvania State University. By 1993 she was elected to a three-year term as vice president there. Later that year, NASA appointed her chief scientist and she was stationed at Langley Research Center near Washington, D.C.

In 1996, Cordova was awarded NASA's highest honor—the Distinguished Service Medal.

She was featured on the public broadcasting television series *Breakthrough: The Changing Face of Science in America* and in the documentary *Life Beyond Earth*.

Dr. Lydia Villa-Komaroff (United States, 1947–)
Third Mexican-American woman in the United States to earn a doctorate in the sciences and a pioneer in the field of cloning. Lydia Villa-Kamaroff made a major scientific discovery essential in the treatment of diabetes.

With curiosity and fascination, Lydia Villa-Komaroff believes that every child starts out a scientist. By the time she was nine, Villa-Komaroff knew she wanted to be a scientist. She is now a molecular biologist and a pioneer in the field of cloning. She has spent more than twenty years studying genes, concentrating on protein synthesis, cell development, and growth mutations.

Growing up in Santa Fe, New Mexico, she was the eldest of six children. Both her parents were teachers. Her father was also a musician who ignited her curiosity to learn when she was only five years old. He brought home the *World Book Encyclopedia* and told her that everything she wanted to know was in those books.

In high school, Villa-Kamaroff won a minority scholarship from the National Science Foundation to attend a summer lab program at a Texas college. In 1965, she enrolled as a chemistry major at the University of Washington in Seattle but was quickly told that women did not belong in chemistry. She switched to biology.

Lydia Villa-Komaroff was listed as a 2003 Most Influential Hispanic by *Hispanic Business* magazine.

In 1970 she moved to the East Coast with the hopes of transferring to Johns Hopkins University, but she came upon another setback. The university was not accepting female students. She enrolled instead at its sister school, Goucher College in Maryland.

That year she also married Dr. Anthony L. Komaroff. After earning her bachelor's degree in biology, they moved to Boston where she went to the Massachusetts Institute of Technology (MIT) for graduate work under Nobel laureate David Baltimore. In 1972, Villa-Komaroff began her dissertation on the polio virus.

Women made up only one-third of her small graduate class. She earned her Ph.D. in cell biology in 1975—the third Mexican-American woman in the United States to receive a doctorate in the sciences. A prestigious fellowship allowed her to continue postdoctoral training at Harvard where she focused on recombinant DNA. When the lab was closed for fear that a supergerm or disease could be created, Villa-Komaroff moved to a lab run by James Watson, the scientist who discovered DNA.

Villa-Komaroff's experiments included trying to clone genes from a silkworm's eggshell, but all her trials seemed futile, frustrating, and filled with scientific failure. When she was able to return to Cambridge, she joined the Department of Molecular Genetics and Microbiology at the University of Massachusetts Medical Center in 1978 and received tenure in 1984. The team had to be sequestered to do its work in insulin cloning that involved gene splicing.

She made a major discovery in 1978—that bacterial cells could produce insulin, a human hormone essential in the treatment of diabetes. It was the first time a human hormone had been synthesized in bacteria, and it was a pioneering step in the study of cures for diabetes.

She moved on to the department of neurology at Children's Hospital and Harvard Medical School in Boston in 1985, while teaching and continuing her research on brain cells in expanded fields of cell and molecular biology. She received funding from the National Health Institutes, the American Diabetes Association, the American Cancer Society, and the March of Dimes Birth Defects Foundation, allowing her to patent several discoveries. Appointed professor of neurology in Northwestern University's medical school in 1996, she oversaw the entire research budget.

In 1995, Villa-Komaroff was featured in *DNA Detective,* a public television documentary that became part of a series on women in science. She was listed as a 2003 Most Influential Hispanic by *Hispanic Business* magazine for her work at Whitehead Institute for Biomedical Research at MIT, where she is chief operating officer and vice president for research.

To promote women and minorities in the sciences, she became a founding member of the Society for the Advancement of Chicanos and Native Americans in the Sciences (SACNAS) in 1973.

Adriana Ocampo (Colombia, 1955–)

The planetary geologist at NASA who first proposed the theory that the impact of the Chicxulub meteorite led to the extinction of dinosaurs, Adriana Ocampo is the recipient of numerous awards for her work as a scientist and for her efforts in community outreach programs.

There were many theories as to the extinction of dinosaurs. Adriana Ocampo was the first to suggest that a ring of sinkholes in the Yucatán peninsula in Mexico was a result of an enormous meteorite that smashed into Earth 65 million years ago. That impact may have created dust and gases that caused acid rain, decreasing the dinosaurs' food supply, which eventually caused them to become extinct.

Ocampo was given a grant to continue her research, and she traveled through Belize and Mexico looking for traces of the crater. Her discovery helped scientists prove that the tremendous impact of the Chicxulub meteorite caused the extinction of more than 50 percent of the Earth's species.

Ocampo is a planetary geologist at NASA. She has worked on several space exploration projects, including the Viking Mission to Mars, the Mars Observer, and the Galileo Mission to Jupiter. Ocampo was appointed coinvestigator on the proposed Hermes Mission to explore Mercury. She was the science coordinator of the Near Infrared Mapping Spectrometer (NIMS), one of the instruments used in the *Galileo*.

While growing up, her ideal playtime was using kitchen utensils and appliances to create spacecraft and colonies on other planets. When her parents bought her a book on space travel and planets, her focus became clear. She wanted to explore space and be an astronaut.

What fascinated her most about the first walk on the moon, however, was its surface, the unusual rocks, soils, and craters. From that moment on, she was hooked on geology.

Although Ocampo had been born in Colombia and raised in Argentina, her father had been to a Harvard program on scholarship and loved the United States. They moved to Los Angeles in 1970 to escape the political unrest in Argentina and to find a space program to enroll her in.

The culture shock disappeared when sixteen-year-old Ocampo learned about the Explorers, a space exploration club that worked with scientists from the Jet Propulsion Laboratory (JPL), a part of the National Aeronautics and Space Administration (NASA) that specializes in space exploration. Ocampo joined immediately and worked at internships at the lab throughout her college years.

She earned a degree in geology with an emphasis on planetary science from California State University in Los Angeles. Her master's and doctorate were from California State University, Northridge, where she began her thesis on the Chicxulub.

Ocampo was invited to work on the Viking Project's first spacecraft landing on the planet Mars as part of its Imaging Team. Her mission was to develop special expertise in the remote sensing of data. Named after the ancient Vikings who set out to explore the New World, the spacecraft took pictures of the moons of Mars. She examined them and collaborated in the creation of an atlas—the first ever—of Phobos and Deimos, the two moons.

> When Adriana Ocampo's parents bought her a book on space travel and planets, her focus became clear. She wanted to explore space and be an astronaut.

To bring North and South America together to talk about space and share their knowledge, she organized conferences in Costa Rica and Chile. Since 1998, Ocampo has worked at NASA headquarters in Washington, D.C., at the Office of Space Science, the Office of External Relations, and the Office of Earth Science. She works on international collaboration in space missions with the European Space Agency.

She designed a first-of-its kind workshop for disseminating planetary science information. The United Nations used her workshop as a prototype for similar workshops throughout the world, in conjunction with the European Space Agency and the Planetary Society.

Ocampo serves on the Society of Hispanic Professional Engineers National Board of Directors and is a member of the Planetary Society

Advisory Council, which shares the latest scientific discoveries with the general public while promoting the need for continued space exploration.

As a member of the Association of Women in Geoscience, the American Institute of Aeronautics and Astronautics, and the Society of Women Engineers, Ocampo mentors girls and Latinos in the sciences. She is a recipient of JPL's Advisory Council for Women Award for outreach and community work and received the Woman of the Year Award in Science from the Comision Femenil organization (1992). She has applied to become a space shuttle mission specialist.

Margarita H. Colmenares (United States, 1957–)

First woman to serve as president of the Society of Hispanic Professional Engineers, first female construction engineer at Chevron, and first woman and Latina to win the prestigious White House Fellowship.

I n high school Margarita H. Colmenares was urged to pursue a career where she could use shorthand and typing. In college, she accidentally stumbled on the field of engineering and decided she would be an engineer.

She went back to a community college to study physics, chemistry, and calculus while working part-time in engineering with the California Department of Water Resources. Five universities offered Colmenares a scholarship.

At Stanford University, she earned a civil engineering degree. By the time she graduated, she was already working at Chevron International Oil Company in a student work program and would continue working there for many years, mostly as an environmental engineer.

At Chevron, she worked in various capacities. In her position as compliance specialist, her territory covered five states, helping the company remain in compliance with environmental regulations. Colmenares was the first female construction engineer at the company and the first woman to serve as lead engineer in a major environmental cleanup project.

In 1989 Colmenares became the first woman to serve as president of the Society of Hispanic Professional Engineers (SHPE). In her position, she formulated an ambitious program that would promote engineering careers. Chevron approved her proposal to be an executive-on-loan so that she could achieve her goals.

> Colmenares was selected as Outstanding Woman of the Year by *Hispanic Magazine*, Role Model of the Year, and one of the 100 Most Influential Hispanics in the Country.

For two years during National Engineers Week, Colmenares was named to the All-Star Team of nationally recognized leaders in engineering. She traveled to more than 100 professional and student NSHE chapters, inspiring 30,000 members to take on leadership roles in their communities. She encouraged students to pursue careers in the sciences and asked government officials to make education a priority.

As her term as president of SHPE came to an end, she applied for the White House Fellowship with Chevron supporting her as an ideal candidate for the program. Candidates come from all sectors—academic, professional, business, government, and artistic—and for one year would work with heads of government departments and agencies in areas that concerned them.

Colmenares was one of sixteen and the only woman selected. She was the first woman and first Latina to win the fellowship since the program's establishment in 1991. She chose to work with the Department of Education.

In 1994, the Clinton Administration appointed Colmenares as director of the Office of Corporate Liaison at the United States Department of Education. The appointment was in line with her lifetime goal—to increase the number of Hispanics in scientific and engineering careers.

Born in Sacramento, California, Colmenares was the eldest of five children. Her parents had emigrated from Mexico and supported her quest for education. At Stanford, she tried to maintain a balanced life and combined work with other passions. She taught and codirected the Stanford Ballet Folklorico.

She was profiled on the PBS series on careers for teenagers, *Choices for Youth*. Her work was featured in an elementary school textbook, *Science Anytime, Margarita H. Colmenares: She Helps Keep the Environment Clean*.

Colmenares was selected as Outstanding Woman of the Year by *Hispanic Magazine*, Role Model of the Year, and one of the 100 Most Influential Hispanics in the Country. She is the youngest recipient of the Distinguished Alumni Award for public and community service from the Community College League of California.

Dr. Ellen Ochoa (United States, 1958–)

First Latina astronaut and the recipient of numerous awards for her scientific achievements and for work in promoting the education of children, especially in the Hispanic community.

In 1990, the National Aeronautics and Space Administration (NASA) selected Ellen Ochoa from more than 2,000 applicants to enroll in the astronaut training program.

Ochoa became the first Latina astronaut and has since logged nearly 1,000 hours in space. Her first space shuttle flight was on the *Discovery* in 1993, where she conducted research on sun radiation levels and its effect on Earth's ozone layer, climate, and environment.

Born and raised in Southern California, Ochoa loved school, especially reading and math. She was a good student and was competitive. In junior high she won the San Diego County spelling bee. A classical flutist in high school, she won an award recognizing her as a top musician, and she entertained thoughts of becoming a professional musician before she ever dreamed about reaching for the stars.

Ochoa graduated valedictorian of her high school and went on to San Diego State University. When she entered college, she did not know what field to pursue. She leaned toward physics or engineering. An engineering professor told her to steer clear of engineering because the classes would be too difficult. She took the lack of encouragement only as a slight detour and then embraced it as a challenge.

Ochoa majored in physics at San Diego State University and went on to earn her master's and doctorate degrees in electrical engineering at Stanford University. She remained an accomplished musician, earning a Student Soloist Award with the Stanford Symphony Orchestra.

By the time Ochoa reached the NASA astronaut training program, she already had an impressive resume. She worked as a research engineer at Sandia National Laboratories and supervised scientists at the NASA Ames Research Center. She co-invented optical techniques for use in space research and she held three patents for those inventions by the time she was in her mid-thirties.

When Ochoa entered the training program, the evaluation and selection process was grueling and competitive. Her degrees and work experience in a technical field were only part of what the program was looking for in potential candidates.

Veteran astronauts interviewed her, assessing her in everyday things like her disposition, the way she communicated, and how she might respond to emergency situations. Selected as one of twenty-three finalists, among only five women, she attended daily seminars for a year in subjects such as oceanography, astronomy, and orbital mechanics. She also participated in simulated shuttle liftoff, flight, and re-entry; weightlessness exercises; and trained to repair equipment and instruments while in pressurized suits underwater.

 Ellen Ochoa made her first space shuttle flight on the *Discovery* in 1993.

All of her training helped prepare her for any number of technical flight assignments. Ellen's space missions have included verifying software used during flight to control the shuttle equipment, using the International Space Station's robotic arm to maneuver space walkers around the station, and collecting data for solar studies.

On her first *Discovery* flight she was allowed to take two personal items. She selected her flute and a picture of her research engineer husband, Dr. Coe Fulmer Miles.

She served as chief of the Astronaut Office, which deals with the International Space Station. She worked on President Bill Clinton's commission on the celebration of women in history. Since her first flights she has had two children and remains committed to promoting the importance of education to children, especially to girls and Latinos.

A member of the Optical Society of America and the American Institute of Aeronautics and Astronautics, Ochoa received the Hispanic Heritage Leadership Award, the Hispanic Engineer Albert Baez Award for Outstanding Technical Contribution to Humanity, the Congressional Hispanic Caucus Medallion of Excellence, and the Women in Aerospace Outstanding Achievement Award. She has earned seven achievement awards from NASA, such as the Exceptional Service Medal and the Outstanding Leadership Medal.

Television: News Shakers and Makers

Cristina Saralegui (Cuba, 1948–)

Emmy Award–winner Cristina Saralegui is the first and only Hispanic to host daily television programs in two languages and the only Latina to run a television variety talk show, a radio show, and magazine simultaneously.

Give Cristina Saralegui an hour, a taboo subject, and an audience and she will provide pure unadulterated entertainment. Known as "the Latina Oprah," or "Oprah with Salsa," the Havana-born Saralegui hosts *El Show de Cristina*, reaching more than 100 million viewers worldwide.

When the show first started in 1989, finding guests that would be willing to talk about controversial issues was her first hurdle. Another issue was dealing with conservative and influential entities that thought she might threaten traditional values.

Saralegui also had to face racism directed at her. Initial responses accused her of being too white to represent Hispanics. Saralegui quickly countered with a simple statement that Latinas are beautiful in every shade of colored skin.

After the first show, Cristina said she received letters that she would not show her pastor, gynecologist, or husband. It was not difficult to get guests to come on the show after that.

The visionary Saralegui is the only Latina to have a television variety talk show, a radio show, and magazine simultaneously running. She is the first and only Hispanic to host daily television programs in two languages, English and Spanish. The show has won ten Emmy awards.

> Initial responses accused her of being too white to represent Hispanics. Saralegui quickly countered with a simple statement that Latinas are beautiful in every shade of colored skin.

El Show de Cristina was a second career for the outgoing, yet hard-hitting, Saralegui. With a background in creative writing and twenty years in the publishing business, she already knew how to interview, hit a compassionate note, and give people a forum where they could speak up about taboo subjects. Her roots were in journalism.

As an heir to her family's publishing business, which produced magazines such as *Bohemia, Carteles,* and *Vanidades,* Saralegui took after her publishing guru grandfather, Don Francisco Saralegui. Don Francisco, also known as "the Paper Czar," inspired her to try publishing as a living.

When the family left Cuba in 1960 and settled in Miami, Cristina was only twelve years old. She attended the University of Miami, studying communications and creative writing.

She became an intern at *Vanidades,* a magazine her grandfather had created back in Cuba. She had to teach herself to write in Spanish since her later education had all been in the United States and in English.

Working at several publications, she proved her own innate talents for writing and editing. She went on to become the editor-in-chief of *Cosmopolitan en Español.* After ten years, she left the print journalism world to produce and host her own television show on Univision, a Spanish-language network.

A radio segment called *Cristina Opina* (Cristina's Opinion) allows her to share motivational and inspirational messages with her audience. As a spinoff from the show, she copublishes *Cristina La Revista* (Cristina the Magazine).

She and husband, Marcos Avila, started an AIDS awareness foundation called Arriba la Vida/Up with Life. She is a member of the National

Council of the American Foundation for AIDS, and is on the board of the National Association of Hispanic Journalists.

Saralegui received the Outstanding Communicator of the Year Award from the National Organization of Women in Communication for bringing the concerns of the Latin community to mainstream media. She has also received the Corporate Leader Award from the National Network of Hispanic Women and the Distinction for Leadership and Communications and Broadcasting Award from AMFAR (American Foundation of AIDS Research) for her commitment to AIDS education in the Spanish-speaking world.

Saralegui sees her parents, who have been married for sixty years, as role models. Her family is her foundation, and the closeness of her husband and three children all inspire her.

Sonia Manzano (United States, 1950–)

One of the most well known Latina actresses in children's television, Sonia Manzano has served as a positive influence for millions of children in her role as "Maria" on Sesame Street *and as a member of the show's Emmy Award–winning writing staff.*

S onia Manzano's biggest fans are about three feet tall. Her best friends are the furry and feathered creatures that live on Sesame Street. Living peaceably as one of the few humans alongside Big Bird, Kermit, Elmo, Bert, and Ernie and the rest of the loveable cast, Manzano is best known for her role as "Maria" on the public television children's show.

Sesame Street is shown in over eighty countries spanning six continents. As one of the most visible Latina actresses on children's television, Manzano has been a positive role model since she joined *Sesame Street* in the 1970s. She was nominated twice for an Emmy Award as Outstanding Performer in a Children's Series.

Manzano also writes scripts for the series and has shared fifteen

Emmy Awards with the writing staff. Being able to provide a more honest portrayal of Hispanic culture brings Manzano great satisfaction because when she was growing up, there were no Hispanic images in television or in the media.

> Manzano teaches more than numbers and ABCs. *Sesame Street* is about life. Honest portrayals of human characters are balanced with the wisdom and compassion the furry creatures exhibit toward one another.

The beauty of bilingualism and biculturalism mixed with having friends from all walks of life keep the show fresh. One of the scripts she enjoyed helping to write was on her character's relationship and marriage to "Luis" (Emilio Delgado) and the birth of their TV daughter.

Manzano teaches more than numbers and ABCs. *Sesame Street* is about life. Honest portrayals of human characters are balanced with the wisdom and compassion the furry creatures exhibit toward one another. When Manzano began playing Maria, the character was just a teenager. She went through a hippie and feminist phase, and now is grown up, married, and has a family of her own. Real-life topics cover death, marriage, and pregnancy and everything in between.

Manzano has also written for Nickelodeon's Peabody Award–winning children's series *Little Bill*. The first of her two children's picture books, *No Dogs Allowed!* is a 2004 release. She also writes a parenting column on the *Sesame Street* workshop Web site and has written several *Sesame Street* videos. She enjoys doing voice-overs, such as the voice of Elmo on *Sesame Street*.

Manzano grew up in the South Bronx. Her teachers encouraged her to audition for the High School for the Performing Arts in New York. She was accepted and later received a scholarship to Carnegie Mellon University in Pittsburgh, Pennsylvania, where she earned her degree in drama. Her master's degree is in education. While in college she was cast in the original New York production of the off-Broadway show, *Godspell*. Soon after, she was cast as "Maria" on *Sesame Street*.

She has appeared onstage in *The Living Room* (directed by Jose

Ferrer) and *Happy New Year*. She directed and starred in *Appearing in Person Tonight: Your Mother*. In 2002 she made a return to Broadway in *The Vagina Monologues*. She enjoys her experimental work as a member of the Ensemble Studio Theatre.

She has received awards from the Association of Hispanic Arts, the Congressional Hispanic Caucus, the National Hispanic Media Coalition, and the Committee for Hispanic Children and Families. In 1997, Manzano was keynote speaker for Hispanic Heritage Month at the Library of Congress in Washington, D.C.

Maria Hinojosa (Mexico, 1961–)

CNN's first correspondent of urban affairs, Maria Hinojosa is the recipient of numerous awards for her outstanding work in radio and television as a host, correspondent, and producer. She is also the author of several books.

Maria Hinojosa always felt invisible as a Latina growing up in her Chicago, Illinois, neighborhood. She had no one to relate to, no role models at the forefront, and no faces on the television screen that were similar to her own.

Now a hard-hitting journalist with heart, Hinojosa goes behind the scenes to get to the real stories. As the first CNN correspondent assigned to urban affairs, Hinojosa feels compelled to tell the stories of immigrants like her, who came to the United States and felt like lost souls.

She draws from that sense of invisibility and is determined to cover the news and people in angles that not many other reporters will. She became a journalist because she wanted to see more diversity and to project a different reality on mainstream media.

The rich cadence of Hinojosa's voice also carries over the airwaves of *Latino USA*, a national radio program that she hosts. When she covers a Latino community, she wants the public to know that she isn't "ghetto-izing" herself but is simply telling an "American" story, told from a different viewpoint, giving perhaps, a new perspective.

She has covered community stories like hunger in the suburbs, camps for homeless kids, and teenage pregnancy, but she's also covered hard-hitting pieces such as the aftermath of September 11 and its effect on families, Mexico–U.S. border issues, the *Columbia* shuttle disaster, and the development of AIDS resources.

Her physician father and social worker mother instilled in her the need to remain connected with her roots. To maintain that strong connection, her family spent time in Mexico every summer. From these trips, Hinojosa learned to embrace her heritage, but they also made her acutely aware of the socioeconomic disparity of the life surrounding her, whether she was in Mexico, Chicago, or other parts of the world.

Whether she covers the black, gay, or business community, a gang member, someone who is HIV-positive, or someone crossing the border without papers, Hinojosa's goal is the same: She tries to get in touch with the humanity of her interviewees because she wants to make them feel "visible."

At Barnard College in New York City, she majored in Latin-American studies, women's studies, and political economy. She gained her first radio experience as host and producer for Columbia University Radio's *Nueva Canción y Demás*. The show started out as a bilingual venture but turned into a monolingual Spanish show covering the arts, politics, and activism.

🐦 Hinojosa tells the stories of immigrants like her, who came to the United States and felt like lost souls.

Prior to CNN, she worked at National Public Radio (NPR) as a general assignment correspondent. She hosted *Visiones*, a public affairs talk show and was the first Latina to host *New York Hotline*, a live prime-time talk show.

She produced several news shows including *Where We Stand with Walter Cronkite, The Osgood File,* and *Newsbreak*. She has also penned several books, including *Raising Raul: Adventures Raising Myself and My Son* and *Crews: Gang Members Talk with Maria Hinojosa,* which grew out of an award-winning news story she covered.

Hinojosa was named one of the Most Influential Working Mothers in America by *Working Mother* magazine, and one of *Hispanic Business* magazine's 100 Most Influential Latinos in the United States. She was presented the Robert F. Kennedy Award for her NPR story, "Manhood Behind Bars." She received the Latino Heritage Award from Columbia University, the Associated Press Award, and the National Association of Hispanic Journalists Radio Award. The National Council of La Raza awarded Hinojosa the Ruben Salazar Award in recognition of her dedication to promoting a positive portrayal of Latinos.

Giselle Fernandez-Farrand (Mexico, 1964–)

A successful news correspondent, anchor, talk show host, and producer who has won five Emmy Awards and started her own production company, Giselle Fernandez-Farrand's skill as a correspondent garnered her a coveted interview with Fidel Castro.

"There are no coincidences in our lives."
— Giselle Fernandez-Ferrand, *www.soymujer.com*

Five-time Emmy Award–winning news correspondent Giselle Fernandez-Farrand has taken leaps of faith throughout her journalistic career, redefining herself personally and professionally with each step.

She has worked as a news anchor for all major United States television stations, covered entertainment on *Access Hollywood,* and hosted the A&E Network History Channel.

An interview she conducted with Cuban dictator Fidel Castro launched her into the spotlight. Castro had been impressed with her coverage of Cuban immigration crises, the unrest in Haiti, and the United States invasion of Panama. It was his first English-language interview in two decades.

Similar assignments earned her respect and recognition. Her journalistic career has taken her from local to national television journalism, from lighthearted daily entertainment news magazines, to Web sites celebrating women. She has produced heart-wrenching and inspirational documentaries dealing with everything from world policy to metaphysics.

> ✎ Fernandez-Farrand's love of journalism, of digging for stories, came literally from digging for historical facts and gathering mystical Mexican folklore while traveling throughout Mexico with her mother, who was researching her doctoral thesis.

Fernandez-Farrand hosts a talk show program for Sí TV called *Café Olé with Giselle Fernandez,* featuring music, film, and television celebrities. She hopes to take the upbeat show to English-language stations in order to broaden Latino-themed programming in mainstream television.

Promoting health, wellness, business, family, and general empowerment for women, especially Latinas, she has developed Web sites such as *www.soymujer.com, www.lastories.com,* and *www.daringdames.com.* She also writes guest columns for health and women's magazines.

Born in Mexico, she refers to herself as "the original Kosher Burrito" because her mother is Jewish and her flamenco dancer father inspired her passion for her roots. Her love of journalism, of digging for stories, came literally from digging for historical facts and gathering mystical Mexican folklore while traveling throughout Mexico with her mother, who was researching her doctoral thesis. Interviewing hundreds of villagers about mysticism, mythology, and Mexican traditions ignited Fernandez's journalistic curiosity.

Fernandez-Farrand earned a journalism degree from Sacramento State University, where she took advantage of the many radio internships available. Directly after graduating from college, she landed her first television job in Colorado. She worked in Los Angeles, Miami, Chicago, and New York.

It was through her work that she became involved with charities, which gave more clarity and direction to her life. She is an advocate and spokesperson for breast cancer research, education, and treatment. She is a member of the Smithsonian National Board for Latino Initiatives. Through her work on the board of trustees for Children's Hospital Los Angeles, she learned of the plight and heartache associated with young cancer patients and their families and friends.

Getting to know one such victim, Dustin "Dusty" Maraz, inspired her to leave the broadcast world she knew. She felt it was her destiny to tell his story of inspiration, hope, and eventual heartache. He was the first subject in her Web site *www.lastories.com,* which features people living in Los Angeles. With help from her husband, she turned Dusty's story into a documentary.

Taking another leap of faith, Fernandez-Farrand stepped out of the hard-news spotlight to develop programs for cable network television and produce documentaries, a desire that had been burning in her for a long time. She finds creative freedom and innovative ways to tell stories through these projects. Her production company, Skinny Hippo Productions, has since taken flight.

Nely Galán (Cuba, 1964–)

Television anchor, talk show host, and producer Nely Galán is the founder of Galán Entertainment and is a pioneer in integrating Latino television programming with the American mainstream market.

Being picked on while growing up because she was "different" could have had a negative effect on Nely Galán, but her mother's words always rang in her ears: "You have the best of both worlds."

Galán took the words to heart when she went to work in television, where being bilingual and bicultural were great assets to her career. At twenty-two, she became the youngest television station manager in the United States, and shortly thereafter, the youngest president of entertainment for Telemundo.

Dubbed "the Tropical Tycoon" by *New York Times Magazine,* Galán was unwilling to be a token Hispanic and instead considered herself a self-made businesswoman with vision and negotiating power. *Entertainment*

Weekly cited her as one of the most powerful young executives in Hollywood.

> 🖏 Galán was unwilling to be a token Hispanic and instead considered herself a self-made businesswoman with vision and negotiating power.

Her meteoric rise in television included hosting her own syndicated talk show—*Bravo*, which aired in English and Spanish versions—by the time she was twenty-seven. At CBS, she accepted an offer to be an anchorwoman as long as she could host a television talk show and retain the rights to *Bravo*.

She started Galán Entertainment when she was thirty years old. It is one of the leading U.S. entertainment companies to integrate Latino content with the American mainstream market. She has hosted, developed, or produced programs on syndicated, cable, and network television, such as HBO, PBS, E! Entertainment, Fox, and CBS, as well as Telemundo.

Galán is a pioneer in getting American broadcasters to tap into the huge English-speaking Latino audience. She wants television programming to focus on U.S.–born Hispanics and to bridge the gap between Hispanics who watch Spanish shows and those who prefer English-language shows. Staying true to her vision has not always been easy.

Born Arnely Alvarez, Galán was the only Latina in an all-girl Catholic school. As a sophomore she wrote a paper about what it was like being a child of immigrants. The school decided that because she was fourteen years old, she could not have written the piece. They accused her of plagiarism. Her parents could not help because they did not speak English.

Galán fought the accusation by writing an article on why parents should not send daughters to an all-girl Catholic school and submitted it to *Seventeen* magazine, which bought and published it. She was promptly expelled. Humiliated for herself and her parents, who had struggled to send her there, she decided to fight the decision, even against her mother's wishes. She went to the school board and presented her case—they couldn't expel her because of what she had written against them. She won and settled out of court, and was able to graduate early.

111

Standing up for what she believes in gives her strength and direction. Galán Entertainment continues to look for more empowering projects for the Latino community. When entrepreneur Christy Haubegger approached her with the idea of starting a national bilingual magazine, Galán invested in the project with several others. In 1996 the magazine was launched. Today *Latina* magazine has a circulation of 350,000.

Lisa Guerrero (United States, 1964–)

At one point the only woman to work simultaneously as a sportscaster and an actress, Lisa Guerrero has achieved many "firsts" for women in sports news.

> "If you look good, people assume you aren't credible. It's a battle you'll always fight if you're on TV and a female. The bottom line is: I know my sports."
>
> —Lisa Guerrero

When her mother died, Lisa Guerrero was only eight years old. Her father enrolled her in theater therapy to help her cope with the devastating loss. It helped. It also sparked a passion for acting.

As she grew older, her father signed her up for team sports like basketball, volleyball, and softball—where she excelled as a pitcher and first baseman. Sports brought out the best in her.

If there was one thing Guerrero loved, it was sports. She knew them inside and out and could debate stats, names, and the history of any given team or athlete. Until 2004, she was a sideline reporter for ABC's *Monday Night Football*.

In 1999 Guerrero was hired by Fox Sports Network as an exclusive broadcast journalist for *Fox Overtime* and *Fox Extra Innings*, and she served as a cohost on *Sports Geniuses* and other shows before landing "the big one."

Guerrero was the national sports update anchor and the only woman on Fox's *The Best Damn Sports Show Period*. She has scored virtually impossibleto-get interviews, including Bobby Bonds and Dennis Rodman. She even made Rodman, the bad boy of basketball, cry in an interview.

Even as a self-described "girly-girl," she built her reputation as one of the most capable female reporters in sports. She is the only woman to ever host a NFL team magazine show, *Chargers Magazine,* and at one time was the only Latina sportscaster in Los Angeles, California.

> Even as a self-described "girly-girl," Guerrero built her reputation as one of the most capable female reporters in sports. She is the only woman to ever host a NFL team magazine show, and at one time was the only Latina sportscaster in Los Angeles, California.

When she won a spot on Aaron Spelling's daytime drama *Sunset Beach* and a sportscasting job with KCBS on the same day, she would become the only woman working simultaneously as an actress and as a sportscaster. For one year, she was a soap opera villain working Monday through Friday using her father's last name, Coles. On the weekends, she worked as a sports reporter using her mother's name, Guerrero.

She also had a regular reporting gig on *EXTRA!* a television entertainment magazine.

Guerrero finally decided to go full time with sports broadcasting because of the opportunities. Speaking Spanish and English gave her an edge on getting the scoop on Spanish-speaking athletes.

On *The Best Damn Sports Show Period,* she would not compromise her femininity to prove she knew her stuff. She refused to change her appearance at the suggestion of a network executive who thought she should look more conservative by wearing suits and no makeup and by limiting her smiling. The president of the station backed her, however, and accepted her personal style.

When she once went fifty-one consecutive weeks without a day off, she was recognized as "the hardest working person in sports" by the *Los Angeles Times.* The recognition meant a lot—because it was based on her work ethic, not on her being a woman.

Guerrero took the roundabout way of getting her coveted position as a sports anchor. She started as a cheerleader for the Los Angeles Rams, then worked as a choreographer for a cheerleading team. She was a sports marketing executive in the World League of American Football and the International Basketball Association.

When she made it to Hollywood, she modeled, appeared in more than 200 commercials, and appeared on television shows like *Cybill, In the Heat of the Night, Matlock,* and *Frasier.* Her movie appearances include *Batman Returns, Fire Down Below,* and *Love Potion No.9.*

Maria Elena Salinas (United States, 1964–)
An Emmy Award–winning veteran journalist of television news, Maria Elena Salinas has interviewed dozens of world leaders and is one of the few syndicated columnists of Hispanic descent in the United States.

For more than twenty years, Maria Elena Salinas has shown her loyalty to the Univision television network as anchor of *Noticiero Univision.* Audiences, in turn, trust her news coverage. The Emmy Award–winning bilingual journalist remains a highly acclaimed and respected veteran of television news. Salinas has reached millions of Hispanic viewers in the United States and in almost twenty Latin-American countries.

Her coverage has spotlighted dozens of world leaders for over two decades. She has had exclusive interviews with President George W. Bush, former Presidents George Bush and Bill Clinton; Mexican Presidents Carlos Salinas de Gortari, Ernesto Zedillo, and Vicente Fox; Chile's Augusto Pinochet; Panama's Manuel Noriega; and Nicaragua's Daniel Ortega and Violeta Chamorro. She covered Pope John Paul II's trips and Princess Diana's death, live from London. Her work has earned her three Emmys and countless journalistic recognitions.

Born in Los Angeles, California, to Mexican immigrants, she began
her journalism career as a radio commentator. Her insightful reporting of

the growing Hispanic community of Southern California launched a journalism career that she cherishes.

🖎 Salinas has reached millions of Hispanic viewers in the United States and in almost twenty Latin-American countries.

In 1981, she made the transition to Spanish-language television news coverage when she transferred to KMEX-TV, a Univision affiliate in Los Angeles.

As a cohost to the prime-time television news magazine *Aquí y Ahora* Salinas brings viewers in-depth consumer reports and hard-hitting interviews. In *Noticias Univision Presenta* she focuses her one-hour features on items affecting the Hispanic community.

Her journalism expertise has given her presence in other arenas. She is heard daily on Radio Unica and is one of the few syndicated columnists of Hispanic descent in the United States. She writes stories in both Spanish and English that are featured in more than forty-five daily newspapers across the country. She also writes a weekly column for Univision.com.

Heading up a campaign to help motivate Hispanic children to stay in school, Salinas established a scholarship in her name, which is matched by Univision. It is awarded to an outstanding journalism student pursuing a career in Spanish-language media and offers an internship at a Univision network station.

Salinas has received excellence in journalism awards from the National Association of Hispanic Journalists, the National Association of Hispanic Publications, and the California Chicano News Media Association. She was cited as Journalist of the Year 2002 by Hispanic Media 100.

Salinas was featured as one of *Hispanic Magazine*'s 100 Most Influential Hispanics in the United States and named one of the top 15 Most Influential Hispanics in an Hispanic Voter Trends poll.

Daisy Fuentes (Cuba, 1966–)

The first Latina VJ for MTV and the first to appear on both the Spanish-language and original version of MTV, Daisy Fuentes is a well-known model, actress, host, and emcee.

As a pop culture icon, Daisy Fuentes is hip, attractive, and in the know. Modeling may have made her face recognizable the world over, but her career took off when she became the first Latina VJ (video jockey) for MTV, the cable television music network.

She was the first VJ to appear on both the Spanish-language and original MTV. The gig has made Fuentes a natural with a microphone in her hand and she appears regularly on talk shows, variety shows, sitcoms, and beauty pageants.

Fuentes has interviewed hot bands, singing sensations, celebrities, beauty queens, fitness gurus, and athletes. A bilingual gem, she travels to Latin-American countries where MTV Latino is syndicated, such as Mexico, Paraguay, and Venezuela.

Born in Havana, Cuba, Fuentes was raised in Madrid and came to the United States when she was seven. The transition to an Anglo community was not easy at first, but she blossomed, even becoming the first Latina homecoming queen for her high school.

In college, she studied journalism and communications and in 1988, she got her first television break as a weather girl. Working her way up to reporter and anchor for the evening news of Univision's New York affiliate station, she built up her courage to send in a demo tape to MTV. MTV was sold on her television presence and bilingual capabilities, and she quickly made her mark on the Latino television community as host of MTV Internacional.

MTV was her launching pad. She went on to host several MTV programs including *One on One with Michael Jordan* and *Fashionably Loud*. She had her own talk show, *Talk All-Stars*, on CNBC and became cohost of the family show *America's Funniest Home Videos*. She has appeared in several television shows, including sitcoms and soap operas such as *Larry Sanders*, *Cybill*, *MAD TV*, and *Loving*.

🔹The transition to an Anglo community was not easy for Fuentes at first, but she blossomed, even becoming the first Latina homecoming queen for her high school.

A vivacious and charming on-air personality with a sense of humor, she has emceed the Miss Universe Pageant, American Music Awards, Latino Laugh Festival, *Billboard* Latin Awards, the Alma Awards, *Dick Clark's New Year's Rocking Eve*, World Music Awards, MTV U.S. Top 20 Countdown, and the MTV Video Music Awards.

As an icon for fashion, Fuentes has also hosted shows like *Styleworld* on the Women's Entertainment Network. The show features exotic locations and their local attractions, specialty shops, boutiques, artists, and restaurants.

Representing the Revlon cosmetics and fragrance lines, Fuentes was already used to the spotlight before she went on international television. She has appeared on magazine covers such as *Vanidades* and *Harper's Bazaar, Cosmopolitan en Español, Fitness, Latina,* and *Shape*. She has also produced exercise videos and swimsuit calendars.

Fuentes realizes that being a Latina celebrity in mainstream America brings with it responsibility. Honored as an Outstanding Woman in Media by the Latin Coalition for Fair Media, she brings visibility to the Hispanic community in a positive way.

Fuentes uses her position and voice to heighten awareness of various health issues and organizations. She works with the Pediatric AIDS Foundation, St. Jude's Hospital, and the Starlight Children's Foundation, which makes the wishes of seriously ill children come true. As a daughter of a breast cancer survivor, Fuentes is also active with the University of California Los Angeles/Revlon Breast Cancer Research campaign.

Activists, Leaders, and Politicians: Taking a Stand

La Pola (Policarpa Salavarrieta)
(Colombia, 1795–1817)

A national heroine of Colombia who worked as a spy in the resistance movement against Spanish rule, La Pola gave her life in the fight for Colombia's independence.

A seamstress turned spy, La Pola was young but her ideals for justice and political equality were ageless. A rebel, she fought passionately for her people's freedom from Spanish rule.

Born in a small mountain village in Colombia, La Pola was a seamstress by the time she turned fifteen. Her older brothers, who were studying to be Augustinian monks in the regional capital of Santa Fe, influenced the political beliefs of La Pola and her sister. They warned her that Spanish rule was wrong and that many of their people suffered at their injustices.

Spain ruled the land with racial divisions, and there was not much of a chance for those born as Native Americans, blacks, or mestizos to hold more than menial jobs. Creoles could work with the church or government, but could never rise above their stations, either.

Her family grew restless from Spanish oppression, believing they should have the same opportunities as the Peninsulars—Spanish-born whites who were the highest-ranking ethnic group. La Pola was convinced that her brothers were right about Spanish rule.

Because she was an exceptional seamstress, La Pola was able to find many jobs in Bogotá. She worked her way up the ranks to work in the houses of Spanish royalist families there. She projected intelligence, high morals, and patriotic ideas, had connections and referrals by her godparents.

Soon after she moved to Santa Fe, she immediately connected with the resistance movement, the armies assigned there, and the guerrillas from Casanare. La Pola gained contacts within the Spanish troops and urged Creoles who had joined them to mutiny.

With her ability to read and write, La Pola served as a strong resource, a true force to be reckoned with and a go-between. She joined an underground network that assisted Creole guerrillas with food and shelter while keeping them informed. It was easy for her to work quietly in many homes while listening for news about troop movement. Any information she heard while at her jobs, she passed on to the revolutionaries.

In 1810, the Creoles overthrew the royal government. For a few years they governed themselves in peace but the Spanish returned and took control again with a vengeance, imposing martial law. Hundreds of Creoles who were considered revolutionaries were executed without trial.

   At the age of twenty-two, La Pola worked to free the Creoles from Spanish rule and empower them with a voice in their government and in their destinies.

It was not long before the Spanish had a list of spies. La Pola, who was only twenty-two at the time, knew the risks but it did not stop her from trying to free her people from Spanish rule and empower them with a voice in their own government and in their destinies.

Within a short time she was arrested and sentenced to death by firing squad. She did not fear death, but rather thought it an escape from the tyrannical troops. She was shot in the town square as a "republican agent."

Two years after her death, the rebels took control of their land once again. Today there is a statue of La Pola in Bogotá, a tribute to her as a great patriot, a national heroine, and a martyr for freedom.

Jovita Idar de Juárez (United States, 1885–1946)

A prominent journalist and civil rights activist, Jovita Idar de Juárez founded the first Mexican-American women's political organization, La Liga Femenil.

> "Educate a woman and you educate a family."
> —Slogan of La Liga Femenil Mexicanista

Lynchings and beatings of Chicanos were a common occurrence on the Texas-Mexico border. In the early 1900s, Mexicans and Mexican Americans living in that area were poorly treated, whether they were looking for a job, an education, or legal justice. Discrimination was brutal.

Jovita Idar was an interpreter, educator, and political activist. She was also one of the most prominent journalists in Spanish-language newspapers in South Texas and turned to journalism to publicize the poverty and prejudice practiced against Mexican Americans. She wrote numerous articles on education and on preserving Mexican heritage. She followed in the footsteps of her father, a liberal journalist who owned a newspaper.

She founded La Liga Femenil Mexicanista in 1911 to oppose lynching and promote equal education for women.

In 1911, Idar helped her family organize the First Mexican Congress, El Primer Congreso Mexicanisto, held in Laredo, Texas. Mexican-American leaders, including women, came to speak, share their experiences, and find solutions to numerous injustices, including the abuses of the criminal justice system. The congress addressed community issues like education, labor, and economics.

From the congress grew La Liga Femenil Mexicanista (Mexican Feminist League), the first Mexican-American women's political organization.

Idar was elected the first president. The group focused much attention on educating children of the poor and working toward equal rights for women.

Idar also organized a medical relief group, the White Cross, to help people injured in the Mexican Revolution (1911). She traveled throughout northern Mexico with revolutionary forces as a nurse.

✂ In 1911, Idar helped her family organize the First Mexican Congress, El Primer Congreso Mexicanisto, held in Laredo, Texas.

Idar was one of eight children born to Nicasio Idar, a small newspaper publisher, and his wife, Jovita. In 1903 she earned a teaching degree from the Holding Institute, a Methodist school, but quit her job when she could not improve the poor conditions of the school.

She joined the family newspaper, *La Crónica*, along with her two brothers. It criticized anti-Mexican discrimination, lynching, and poor social conditions while supporting the Mexican revolution.

She later joined the newspaper *El Progreso* as its editor. She reported on the atrocities committed by the Texas Rangers against Mexican immigrants and she wrote emotionally about the lynchings she witnessed. She also noted that more than 300 Mexicans were executed without benefit of trial or formal charges in the 1920s. She addressed the rising tension and hatred between Mexicanos and Tejanos.

El Progreso was shut down after she wrote an editorial criticizing President Woodrow Wilson's dispatch ordering U.S. army troops to the Texas-Mexico border. It offended the United States Army and the Texas Rangers and they moved in to shut her down. She stood in the doorway to keep them at bay, but they eventually prevailed.

She headed back to *La Crónica*, which she ran after her father died in 1914. In 1917 she married Bartolo Juárez and moved to San Antonio where she became editor of *El Heraldo Cristiano*, a Methodist newspaper.

Idar continued her activism throughout her life, running a free kindergarten, supporting the Democratic Party, and interpreting for Spanish-speaking patients at the county hospital.

La Pasionaria—Dolores Ibarruri (Spain, 1895–1989)

A legendary leader and founder of the Spanish Communist Party who dedicated her life to civil rights, La Pasionaria was elected to Parliament at age eighty-one.

As her country's civil war raged on, Dolores Ibarruri embraced the war cry of Emilio Zapata, made famous during the Mexican Revolution: "It is better to die on your feet than to live on your knees!"

A fiery, legendary leader known as "La Pasionaria" (the Passion Flower), Ibarruri was a founder and leader of the Spanish Communist Party. As a member of the Partido Socialista and a Republican supporter during the Spanish civil war, she was an impassioned speaker and helped many escape Spain when their lives were threatened for supporting the republic.

Ibarruri used her pseudonym when she penned articles for several communist newspapers, citing political injustices and fighting for civil rights, especially for women and those working in labor unions. She called for women to defend the Republic and she tried to defend women's rights in return. In 1934, she organized a women's group called Agrupación de Mujeres Antifascistas.

During a radio broadcast, she added to Zapata's motto, saying, "It is better to die the widow of a hero than the wife of a coward." Her passion made her a convincing speaker.

She herself was from a poor family. Born the eighth of eleven children, Ibarruri knew the disappointments and tragedies that befell the poverty-stricken. Unable to attend school to be trained as a teacher because of finances, she became a seamstress.

When Ibarruri married Julian Ruiz, a miner, and had six children, she felt doomed to the same life cycle. Four of her children died and she felt that it was because of inadequate medical care and because she was unable to provide them with basic nourishment. Her husband was an active trade unionist and was arrested and imprisoned for leading a strike, which limited their income further.

It was because of her children and husband that she raised her voice and was determined to have it heard. She wanted solutions and a way to improve their lives.

She joined the Communist Party and was elected to the Provincial Committee of the Basque Communist Party. Her visibility and popularity grew as she confronted the issues head-on.

When she took on the job as editor of the left-wing newspaper *Mundo Obrero*, it helped her to campaign for land reform and union rights, and to improve women's conditions.

The fire grew hot as Ibarruri spoke out more and she became a political target. In September 1931, she was arrested for hiding a Communist friend who was wanted by the authorities, but she believed that was just an excuse to imprison her for her audacity and activism. She was released briefly before being re-arrested and wasn't released again until January 1933.

🔖 Known as "La Pasionaria" (the Passion Flower), Ibarruri was a founder and leader of the Spanish Communist Party.

In 1934, she led the First Congress of the Committee of Women, followed by the worldwide Congress of Women in Paris. She sent her remaining children to Russia to study and to keep them safe from the war-ravaged country. When the republic lost the vote Ibarruri fled the country in the mass exodus of Communist sympathizers to be with her children.

She did not sit idle in Russia, but worked her way up the Communist Party ranks to become secretary general in 1942 and president in 1960. She was awarded the Lenin Peace Prize. When she voiced her opinion against the Red Army invasion of Czechoslovakia, however, her outspoken passion once again threatened her safety.

In 1977, after thirty-eight years (and the death of Francisco Franco), she returned to Spain, the land she loved and fought for. She was elected to Parliament in Spain's first elections in forty years. Even though she was eighty-one years old and never had formal training or an extensive background in politics, the masses adored her almost like a saint.

She died in 1989 from pneumonia, an ailment she had been plagued with but never had treated. She was ninety-three and a picture of incredible courage and self-sacrifice.

Felisa Rincón de Gautier (Puerto Rico, 1897–1994)
The first woman elected mayor of San Juan, Puerto Rico, and a pioneer in the fight for women's rights, Felisa Rincón de Gautier served as goodwill ambassador under four United States presidents and received numerous prestigious awards from countries around the world for her efforts.

So loved was Felisa Rincón de Gautier as the first female mayor of San Juan, Puerto Rico, she was re-elected to the post four times. From 1946 to 1968, "Doña Fela" was the people's mayor.

She made politics accessible, personal, and real. She served as a United States goodwill ambassador under four North American presidents. She helped Puerto Rico Governor Luis Muñoz Marín establish the Popular Democratic Party in the 1930s.

Rincón de Gautier opened the doors of the government to the people, literally. She held weekly open houses to hear grievances and see constituents. She was a pioneer in the movement of political rights for women, and helped women win the vote in 1932. She sought community reform and was able to improve housing, schools, sanitation facilities, and roads. She opened the first municipal centers for elder care, legal aid, and medical assistance centers and even helped form a Little League. She expanded care for the underprivileged and established the first day care programs that would serve as the model for the Head Start program in the United States.

To bring something special to the tropical holidays, her trademark gift was importing snow for children's Christmas parties. She also hosted a Feast of the Three Kings party for thousands of children and provided each of them with presents.

Her mother died when she was eleven and she dropped out of high school to help her lawyer father, Enrique Rincón Plumey, with her seven siblings until finances improved. During the 1930s Rincón de Gautier moved to New York and worked as a seamstress in a fashionable Fifth Avenue shop, learning the trade and honing her acute business sense, and saving money. When she returned to Puerto Rico, she was able to open a series of clothing and flower shops.

Rincón de Gautier's husband, Genaro A. Gautier, served as assistant attorney general of Puerto Rico and the secretary general of the Popular Democratic Party. She was president of the party's San Juan committee. By the 1940s she was approached several times to become city manager. She declined until 1948, when she was elected to the position.

Though she was criticized for employing so many of her relatives, it did not affect her popularity. She was re-elected four times, serving as mayor for twenty-two years.

Worldwide recognition came when she traveled to South and Central America on behalf of the United States Department of State, in 1953 and 1956. She spoke about education programs and the unique relationship between the commonwealth of Puerto Rico and the United States.

Rincón de Gautier's trademark holiday gift was flying in snow for children's Christmas parties.

She transcended political and geographical barriers to be recognized for her goodwill efforts by many countries. In 1960, she was Puerto Rico's delegate to the United States Democratic National Convention. She was awarded the Gold Medal of Honor, the Don Quixote Medal, the Simon Bolivar Medal, and the Medal of Isabella the Catholic Queen from Spain. She received Ecuador's Gold Medal of Honor, the French Joan of Arc Medal, the Israeli Order of Merit, the Vatican's Pope Pius XII Medal, and the Cruz del Santo Sepulcro de Jerusalem.

Eleanor Roosevelt presented Rincón de Gautier the Hebrew Philanthropic Award in 1961. She won the 1953 Woman of the Year award   125 from the League of American Women and was recognized as the Woman of the Americas by the Union of American Women.

Rincón de Gautier continued to serve as a delegate to national conventions until 1992 when she made her last political appearance at the age of ninety-five.

Luisa Moreno (Guatemala, 1906–1988)

Civil rights activist and trade union leader who organized the first Latino civil rights assembly and was the first female vice president of UCAPAWA.

When Luisa Moreno went to work at a Spanish Harlem sweatshop to help support her family during the Great Depression, she was outraged and appalled to see the working conditions and how minorities suffered under segregationist policies.

She united Latinas to stand up against police brutality in New York City and urged them to join La Liga de Costureras, a garment workers' union. It would be the start of Moreno's lifetime commitment to securing civil and human rights. As an advocate for better working conditions, Moreno became a full-time labor organizer and focused the spotlight on the deplorable and unfair working conditions in sweatshops, canneries, factories, and agricultural fields in the 1930s and 1940s.

In 1930 Moreno joined the Communist Party of New York because it aligned with her progressive ideals in organizing workers and fighting for better living conditions, desegregation, relief aid, and against deporting Mexicans without just cause.

Over the years, she worked with the International Ladies Garment Workers Union, the American Federation of Labor (AFL), and the more radical Congress of Industrial Organizations (CIO). Although Moreno worked for many ethnic groups, her focus was on Mexican Americans and more specifically, Latinas. She helped start unions for people in the Pecan Shellers Strike in Texas, cotton workers in south Texas, beet workers in

Colorado and Michigan, and cannery workers in California.

Born Blanca Rosa Lopez Rodriguez to a wealthy Guatemalan family in 1907, Luisa came to Oakland, California, in 1928 to attend the College of the Holy Names, a private school. Upon returning to Guatemala, she worked at various newspapers, which fueled her interest in social reform.

She returned to the United States, adopting the name Luisa Moreno to spare her family embarrassment. They felt she was tainting the family name because of their opposing political viewpoints. She chose her new name in honor of a famous Mexican labor organizer, Luis Moreno.

While working as a reporter in Mexico, Moreno met and married Mexican artist Miguel Angel de Leon. They moved to New York where her baby, Mytyl, was born and Moreno began her union work. In 1935 they divorced. She moved back to California where she was able to help secure higher wages, equal pay for equal work, and benefits for female cannery workers. Women made up 75 percent of the cannery work force.

> Although Moreno worked for many ethnic groups, her focus was on Mexican Americans and more specifically, Latinas.

Moreno initiated El Congreso de Pueblos Que Hablan Español (the Spanish-Speaking Peoples' Congress) in 1938, which was the first Latino civil rights assembly. Delegates from across the country met in Los Angeles to discuss better education, health, and employment opportunities on a national level.

She became the first woman vice president with the United Cannery, Agricultural, Packing, and Allied Workers of America (UCAPAWA), an organization that allowed Mexican workers to be represented among the 70,000 members. She was also the first Latina member of the California CIO Council.

Moreno married Gray Bemis, a U.S. Navy sailor she had met while on an organizing trip to San Diego. They entertained ideas of retirement. She began writing a book about organizing unions while settling down in their apartment by the beach. Still, she was sought after for her experience with civil rights.

She spoke in Washington, D.C., in 1940, addressing the mass deportation of Latinos during the Depression. Many had been legal residents when they were deported but had no papers to prove it. Moreno fought for their rights and legal representation.

Moreno applied for U.S. citizenship in 1948. She was offered citizenship only if she testified against Australian labor leader Harry Bridges. She refused, knowing she would be a "free woman with a mortgaged soul." She was accused of being a Communist, and underwent hardship and betrayal but refused to denounce her stance, citing protection under the Constitution. The repercussions were great.

Despite the support of journalist Carey McWilliams and editor Ignacio Lopez, she was deported to Mexico in 1950. She continued to organize workers in Mexico, Cuba, and Guatemala. When Bemis died from emphysema, she was heartbroken and eventually moved back to her native Guatemala, where she wrote her autobiography. She died after suffering two strokes.

Minerva Bernardino (Dominican Republic, 1907–1998)

An ambassador to the United Nations and cocreator of the Commission on the Status of Women at the United Nations, Minerva Bernardino was the first woman vice president of the Economic and Social Council of the United Nations and was a pioneer in equal rights for women.

Minerva Bernardino shared a passion for human rights alongside United States First Lady Eleanor Roosevelt. At the United Nations General Assembly in 1946, Bernardino joined Roosevelt and three other female delegates to write an "Open Letter to the Women of the World."

She believed that the power of words would liberate women. The open letter asked women to take a more active role in politics and government in order to seek equal rights.

Bernardino was instrumental in changing the wording in many official United Nations documents to include the term *women*. Changing that term changed the lives of thousands of women.

Bernardino was also cocreator of the Commission on the Status of Women at the United Nations. The commission worked to formalize women's political rights and started targeting any violence against women. Twenty years later this movement would be celebrated under the United Nation's Decade for Women (1975–1985).

Bernardino wanted more commitment from governments and human rights organizations to stand by women. The commission came up with the slogan "A life free of violence: It's our right," which became the motto for the UN Campaign for Women's Human Rights.

Bernardino was a pioneer of Latin-American feminists and ahead of her time. She had grown up in a very forward-thinking home as one of seven children. Her mother was progressive, her grandfather was a provincial governor, and her father wanted her to be independent.

Orphaned at the age of fifteen, she had no qualms about working, and started her civil service career. She fought for women's and children's rights, and she worked to establish peace in the Dominican Republic.

In 1929, she was already active in the women's rights movement in the Dominican Republic where she led the Acción Feminista Dominicana, which fought for expanded rights in the 1942 constitution.

 Bernadino used the power of words to motivate women to take action in politics and government.

As the ambassador to the United Nations from the Dominican Republic in 1950, Minerva Bernardino started a career dedicated to advocating international women's rights. After the World War II horrors of the Holocaust, the United Nations approved the Universal Declaration of Human Rights in 1948.

When Bernardino was a delegate at the 1945 Conference for the Charter of the United Nations, she was only one of four women to sign the

129

United Nations Charter. Bernardino was a driving force in getting the group to include the words "Equal Rights for Women" within the charter. The freedom-fighting women also managed to change the term "Universal Declaration of the Rights of Man" to "Universal Declaration of Human Rights" and the phrase "Free Men" to "Free Human Beings" in the United Nations Covenant of Human Rights.

Bernardino was active in the United Nations Children's Fund and was the first woman vice president of the Economic and Social Council of the United Nations. She became chair of the Inter-American Commission on Women from 1944 to 1949, the first official body to promote women's rights.

She was awarded the Hispanic Heritage Award for excellence in education in 1995. In 1997, the fiftieth anniversary of the United Nations Commission for the Status of Women, she was honored for her role in creating the commission.

Emma Tenayuca (United States, 1916–1999)

A labor organizer and strike leader who served as director of the Communist Party in Texas and organized the first successful strike of Mexican women pecan shellers, Tenayuca was one of the most respected unionists of her time.

Emma Tenayuca was moved by the hard-working families struggling to feed their children in San Antonio, Texas. With an unconditional commitment to justice and compassion, she became known as "La Pasionaria de Tejas" (the Passion Flower of Texas).

At a time when women and Mexicans in America had no voice, she grew to be one of the most respected and dedicated unionists, a natural-born leader and humanitarian.

When the Southern Pecan Shelling Company, the largest local industry at the time, announced in 1938 that it would reduce wages from six cents a pound to three cents, the thought was inconceivable. The workers already lived in poverty.

Tenayuca was only twenty-one when she organized what would go down in history as the Pecan Shellers Strike, the first successful strike of the underpaid and mistreated Mexican women pecan shellers in 1938. According to historian Don Carleton, it was "an important landmark in the history of the Mexican-American struggle for economic and social justice."

> Tenayuca organized the Pecan Shellers Strike of 1938—"an important landmark in the history of the Mexican-American struggle for economic and social justice."

Thousands went on strike at 130 plants throughout the city. The resistance was unbelievable. Hundreds of picketers were tear-gassed and beaten, arrested, and kept in deplorable conditions. Thirty-three women were placed in a jail cell designed to hold six.

Even though Tenayuca was singled out for being a troublemaker and a Communist agitator, she persisted and led in negotiations that lasted several months.

An arbitration board finally recognized the union and they won a minimum wage of twenty-five cents an hour, established by the Fair Labor Standards Act. It was a short-lived victory. The company elected to close its doors rather than pay the increase. The company eventually reopened but it mechanized the plants, which displaced thousands of Mexican workers. Tenayuca continued to help workers.

Tenayuca had lived with her grandparents while growing up, to ease the burden of eleven children on her parents. Often she visited the Plaza del Zacate, where radical political representatives came to speak and to hear family grievances. It was there that she first saw the struggles of working-class people.

She was only sixteen when she became involved with the labor movement and nineteen when she was elected as an official of the United Cannery, Agricultural, Packing, and Allied Workers of America (UCAPAWA), a union chartered by the CIO. Instrumental in forming two local chapters of the International Ladies Garment Workers Union, she was jailed numerous times for her beliefs, but her dedication never wavered.

Reading the works of Tolstoy and Marx while in high school influenced her to join the Communist Party in 1937. She married Homer Brooks, leader of the Texas Communist Party, and had one son. In time, she was named director of the Communist Party for the state. She was "red-baited" in a *Time* magazine article that described her as "a slim, vivacious labor organizer with black eyes and a Red philosophy."

In 1939, Tenayuca tried to hold a meeting of the Communist Party, but more than 5,000 anti-Communists stormed the auditorium. Known as "the Municipal Auditorium Riot," she barely escaped with her life. Thereafter, she was hounded by death threats and was blacklisted, leaving her unable to find work. Fearing for her own safety, she was forced to leave Texas because of the anti-Mexican, antiunionist, and anticommunist hysteria.

In San Francisco she earned her teaching certification from San Francisco State College. Later she earned a master's degree in education from Our Lady of the Lake University. When she returned to San Antonio in the late 1960s, she began a second career as a teacher.

Eva Perón (Argentina, 1919–1952)

The ambitious, politically savvy, and controversial first lady of Argentina fought for human rights and was an integral force in achieving equal rights for women and women's suffrage in Argentina.

If ever there was a controversial political leader, Eva Perón—Evita—was it. Charismatic and colorful, she was "the Cinderella of Argentina."

As the first lady of Argentina, she was committed to the poor and the working class but she owned more than 100 furs, Christian Dior dresses, and expensive jewelry. She was adored by many, feared by some, hated by others.

Perón was one of five illegitimate children born to Juana Ibarguren and Juan Duarte, a deputy justice of the peace. Although he acknowledged them as legally his, when he died they were not allowed into the funeral. "Eva Maria" saw the disparity between the rich and the poor and made up her mind that she would one day be a famous actress to leave her poverty well behind her.

She headed for Buenos Aires when she was fifteen. She modeled for magazines and became moderately successful as an actress onstage and in film but found some celebrity status with radio. She starred in *Heroines of History*, a biography series she started that featured illustrious women like Elizabeth I of England, Sarah Bernhardt, Isadora Duncan, and Catherine the Great. The show ran until 1945.

The radio would serve her well as she made a segue into politics. She was only twenty-four when she met Colonel Juan Domingo Perón at an earthquake relief fundraiser in 1944. He was the minister of war and secretary of labor. He was forty-eight, charming, and intelligent. They both came from working-class roots. There was an instant chemistry between them and they married in 1945.

Evita worshipped and loved him and became the driving force behind their rise to power. They traveled the countryside and working-class neighborhoods where he pledged himself to be a man of the people. Making "impromptu" speeches in the streets full of cheering crowds, he urged opposition to the current government.

 Eva Perón was adored by many, feared by some, hated by others.

Juan Perón's rule came to depend on Evita's popularity. Using her talents as a great actress and orator, she plugged him on the radio with her emotion and won over thousands. With her brilliant campaigning he was elected president in 1946.

They became the voice of the working class. She was given her own office in the capital. He appointed her to a variety of positions, including head of the Radio Association of Argentina and director of the Social Aid

Foundation, a state charity for the poor. Perón advocated minimum wages, decent working conditions, and regular raises. She kept a pile of money on her desk to give to visitors.

The Peróns ruled with an iron fist, however, creating fear and repression when they jailed anyone who opposed them. They controlled information by censoring radio and newspapers.

Despite her success, Perón never gained social status within high society. When the Sociedad de Beneficencia, a social group in charge of Argentinean charities, refused to make her honorary president—a first lady tradition—she cut funding to the group.

> Perón advocated minimum wages, decent working conditions, and regular raises. She kept a pile of money on her desk to give to visitors.

Still, to some she was known as the Lady of Hope. As the unofficial minister of labor and health, she formed a charitable foundation to help build schools, hospitals, orphanages, and homes for the elderly and for unwed mothers. Evita became the voice of the feminist movement—working for women's right to vote, equal pay for equal work, divorce rights, and civil equality. She formed the Association for Women's Suffrage, and Argentine women won the vote in 1947.

At home she was revered by millions and she wanted that popularity abroad. However, when Evita traveled to Europe, only Spain welcomed her, in an effort to improve trade relations. She was coolly greeted in France and by the pope, and was not invited to Buckingham Palace. The United States publication *Time* magazine revealed that she was an illegitimate child. She banned the magazine from Argentina for four months.

Evita died of cancer at the age of thirty-three. When her death was announced on the radio, she was hailed as "the Spiritual Leader of the Nation." Lines stretched for thirty blocks in every direction for two days as the dense and wild crowds gathered in the streets of Buenos Aires to mourn her death. Juan Perón had promised he would not allow her to be forgotten. Before she could be placed in a gigantic mausoleum that was being built for her, her perfectly embalmed body disappeared for almost fifteen years. It turned up in Italy under a false name. In 1976 her body was returned to Argentina and properly buried. Within three years after she died, Juan Perón fell from power.

Josefina Fierro de Bright (Mexico, 1920–)

This labor union organizer and civil rights activist organized the Mexican-American underground railroad and served as executive secretary of El Congreso.

Americans feared losing their jobs to Mexicans during the Depression and in an act of panic, repatriation was launched. The United States deported Mexican Americans even though they were citizens and had lived in the United States all their lives.

Josefina Fierro de Bright organized an underground railroad reminiscent of Harriet Tubman's. In the 1930s and 1940s, she started the intricate underground system that returned hundreds of Mexican Americans who had been illegally deported to Mexico by the United States.

Fierro de Bright fought for their rights time and again. In 1943 she single-handedly negotiated with Vice President Henry Wallace, appealing to the Roosevelt administration to make Los Angeles out of bounds to military personnel during "the zoot suit riots."

The sailors and Anglo civilians who hunted down and beat up Mexican Americans also raped dozens of Mexican-American women. This ignited the macho spirit of the Mexican-American men, who did not want gringos near their women. The administration ordered all military personnel to stay out of Mexican districts in Los Angeles, which helped bring an end to the violence.

The riots were not her first experience dealing with racism. When Fierro de Bright and her family served meals to migrant workers, it exposed her to the injustices of farm labor camps at an early age. She abandoned her studies at UCLA to become a labor union organizer.

She served as executive secretary of El Congreso de Pueblos de Habla Español (the Spanish-Speaking Peoples' Congress), one of the first national Latino civil rights organizations in the United States. The congress held a national conference in 1939 that included more than 1,000 delegates from almost 130 organizations. After the conference, the organization drafted a comprehensive platform to deal with injustices.

> When Fierro de Bright and her family served meals to migrant workers, it exposed her to the injustices of farm labor camps at an early age. She abandoned her studies at UCLA to become a labor union organizer.

From her position, Fierro de Bright organized protests against racism in the Los Angeles, California, school system, against the exclusion of Mexican-American youths from public swimming pools, and against police brutality.

In 1942, she was one of the key figures in organizing the Sleepy Lagoon Defense Committee on behalf of seventeen Chicano youths who were unjustly accused of murdering another youngster and were held without bail and with little evidence. The grass-roots efforts and unyielding protests paid off even though it took two years. The convictions were overturned and all the young men were acquitted and freed.

Fierro de Bright was instrumental in the coordination of El Congreso's support for Spanish-speaking workers in various unions. She worked with other labor organizers such as Luisa Moreno, Emma Tenayuca, and Bert Corona, promoting activism from a grass-roots level.

Dr. Antonia Pantoja (Puerto Rico, 1922–)

The first Latina recipient of the prestigious U.S. Presidential Medal of Freedom Award, Antonia Pantoja founded the Puerto Rican Forum and ASPIRA, as well as numerous other organizations dedicated to the education and empowerment of disadvantaged youths.

"One cannot live a lukewarm life. You have to live with passion."
—Dr. Antonia Pantoja

hen she moved to New York and started working as a factory welder in 1944, Antonia Pantoja saw the blatant racism and discrimination against Puerto Ricans. They needed leadership and vision to help them restore their dignity. They needed to learn about their rights and political power.

Pantoja had come to the United States to pursue her education, and she saw education as an answer to many problems. She earned her master's of social work degree in 1954 and a doctorate nearly twenty years later.

She began teaching with a profound interest in addressing the needs of disadvantaged children. In the 1950s she led a group of young Puerto Rican activists to seek innovative solutions to the high dropout rates and the debilitating unemployment. They had to become active in their own destinies.

She helped build numerous institutions that offered support. In 1961 Pantoja organized the ASPIRA ("strive") Club in New York. ASPIRA brought Latino students together to educate them and develop their leadership skills. They worked with educators and social work professionals who shared Pantoja's concern for the high dropout rates among Puerto Rican students. ASPIRA grew into a national organization dedicated to empowering communities and Puerto Rican youths in particular.

In 1952, she helped found the Puerto Rican Association for Community Affairs (PRACA), the first Puerto Rican civil rights advocacy organization. It focused on leadership development and women's issues.

In 1957 she formed the Puerto Rican Forum, a think tank to come up with special projects to address the community's needs. It turned into the National Puerto Rican Forum, a service organization that has trained nearly 1 million Hispanics and helped them find employment.

She was a pioneer for the advancement of bilingual education, and advocated litigation against the New York City Board of Education in 1972. It resulted in a landmark case mandating bilingual education in the school system.

As a professor at the Columbia University School of Social Work, she learned of resources that could help communities. In 1970, she wrote a grant proposal and secured funding to establish the Puerto Rican Research and Resource Center, an organization devoted to data collection and policy development.

Dr. Pantoja moved to California for health reasons, and she became an associate professor of social work at San Diego State University. She founded the Graduate School for Community Development, an institution that serves communities and neighborhoods throughout the nation by helping citizens develop their own problem-solving skills.

In 1973 she founded Universidad Boricua, a Puerto Rican research center and bilingual university, and in 1985 launched Producir, a project that enables rural communities to create cottage industries, generate employment, and provide services.

When she returned to New York in 1998, she wrote her autobiography, *Memoir of a Visionary: Antonia Pantoja,* published by Arte Publico in 2002. It is a model of commitment and vision.

In 2001, she helped found the Latino Educational Media Center, which disseminates media information on the Latino experience in the United States.

> In 1958 Pantoja organized the ASPIRA ("strive") Club in New York. It brought Latino students together to encourage growth and leadership skills.

Pantoja was the first Puerto Rican Latina to receive the Presidential Medal of Freedom Award, which she received in 1996 from President Bill Clinton. It is the highest honor bestowed upon a civilian by the United States government. Only three other Puerto Ricans have received the honor.

The Mirabal Sisters (Dominican Republic, 1924–1960; 1926–1960; 1936–1960)

National heroines of the Dominican Republic who were assassinated for their involvement in the resistance movement against the dictator Rafael Trujillo, the martyrdom of the Mirabal sisters led to a revolution and the assassination of Trujillo.

Their code name was Las Mariposas, "the Butterflies." Patria, María Teresa, and Minerva Mirabal belonged to the underground resistance, leading clandestine activities against President Rafael Trujillo's oppressive dictatorship in the Dominican Republic.

Their mission was to restore democracy and human rights to the island nation. They were symbols of dignity, strength, and inspiration.

The risk was great. Resisters to the government "disappeared" suddenly at the hands of the secret police. Others were imprisoned, tortured, or brutally killed. Yet, the Mirabal sisters believed freedom was worth the risk.

In November 1959, Trujillo announced that his two main problems were the Church and the Mirabal sisters. Within a year, all three sisters were brutally murdered.

They grew up in a family of privilege, daughters to Enrique Mirabal Fernandez and Mercedes Reyes Camilo (known as Chea), who owned a farm, coffee mill, meat market, and rice factory. Patria was born on the anniversary of the Dominican Republic's independence. Her name meant "fatherland" and signified patriotism. She married Pedro Gonzalez, a farmer, and had four children.

Minerva was incredibly intelligent and loved to study, memorizing French poetry at the age of seven. She was a fan of Pablo Neruda and Pablo Picasso. Her husband was Manuel "Manolo" Tavarez Justo. They had two children.

The youngest, María Teresa, was a math genius. She married engineer Leandro Guzmán and had one daughter. She loved following in Minerva's footsteps.

Their family's status ensured political favor with the dictator—but only if they ignored the government's rampant corruption and disregard for human rights. The Mirabal sisters thought him contemptible. When Minerva rebuked Trujillo's advances, it humiliated and angered him. He began his relentless harassment of the Mirabal family.

Minerva refused to write a letter of apology for leaving one of Trujillo's parties early. She and her mother were imprisoned. Their father was once imprisoned for not buying Trujillo's book. Minerva was denied access to the university because she wrote a thesis paper supporting basic human rights and the need for a change in government to secure those rights. When it was leaked that the sisters were behind a takeover plot, all three of their husbands were jailed.

The Mirabal sisters were symbols of dignity, strength, and inspiration.

No matter how many times Trujillo jailed them or how much of their property he took, Minerva, Patria, and María Teresa would never agree with his politics. Their family understood.

In 1960 the sisters went to visit their husbands in jail, but they did not make it home. Their jeep was found in a ravine. The story goes that Trujillo's men ambushed the women and pulled them from their jeep into the sugar cane fields, where they handcuffed, strangled, and clubbed the sisters to death. They then put the women's bodies back in the jeep and pushed the vehicle over the edge of the mountainside in order to make it look like an accident.

Patria was thirty-six years old, Minerva was thirty-four, and María Teresa was twenty-four.

The murder was the last straw for the Dominican people. The revolt took root and started Trujillo's downfall. Within one year, Trujillo was assassinated.

The Mirabal sisters were national martyrs. Elsa Nuñez painted their images on the Obelisco del Malecón. The title of the painting is "A Song to Liberty." Ironically, Trujillo had ordered the construction of the obelisk as a shrine to himself.

Dedé (Bélgica), the remaining Mirabal sister, tends the museum that commemorates her sisters. Julia Alvarez wrote a historical fiction novel based on their story, titled *In the Time of the Butterflies*, which was made into a movie produced by and starring Salma Hayek.

At the first Latin-American and Caribbean Feminist Meeting in Colombia in 1981, the day of their death was declared International Day Against Violence Toward Women. It is celebrated on November 25, the anniversary of their death.

Violeta Chamorro (Nicaragua, 1929–)

The first woman president of Nicaragua, Violeta Chamorro was the country's first democratically elected president in almost 200 years.

> "The biggest desire since my husband died for this flag and bequeathed it to me, is to fight for democracy."
>
> —Violeta Chamorro,
> 1991 acceptance speech for the Democracy Award

Violeta Chamorro wanted simply to restore democracy to her native Nicaragua. After an eight-year-long civil war with unbelievable bloodshed, she hoped her election as the first female president of Nicaragua might bring peace and freedom for her people, who for too long had suffered at the hands of splintered radical political groups. However, her influence went beyond Nicaraguan borders. She was also the first woman to ever govern a Central American country.

Born Violeta Barrios, she was the daughter of a wealthy cattle rancher and landowner. She was educated in the United States. She dropped out of college in Virginia and returned to Nicaragua when her father died.

In 1950 she married Pedro Joaquin Chamorro Cardenal, the *La Prensa* publisher who had inherited the newspaper from his father. He was also the descendant of influential Nicaraguan statesmen.

Outspoken in his political beliefs and in the freedom of the press, he regularly opposed the practices of the Somoza dictatorship. He was repeatedly jailed and threatened. In 1957, the Chamorro family escaped to Costa Rica where they lived for several years.

When Pedro returned to Nicaragua in 1960, he continued to voice dissent against Somoza's sons. He was assassinated in 1978, and his death touched off a civil war in the country.

Chamorro assumed control of *La Prensa* as publisher after the assassination and maintained an oppositional stance against Somoza. She contributed money to an antigovernment organization known as the Sandinista National Liberation Front (FSLN), which defeated the Somoza regime in 1979.

Chamorro became one of the five-member civilian executive "junta" in the new government, but grew disillusioned within a year, as the FSLN became more aligned with socialist views under the leadership of Daniel Ortega. He expelled her and other members from the board and consolidated his power over the nation. Angered with his betrayal and the authoritarian nature of the new regime, Chamorro became a constant vocal critic of the Sandinista regime from 1980 to 1990, using *La Prensa* as the vehicle. She also took out a full-page advertisement in the *New York Times,* denouncing Ortega's rule while trying to secure support from the United States in her mission to restore democracy.

Another civil war erupted. In 1987, Central American presidents intervened to bring Nicaragua's war to an end. After agreeing to disarmament, a free press, and free elections, the National Opposition Union chose Chamorro as their presidential candidate.

As the president of Nicaragua, Chamorro brought hope for a democracy and better relations with the United States.

She defeated Ortega in the first democratic election Nicaragua had seen in almost 200 years, and she was inaugurated in 1990. As the president of Nicaragua, Chamorro brought hope for a democracy and better relations with the United States.

Seeing the unemployment, poverty, and aftermath of the brutal war, she promised to help reform the country's troubled economy, negotiate a truce to end the civil war, grant amnesty to political prisoners, restore private property, advocate no censorship of the press, reduce the military, and decrease human rights violations. Although the Sandinistas blocked her efforts repeatedly, she persevered until her term ended in 1995.

In 1991, the United States National Endowment for Democracy presented Chamorro with the Democracy Award, which is given to representatives of different countries for their contributions toward democracy.

Dolores Huerta (United States, 1930–)

Cofounder and first vice president of the United Farm Workers Union, Dolores Huerta was the first Latina inducted into the National Women's Hall of Fame.

"I think we showed the world that nonviolence can work to make social change."

—Dolores Huerta

Dolores Huerta was known as "the Dragon Lady," a nickname bestowed upon her by landowners who had to face her when she fought for the rights of migrant workers.

Her direct approach made it clear that their derogatory sexist and racist remarks and questionable actions were unacceptable.

For more than half a century, Huerta has dedicated her life to the struggle for social justice and dignity for poor migrant farm workers. She is the most prominent Chicana labor leader and civil rights activist in the United States.

She is the cofounder and first vice president of the United Farm Workers (UFW), the first successful union of agricultural workers in the history of the United States. Sometimes she was known as Dolores "Huelga," or "strike," for the numbers of strikes she organized.

Born Dolores Fernandez in New Mexico, she was raised in California's San Joaquin Valley with two brothers, two sisters, and a divorced mother, who worked in a cannery and as a waitress to make ends meet during the Depression. Still, Huerta was involved with youth activities; took piano, violin, and dance lessons; sang in choir; and was an active Girl Scout. She spent her free time with her grandfather, who called her "seven tongues" because she talked too much. This ability would later become her greatest asset.

During the 1940s their financial situation improved. They owned a restaurant and a hotel boarding house where they often let poor farm workers stay free. She and her brothers worked there, learning to appreciate all different types of people in an ethnically diverse neighborhood. Huerta saw that they worked very long hours for very little pay and absolutely no benefits. They would sometimes get paid fifty cents per bucket of what they had picked, sometimes, twenty cents. Some farm owners would deduct from workers' pay if they drank their water during the day. Huerta promised she would make their lives better.

Huerta might have been inspired by her mother's compassion and her father's activism. She had stayed in touch with him when he worked as a coal miner and later with labor unions. He returned to school and earned a college degree. He won election to the New Mexico state legislature where he worked for better labor laws.

For more than half a century, Huerta has dedicated her life to the struggle for social justice and dignity for poor migrant farm workers.

Huerta earned a teaching degree but found she wanted to help the kids who arrived to school barefoot and hungry. She turned to community work and social activism.

In the 1950s, she became a founder of the Stockton, California, chapter of the Community Service Organization (CSO), which opposed segregation and lobbied for better working conditions. They registered people to vote and organized citizenship classes for immigrants.

Farm workers' living and working conditions concerned her most. She joined forces with César Chávez and established the National Agricultural Workers Association in 1962, which became the infamous United Farm Workers, with more than 100,000 members.

Elected vice president in 1972, she devised strategies for the strikes and leading workers on the picket lines. They fought for workers' rights to minimum wages, paid holidays, unemployment insurance, and pensions. She marched 300 miles to the state capital to call attention to their struggle. After a successful nationwide boycott of California grapes, lettuce, and Gallo wines in 1978, she was the first to negotiate a bargaining contract between the UFW and California farm owners.

Married and divorced three times, Huerta had eleven children. Her extended family offered support whenever she was arrested—which was more than twenty times. In 1988, she was injured in an unprovoked beating by police officers. With broken ribs and a ruptured spleen, she underwent emergency surgery. People were outraged and caused the San Francisco Police Department to change its rules regarding crowd control.

Huerta helped found KUFW—Radio Campesina, the union's radio station in California. She is honored in countless murals and corridos (ballads). She has worked as vice president for the Coalition for Labor Union Women and as vice president of the California AFL-CIO. She is a board member for the Fund for the Feminist Majority.

She is a recipient of the American Civil Liberties Union Roger Baldwin Medal of Liberty Award, the Eugene V. Debs Foundation Outstanding American Award, and the Consumers' Union Trumpeter's Award. In 1998 *Ms.* magazine listed her as one of three Women of the Year, and the *Ladies Home Journal* listed her among the 100 Most Important Women of the Twentieth Century.

Huerta received the 2000 Leadership Award from the Hispanic Heritage Awards. She was honored by the California State Senate with the Outstanding Labor Leader Award, received the Woman of Courage Award from the National Organization for Women, and was the first Latina inducted into the National Women's Hall of Fame.

Maria de Lourdes Pintasilgo (Portugal, 1930–)

Foremost an activist for women's rights, Pintasilgo served as a member of the European Parliament, as ambassador and prime minister of Portugal, and has held numerous other political and social offices. She is currently on the Council of Women World Leaders.

Women being persecuted. Women and voting rights. Women and equality. In her position as prime minister of Portugal and other influential political offices she has held, Maria de Lourdes Pintasilgo saw an opportunity to keep women's rights at the forefront of her agenda. She does so with theology, Christian spirituality, and connections in nongovernmental organizations.

Pintasilgo's approach has been called Christian feminism. The label is secondary. She has worked to promote women and their rights through political, religious, cultural, economic, and social reform at an international level. Issues relate to identity, citizenship, and contributions of women in different fields.

While working as prime minister from 1979 to 1980 and as a member of the European Parliament, Pintasilgo often found international resources and networking support systems for women. Linking women's organizations like the Women's Liaison Group with religious entities like the Ecumenical Council of Churches offered different resources on discrimination and alternatives to family law and working women.

> Pintasilgo has worked to promote women and their rights through political, religious, cultural, economic, and social reform at an international level.

Before becoming involved in politics, Pintasilgo received training as an industrial engineer and worked as a researcher with the National Nuclear Energy Commission. In light of her background, she was asked to join the Council of Women World Leaders. As a council member, she helps encourage women to enter politics and serves as a resource for women in leadership positions. She is one of fifteen council members.

The organization provides a network between current and former women leaders. They seek practical solutions to national problems through fact-finding missions and debate among policy experts and advisers. Council members must be available to newly elected leaders and to mentor young women in leadership roles. The organization is based in the Kennedy School of Government at Harvard University.

Other political responsibilities have helped Pintasilgo remain in touch with communities and outreach efforts. She served as minister of Social Affairs (1974–1975), state secretary for Social Security, and ambassador of Portugal to UNESCO (1976–1979). She was also a member of the Portuguese delegation to the United Nations General Assembly. Her political aspirations also led her to run for president of Portugal in 1986.

Her books include *The New Feminism: To Think the Church Anew* and *Caring for the Future: Making the Next Decades Provide a Life Worth Living.*

Pintasilgo has been president of the Independent Commission on Population and Quality of Life. She is a member of the National Council for Life Sciences, and is a mentor of the project Towards an Active Society.

Lourdes G. Baird (Ecuador, 1935–)
A retired U.S. district attorney and district court judge, Baird has worked on many high-profile cases in California.

Lourdes G. Baird was in her mid-thirties when she decided to go back to school and study law after raising her three children. Hesitant about her decision because she was older than most of the students around her, the trepidation disappeared once she was accepted into law school. It was a match made in heaven.

She started on the fast track when she graduated with highest honors from the University of California at Los Angeles in 1973 with a degree in sociology. Three years later she graduated with honors from UCLA's law school and passed the bar the first time out when she was forty-one years old. She would eventually become the first Hispanic woman to serve as a judge in the Central District of California.

The journey to her coveted position started in 1990 when Republican Senator Pete Wilson and President George H. Bush nominated Baird as U.S. attorney of California's Central District even though she was a Democrat. One month after her nomination, she was approved by the Senate. She was fifty-five years old. Her three grown children watched her get sworn in.

Anxious to get to work in one of the most notorious districts for criminal activity, Baird would oversee seven counties and 14 million people. Her jurisdiction was known for the highly sensitive cases that came to its table. The case of Rodney King, a black motorist who was viciously beaten by officers from the Los Angeles Police Department, was one such prominent contemporary case.

The officers were initially acquitted and a riot erupted in which more than fifty people were killed and $800 million in damages resulted. Baird led the new prosecution against the police officers and obtained two convictions.

Baird is a woman of strong convictions. She is tough but fair—qualities that helped make her one of the most respected jurists in the United States. She had a short stint in private practice, served as a municipal judge on the Los Angeles Superior Court and taught law at Loyola University in Los Angeles.

> ⚜ Lourdes G. Baird is a woman of strong convictions. She is tough but fair—qualities that helped make her one of the most respected jurists in the United States.

Baird became a federal judge of the U.S. (Central California) District Court in 1992, where she served until her retirement in early 2004.

Baird belongs to the California Women Lawyers Association, the National Association of Women Judges, and the Latino Judges Association. She was president of the UCLA School of Law Alumni Association and was named 1991 Alumnus of the Year by the UCLA School of Law and Woman of Promise by the Hispanic Women's Council.

Vilma Martinez (United States, 1943–)

A civil rights activist and attorney, Martinez helped establish MALDEF as a national force during her tenure as general counsel and president.

ilma Socorro Martinez was fast becoming bitter. She hated the racist remarks and the discrimination her parents endured in their Texas hometown. Because of her skin color and ethnicity, she also endured the humiliation and helplessness caused by discrimination.

High school counselors recommended she go to vocational school instead of college, even though she was in the National Honor Society. Teachers referred to her as Spanish instead of Mexican-American to spare her feelings. There were many other such incidents that fueled her anger.

Her mother gave Martinez the best advice: If she let others destroy her that way, no one would listen to what she had to say. She had to channel her bitterness into something constructive. Because of the treatment she had received while growing up, Martinez vowed to work in civil rights to give minorities a voice.

After graduating from the University of Texas in only three years, she went to Columbia University's law school on a scholarship. As soon as she graduated, she joined the staff of the Legal Defense and Education Fund of the National Association for the Advancement of Colored People (NAACP). Working on behalf of minorities and the poor, Martinez channeled her energies there, helping victims of race and gender discrimination.

In 1970, her career took a detour when she started working as an equal employment opportunity counselor for the New York State Division of Human Rights. Her job was to draft and implement new regulations to ensure the protection of employment rights.

She joined a private practice in 1971, the same year she heard that an organization like the NAACP was starting up for Mexican Americans. The opportunity to secure civil rights for Mexican Americans on a grand scale was what she had been working toward her whole life. She and Graciela Olivarez, a Notre Dame Law School graduate, were the first women to join the Mexican American Legal Defense and Educational Fund (MALDEF).

In 1973, when she was only twenty-nine, she became president and general counsel of MALDEF.

The cases they took on evoked change throughout the United States and made MALDEF a solid foundation to be reckoned with. They updated the United States Voting Rights Act to include protection of Mexican Americans. Up until then, unfair practices were blatant. Mexican Americans would arrive at polling stations only to find that they had run out of ballots. Many were threatened with fines or jail if they voted. By working with other coalition groups, voting rights were secured for Mexican Americans in 1975.

High school counselors recommended Martinez go to vocational school instead of college, even though she was in the National Honor Society.

Martinez helped win the right for children who did not speak English to receive bilingual education in the public schools. She also won a case against the state of Texas for charging illegal aliens $1,000 per child for attending public school. Some had lived in the United States for years but were undocumented. She worked with the United States Census Bureau and was instrumental in getting the term "Hispanic" on the census and as an official count for the country's population. These groundbreaking cases set the precedent for similar cases across the nation.

Martinez also worked on fundraising and staff recruitment. She secured resources so they could keep their mission in mind, and not worry about meeting the payroll. By the time she left MALDEF in 1982 to return to a large law firm, the organization was operating with a $4.9 million annual budget. More than thirty attorneys now work on cases nationwide.

Martinez was honored with the Jefferson Award for public service from the American Institute, the Medal of Excellence from Columbia University's Law School for her work with civil rights, and the Valerie Kantor Award for Extraordinary Achievement for her work with MALDEF. She cofounded the Achievement Council at the University of California Los Angeles, which 150 seeks to increase the number of minority students attending college.

Linda Chavez-Thompson (United States, 1944–)

The first woman and the first person of color ever elected to a top office of the AFL-CIO, Chavez-Thompson is the highest-ranking woman in the labor movement.

As the daughter of sharecroppers, Linda Chavez-Thompson knew what it was to do backbreaking, low-paying work. She worked in the fields picking cotton in Texas in the summer when she was only ten years old. Her entire family worked all day. The adults earned fifty cents an hour. Children earned thirty cents an hour.

The grueling work planted a seed for her future career. Chavez-Thompson is now the highest-ranking woman in the labor movement. She was the first person of color and the first woman elected to one of the AFL-CIO's three main offices. As executive vice president, she brings over thirty-five years of union work experience to the position.

Born in Lubbock, Texas, she dropped out of high school in the ninth grade to help support her family. In 1963, she married her first husband and started cleaning houses for a living.

Her trade union work began in 1967 when she joined the Laborers' International Union and served as the secretary for the union's local in Lubbock. She started to learn the intricacies of the union. As the only Spanish-speaking official, she also served as a union representative and translator for Hispanic members.

In 1971 she went to work for the American Federation of State, County and Municipal Employees and rose through the ranks, becoming vice president in 1988. She was responsible for advancing legislation, political action, and educational programs. She also conducted every level of grievance procedure for members.

In 1995 she ran for the office of executive vice president of the AFL-CIO and won. She is dedicated to working with other minority groups. She wants to address the needs of workers who are also wives and mothers, and wants to bring more women into leadership positions.

Chavez-Thompson was appointed by President Bill Clinton to serve on the President's Initiative on Race and as vice chair of the Presidential

Committee on Employment of People with Disabilities.

She represents a variety of national organizations, including the National Committee on Pay Equity, the United Way of America, the President's Committee on the Employment of People with Disabilities, the Congressional Hispanic Caucus Institute, and the Labor Heritage Foundation. She served as a vice chair of the Democratic National Committee.

> Chavez-Thompson wants to address the needs of workers who are also wives and mothers, and wants to bring more women into leadership positions.

Chavez-Thompson is a Women's History Month Honoree, and she continues to be an advocate for the rights of Latinos with organized labor.

Antonia Hernandez (Mexico, 1948–)

Former general counsel and president of MALDEF and current president of the California Community Foundation, Antonia Hernandez has dedicated her life and career to protecting the civil rights of Latinos.

> "Everyone is governed by the same laws.
> Everyone is entitled to justice."
>
> —Antonia Hernandez

When students she was working with started staging walkouts because of poor conditions and lack of supplies, Antonia Hernandez changed her mind about teaching. The only way she could really help them was to change the unfair laws that were holding them back.

For thirty years Hernandez has protected the civil rights of the nation's Latinos. According to the United States Census Bureau, there are approximately 38 million Hispanics in the United States. As president and general counsel of the Mexican American Legal Defense and Educational

Fund (MALDEF), a national nonprofit litigation and advocacy organization, Hernandez helped make impressive changes in education, political representation, employment, immigration, and voting rights. At MALDEF, she directed all litigation and advocacy programs, oversaw a $6 million budget, and managed a seventy-five-person staff.

Her parents instilled in her and her six siblings the belief that serving the public interest was a noble thing to do. They valued education. Every one of her brothers and sisters graduated from college.

She developed a strong sense of her cultural roots and identity, which is why she could not sit by and see Hispanic Americans being treated as second-class citizens. She chose to practice law to help Latinos.

Hernandez earned her bachelor's and law degrees from UCLA. She immediately took on a job with the East Los Angeles Center for Law and Justice, which worked on civil and criminal cases, often involving police brutality. She then moved on to the Legal Aid Foundation in 1977, where she became the directing attorney of a local office.

Hernandez took time off to work as campaign coordinator for Senator Ted Kennedy when he ran for the Democratic Party's nomination for president in 1980. She then began working with MALDEF. At this time, she married attorney Michael Stern and had three children.

Her advocacy efforts in California were recognized and she was offered a job at the United States Judiciary Committee in Washington, D.C. She was the first Latina to work for the committee in writing legislation and informing Senate members about civil rights and immigration issues.

> Hernandez was the first Latina to work for the committee in writing legislation and informing Senate members about civil rights and immigration issues.

Hernandez serves on the Senior Advisory Committee of the John F. Kennedy Institute of Politics at Harvard University, the Pacific Council for International Policy, and the Commission on Presidential Debates. She 153 works with the National Hispanic Leadership Conference, the Latino Museum of History, and the Quality Education for Minorities Network.

Hernandez resigned from MALDEF in 2003 to become president and CEO of the California Community Foundation.

Ileana Ros-Lehtinen (Cuba, 1952–)
First woman and first Latino elected to the U.S. House of Representatives.

*I*leana Ros-Lehtinen has been known as a "defender of democracy." She was the first woman and first Latino to be elected to the U.S. House of Representatives. She joined the Congressional Hispanic Caucus and became the only woman, only Cuban-American, and only Hispanic Republican representative.

Ros-Lehtinen founded a private elementary school in Miami, Eastern Academy, serving as principal while earning her master's degree with honors in education. While doing this, she decided to run for Florida's state legislature. She was elected as a state representative in 1982. In 1986 she was elected state senator, during which time she met and married her husband, Dexter Lehtinen, who was also a Florida State legislator. They would be the first married couple to serve simultaneously in Florida's House of Representatives.

She focused on education, children, senior citizens, women and their health, the homeless, victims' rights, and the environment.

She also saw things from the eyes of a Cuban refugee concerned about her native country. As one of the most visible spokespersons against Cuban leader Fidel Castro and the plight of Cuban refugees, she has frequently been called "the darling of the Cuban community."

When her family moved to the United States after the attempted overthrow of Castro in 1961, her father realized they would not be able to return. He gave his heart and patriotism to the United States and so did his children. Ros-Lehtinen was nine years old and she understood.

Ros-Lehtinen ran for the U.S. House of Representatives in 1989 to fill the vacancy of an incumbent congressman. The ensuing election was heated with accusations of bigotry on both sides. The Latino vote was crucial. Ros-Lehtinen won, giving an ethnic balance of power in the Miami area. She was able to heal campaign wounds and went on to win the re-election with 60 percent of the vote.

> As one of the most visible spokespersons against Cuban leader Fidel Castro and the plight of Cuban refugees, Ros-Lehtinen has frequently been called "the darling of the Cuban community."

In her new post she has become a leading figure in shaping foreign policy, especially toward Latin America. She became the first Latina to chair a subcommittee when she oversaw the Africa Subcommittee. She worked on the House Foreign Affairs Committee, even while maintaining ties with the Cuban-American National Foundation. She worked on the Cuban-Democracy Act, which prohibits subsidiaries of U.S. corporations from trading with Cuba. She is a member of the Speaker's Task Force for a Drug-Free America and the Subcommittee on International Operations and Human Rights.

Ros-Lehtinen initiated Florida's Prepaid College Tuition Program, and promotes bilingual education for all.

Rigoberta Menchú (Guatemala, 1969–)

The youngest recipient of the Nobel Peace Prize and founder of the Rigoberta Menchú Foundation, an aid organization for indigenous people. Menchú served as spokesperson for the United Nations International Decade of Indigenous People.

The Menchú family, who were Quiché Indians, lived in the beautiful northern highlands of Guatemala. Their peace was shattered when the military government and plantation owners started taking the land by force, land that had belonged to the indigenous people for generations.

The Menchús fought for the rights of their people—at a huge price. Rigoberta Menchú's brother was kidnapped in 1979, tortured, and burned alive while his family stood by helplessly watching. The following year her activist father and nearly forty others died in a fire at the Spanish embassy while protesting violations of human rights by the military government against the indigenous people.

The horrors did not stop there. Within months of her father's death, her mother, also an activist and a traditional healer in their community, was kidnapped, raped, tortured, and eventually killed. Nearly 200,000 Indians have been killed in the thirty-year-long battle.

Menchú fled the country and lived to write the story of the horrific social injustices. The book brought international attention to the plight of her people.

In 1992 at the age of twenty-three, Menchú won the Nobel Peace Prize for her book *I, Rigoberta Menchú*. She was the youngest person to ever win the prize.

Awarded under much controversy—many thought the rebel movement conflicted with Nobel ethics of commitment to nonviolence—she maintained that she always worked for peace, even amidst the violence wrought upon her people.

She dedicated the award to her father and used the $1 million cash prize to set up the Rigoberta Menchú Foundation to aid indigenous people.

The United Nations declared 1993 the International Year for Indigenous Populations. Menchú became the spokesperson for the United Nations International Decade of Indigenous People (1994–2003).

> In 1992 at the age of twenty-three, Menchú won the Nobel Peace Prize for her book *I, Rigoberta Menchú*. She was the youngest person to ever win the prize.

Their story had to be told. The Quiché Indians were poor and though many owned tiny plots of land, they could not produce enough crops to feed their families. They worked up to fifteen hours a day, eight months a year on coffee or cotton plantations on the coast to supplement their income, often in deplorable conditions.

They lived in crowded sheds with no clean water. Menchú, like many other children, started working at age eight—otherwise she would not eat. Two of her brothers died while working on the plantations, one from malnutrition and the other from pesticide poisoning. When their land was taken, it was the last blow.

Since indigenous people had no rights, Menchú's father became an activist on their behalf, and the family followed suit. They formed the United Peasant Committee. As a leader in the 1970s movement, he was arrested and imprisoned many times for organizing petitions and protests against the military regime.

When her family was killed one by one, Menchú learned Spanish and continued her father's work, including staging a strike with 80,000 supporters who protested for fifteen days. Menchú became a marked woman. She fled to Mexico in 1982 and wrote *I Rigoberta Menchú* with the help of Venezuelan anthropologist Elizabeth Burg. The book was translated into several languages and became required reading in many universities.

Menchú travels the world over to share her story. She continues her search for resolution and peace and urges women and indigenous people to vote so that they can preserve the rights of all Guatemalan people.

Juana Beatriz Gutierrez (United States, 1932–)
Cofounder and director of Las Madres del Este de Los Angeles, Gutierrez started the grass-roots organization to keep her neighborhood safe.

Juana Beatriz Gutierrez has been labeled an eco-pioneer, an environmental activist, a civil rights activist. It was her job as a mother that made her strong enough to fight for the future of her children.

Gutierrez cofounded and is the director of Las Madres del Este de Los Angeles (Mothers of East Los Angeles), a grass-roots organization that works to keep her Los Angeles neighborhood safe. What guides the socially conscious movement is the belief that community empowerment can bring change.

When they were notified that there were plans to build a prison in her neighborhood, Gutierrez and several friends organized an information campaign along with the support of Gloria Molina, a State Assembly representative. Gutierrez could not imagine that kind of environment surrounding her children. She wanted basic safety rights for the children growing up in the neighborhood. They held weekly candlelight vigils. They were persistent in voicing their antiprison stance.

> The daughter of a Mexican farmer, Gutierrez says her leadership skills evolved from her determination to offer her nine children a better life.

Their actions brought widespread media attention and California dropped its plans in 1992. Successful at that, they continued their efforts in making the community safer. Las Madres fought proposals to build a state prison, an oil pipeline, and construction of toxic waste incinerators and treatment plants in the East Los Angeles area. The organization established a lead poisoning education project and a graffiti removal program. Las Madres has since increased its outreach. The group operates a child immunization project, a scholarship fund, and a mentor task force.

When Gutierrez heard of upcoming construction of a municipal waste incinerator and the toxic ash that would result, her group fought against it and stopped its construction. It had been assumed that the low-income neighborhood would not fight against companies or projects that produced pollution-causing agents.

Las Madres started a successful water conservation program that reaped multiple benefits. The organization hired the unemployed to distribute free water-conserving toilets in return for old, water-guzzling ones. The old toilets were smashed to pieces that would be used as underlay for city streets. The money earned for administering the program was used to hire young people to go door to door, urging families to take their children to clinics for immunizations and to be tested for lead poisoning.

Las Madres also established a Community Mobilization Line, which keeps the community informed on health and well-being issues pertinent to children. The line serves as a communication liaison aimed at correcting stereotypical misinformation on barrios and the people that live there.

She started her efforts in 1979 with a simple neighborhood watch program when drug dealers and gangs moved into a park near her house. She learned people have the power to stop unsafe practices in their neighborhoods and keep their communities safe and healthy.

Gutierrez won the 1995 National Mujer Award from the National Hispana Leadership Institute, is featured in the book *Environmental Activists* by John Mongillo and Bibi Booth, and was honored with a 1996 Phenomenal Woman Award from California State University.

Elvia Alvarado (Honduras, 1940–)

Founder of the Federation of Campesina Women and head of the International Relations of the Union of Rural Workers, Elvia Alvarado is an author and worldwide speaker on the plight of the poor in Honduras.

"I would give my life for my people."

—Elvia Alvarado

The peasant women she met on the back roads of Honduras were dying of malnutrition. For them, Elvia Alvarado was tortured, beaten, and jailed for twenty-five days without food or water. Her back carries deep scars and the weight of social justice.

In fighting for the *campesinas'* rights, she was seen as a communist and guerrilla, a threat to the government. Trained and sent by the Catholic Church to organize women's groups to combat malnutrition in rural Honduras, Alvarado had questioned why malnutrition was a problem in the first place.

As she traveled by foot, the reasons became clear. There was a great division among the classes and poverty was more than rampant. Although the *campesinas* helped to produce billions of dollars worth of sugar cane, rice, corn, bananas, beans, coffee, and textiles from the land, their income barely sustained them.

Military and corporate forces and Hurricane Mitch had stripped away their own lands. They suffered from abhorrent practices of sweatshops, no medical attention, and minimal education. Many women who worked in foreigners' factories suffered lung diseases because of the air quality within the facilities.

Opening her eyes to the helplessness of women and children in her country, Alvarado founded the Federation of Campesina Women. She became a passionate voice for the women imprisoned within a machismo society, and were also victims to military authority, corporate exploitation, and unfair employment practices. By speaking with these victims, she saw the need for change.

The majority of the *campesinas* had never ventured far from their villages. Despite Alvarado's second-grade education, her passion and commitment in improving the lives of her people propelled her to become politically aware and savvy.

As head of International Relations of the Union of Rural Workers, Alvarado travels the world and speaks eloquently of their fight against poverty, workers' exploitation, and political oppression. As an organizer, Alvarado works with compassion and determination. She herself worked in the fields, raised a family of eight, and rallied Honduran *campesinas* to understand the importance of a labor movement. She has struggled for years to enforce an agrarian reform law so that they can recover their lands.

Empowered by her vision, she became a "Fair Trade coffee grower." The Fair Trade Certified label guarantees that coffee importers pay a fair price to farmers and work with democratically organized cooperatives. She urges boycotts of products produced at the expense of peasant workers in Central America.

Her book *Don't Be Afraid, Gringo* and the corresponding PBS documentary, *Elvia and the Fight for Land and Liberty,* take her on worldwide speaking tours where she shares her story about the injustices in Honduras and the plight of her fellow *campesinas.*

Janet Murguia (United States, 1960–)
Executive director of the National Council of La Raza.

Janet Murguia's family has a tradition of serving the community—a calling. Murguia serves her community on a grand scale. She became executive director and chief operating officer of the National Council of La Raza (NCLR) in 2004. Established in 1968 to reduce poverty and discrimination and improve life opportunities for Hispanic Americans, NCLR is a private, nonprofit organization. It is one of the largest, most respected, and powerful Hispanic advocacy organizations in the United States.

She had been on the board of directors since 2002 when she was chosen to oversee more than 300 NCLR affiliates in forty states, including Puerto Rico and the District of Columbia.

She is expected to become president of the organization when La Raza founder, Raul Yzaguirre, retires in 2004 after thirty years of service. Murguia's experience in education and politics made her an excellent candidate. She was one of seven children from Kansas, and her family saw education as essential. Four of her siblings have law degrees and two are judges. She earned three degrees from the University of Kansas, one bachelor's in Spanish, one in journalism, and a juris doctorate from the law school.

Murguia worked for five years at the U.S. White House as a legislative aide to President Bill Clinton. She was also deputy director of legislative affairs and served as the senior White House liaison to Congress. During the Gore-Lieberman presidential campaign, she worked as deputy campaign manager with a focus on constituency outreach.

Murguia serves as executive vice chancellor for university relations at the University of Kansas, her alma mater. Listed as one of four "Latinas Making a Difference" by *Hispanic Outlook in Higher Education* magazine, her political and educational experience enhance her work at the NCLR.

She worked in the Office of University Relations, Governmental Relations, and Trademark Licensing at the University of Kansas. She also worked at the public radio station and the Kansas Audio-Reader Network, a radio reading service for the blind and visually impaired. She is also on the board of directors for YouthFriends, a nationally recognized school-based mentoring effort.

> Murguia is listed as one of four "Latinas Making a Difference" by *Hispanic Outlook in Higher Education* magazine.

When the César E. Chávez postage stamp was released in 2003, Murguia helped unveil it. *Hispanic Business* magazine listed Murguia among the 80 Elite Hispanic Businesswomen in the United States and named her one of the 100 Most Influential Hispanics, and *Hispanic Magazine* listed her as one of the 100 Top Latinas.

7

Entrepreneurs: Breaking New Ground

Aliza Sherman (United States, 1945–)

Sherman is the founder of Cybergrrl, Inc., the first woman-owned, full-service Internet marketing company in the world and creator of the first bilingual online network and marketplace for Latinas.

Cyberspace was a place no woman had gone before—until Aliza Sherman ventured into the unknown. A persistent salesperson had urged her to buy a modem along with her first computer, and from that point on everything changed for her.

During those pre-Web days of the 1980s, information was connected only by Bulletin Board Systems containing all text and no images, but the potential power of the Web was imminent. Sherman was fascinated with the information available at her fingertips. She spent hours researching and surfing the new Net.

She found few companies run by women and no networking to help them in their online ventures. This revelation prompted her mission to empower women and girls through technology.

She did not implement her plan right away because she found security in the job she had. She put her vision on a backburner.

All that changed, however, when she and a friend were kidnapped. They were held hostage at gunpoint but managed to escape and identify their captors. Sherman saw the experience as a sign—it was time to change her life's direction and take control of her own destiny.

In 1995, Sherman founded the first woman-owned, full-service Internet marketing company in the world—Cybergrrl, Inc. Sherman was determined to help women and girls learn how to use the Internet, how to create their own Web sites, build strategic alliances, and have access to numerous resources.

She knew that for women to stay competitive in business, they would have to be proficient on the Internet. With the launch of her company, a female online presence had begun. Her logo was "Cybergrrl," a superhero complete with a hot pink cape and the letters CG emblazoned on her outfit.

Sherman started other dot-com companies for women, including Eviva, the first bilingual online network and marketplace for Latinas. It was dedicated to her grandmother, Pascuala Vasquez Enriquez, or "Pequita," who had linked Sherman to her Latina heritage and was an entrepreneurial inspiration when she started her own food business in California and Mexico to support her six children.

❧ Sherman's mission was to empower women and girls through technology.

With a bit of a different slant, Sherman hoped to provide a vehicle to help Latinas get ahead by using the Web, interweaving their cultural influences while dispelling myths about Latinas and business.

Voted as one of the Top 50 People Who Matter Most on the Internet by *Newsweek* magazine, Sherman became a leader in cyberspace innovation and a sought-after online marketing expert in Web design, online marketing, and Internet training.

She was the only woman small business owner on a panel of top technology leaders at a technology summit that landed her on the cover of *USA Today*. She was the first female cover story for *Business Startups* magazine and continued a relationship with the publication as a columnist. She wrote for *Entrepreneur* magazine and penned several books including *PowerTools for Women in Business*, *Cybergrrl@work*, and *A Woman's Guide to the World Wide Web*.

Her networking goals were always foremost. When she found woman-run Web sites, she listed them as links on Webgrrls, the first global Internet networking organization for women. The goal of the sisterhood was to support the few women who had Internet companies, provide opportunities for mentoring and internships, teach new skills, and help women find business partners or clients.

Six Webgrrl women came to the first physical meeting Sherman set up in New York in 1995. Within two years, there were 30,000 members and more than 100 chapters worldwide.

Linda Alvarado (United States, 1951–)

A successful businesswoman who established a thriving business in the male-dominated construction industry, Linda Alvarado was the first Hispanic to become owner of a professional baseball team and was inducted into the National Women's Hall of Fame.

> "What I hope for and long for is the day when people will truly be judged not based on where they came from and their gender, but really on their ability."
>
> —Linda Alvarado, Constructing a Better America,
> *www.usdreams.com.*

Born Linda Martinez in Albuquerque, New Mexico, Alvarado's strong work ethic came from her religious family, whose roots in the state dated back to the 1500s. Her parents, a homemaker mother and a father who worked at the Atomic Energy Commission, had the same expectations from all their children—to excel academically and athletically, despite their occasional run-ins with racism.

Having grown up the only daughter surrounded by five brothers, she was not intimidated by men. In fact, she thrived on her competitive nature, which helped in the business realm, and eventually in the construction industry. Ignoring chauvinistic remarks and unflattering graffiti aimed at her, Alvarado walked onto construction sites determined to succeed in a very macho industry.

Her business savvy and passion for watching construction projects develop from the ground up gave her the impetus to start her own general contracting firm—Alvarado Construction, Inc. Her nontraditional career also led her to become part owner of the professional baseball team, the Colorado Rockies.

Alvarado had a college degree in a nonrelated field when she started working as a contract administrator, working her way up to the construction management group and learning every phase of the construction business. She liked it so much, she returned to school to take classes that included estimating blueprint and critical-path method scheduling.

She earned her credentials as a contractor and was ready to get to work with her new Denver-based company.

Six banks turned down her loan application. Finally her parents loaned her $2,500 and she mortgaged her house to start up. When she bid on potential jobs, however, she was looked at rather incredulously. A woman in a hardhat just didn't look the part and wasn't taken seriously. She was turned down for her inexperience, for being a woman, and for being Hispanic.

> ⟪ A woman in a hardhat just didn't look the part and wasn't taken seriously. Alvarado was turned down for jobs for her inexperience, for being a woman, and for being Hispanic.

When she convinced another construction company to bid on a project with her and got the job, she worked hard to prove her ability. The end result was a fine job that also started her portfolio.

Tenacity and perseverance paid off and opened other doors. She became
the first Hispanic—male or female—to become owner of a professional

baseball team. The investment showed that a woman could thrive in non-traditional fields. She also thought that there were exceptional Hispanic role models in baseball, and seeing a Latina team owner would bring the sport full circle.

Alvarado Construction specializes in commercial, industrial, environmental, and heavy engineering projects throughout the western United States. The company has built huge projects including the Colorado Convention Center, the Navy/Marine Training facility in Aurora, and the High Energy Research Laboratory.

Alvarado was director of the National Hispanic Scholarship Fund and commissioner of the White House Initiative for Hispanic Excellence in Education. She has been recognized twice as the United States Hispanic Chamber of Commerce Businesswoman of the Year and was listed as one of the 100 Most Influential Hispanics in America by *Hispanic Business* magazine (1996). She was inducted into the National Women's Hall of Fame in 2003.

Julie Stav (Cuba, 1955–)

A financial planning and investment guru, successful business owner, bestselling author, and radio show host, Julie Stav is a self-made multimillionaire who has dedicated her career to helping other women and minorities achieve financial success.

"Instead of working for a company, I want you to know how to own the company."

—Julie Stav

Financial Wall Street guru Julie Stav was recently divorced, a single mother, and had forty-four cents in her checking account. She was determined to take control, to invest in herself and her family when she began investing money in the stock market.

When her sister gave her a financial planning book written by a woman in easy-to-understand language, it turned her life around. She   167 became a registered and licensed stockbroker and started her own businesses, Retirement Benefit Systems and Julie Stav, Inc., a marketing communications company. She is now a multimillionaire who shares the wealth.

Stav made it her business to overcome the horrendous fear she had working with numbers. Before long she was making money in the market and found herself helping other women in similar financial straits. Since then she has educated thousands of people through financial planning seminars and investment clubs—powerful and affordable networking systems where members learn marketing basics so that they can start investing.

She writes monthly financial columns for magazines and has her own radio show in both English and Spanish. She is the author of the bestselling books, *Get Your Share* and *Fund Your Future*. Through her PBS financial programs, television appearances, and radio guest spots, she educates her audience to take control of their own destiny, plan their finances, and invest wisely.

Her company targets three groups—women, young people, and Hispanics—but emphasizes the belief that anyone can reach financial goals regardless of debt, age, ethnicity, or income. It does not matter how much money an individual earns. Anyone can learn to make money in whatever profession she chooses.

For those afraid of finances, Stav believes a challenge can empower. She overcame many obstacles herself, which strengthened her character and helped her develop a strong work foundation. Born Julieta Alfonso, her parents sent her alone to the United States when Castro came into power. Stav was just fourteen years old and traveled via a Mexican orphanage to live with her sponsors until her parents could join them two years later.

She started high school in California not knowing one word of English and was given an IQ test—in English—just after she arrived. Her test results came back so low teachers labeled her as mentally retarded. She had always been a high achiever. Her wounded self-esteem was recharged when a teacher who believed in her signed her up for swim team. Everyone was equal in the water. Even though she did not swim well, she worked hard and excelled.

Her father also changed her perception of things when he wrote a letter, in Spanish, to the pope and received a response. Her brother had applied for a job mowing lawns at a Catholic high school and was turned down. Her father asked how they could turn away a fourteen-year-old who wanted to work. Her brother got the job, which helped pay the rent and helped get them both into Loyola Marymount University.

Stav earned a master's degree in education, focusing on bilingual education, which allows students to keep learning while they learn English. Through education and financial savvy, Stav believes individuals from all walks of life should take charge of their financial future so they can have the life they want and deserve.

Christy Haubegger (United States, 1960–)

A graduate of Stanford Law School and founder of Latina *magazine and Latina Media Ventures, Christy Haubegger has dedicated herself to providing Latinas with positive ethnic images and role models.*

When Christy Haubegger was growing up in Houston, Texas, she loved thumbing through magazines but never saw faces similar to hers—olive-skinned, brunette, brown-eyed and with that identifiable Hispanic flair.

She wanted readers to see Latinas like astronaut Ellen Ochoa, basketball player Rebecca Lobo, and actress Jennifer Lopez, women from all walks of life who were successful, beautiful, and capable. Without many ethnic role models in the public eye and with the lack of popular images in the media, she wanted to fill the niche.

Still, she put the idea for a Latina magazine on the backburner so that she could attend Stanford Law School. While there, she got a taste of journalism by joining the editorial staff of the *Stanford Law Review*, eventually becoming senior editor. To help her public speaking and confidence levels, she was a tour guide at the Texas State Capitol.

Upon graduating, she noticed that there were still no magazines for or about Latinas. She decided to act on it. She was only twenty-five years old.

> Haubegger had a dream to fill a niche in the magazine world with beautiful, capable Latinas who could be viewed as role models.

In 1996, Haubegger launched *Latina* magazine, a bilingual publication aimed at the twenty-something crowd. Circulation has grown to 350,000 since its inception. It covers beauty, fashion, health, food ideas, celebrity profiles, and cultural pieces.

It was a long road getting there. Haubegger spent time at different magazines following female editors and publishers, absorbing everything she could about the business and listening when they shared information. She faced nearly 200 rejections from potential investors. Armed with a seventy-five-page business plan, Haubegger knocked on doors until she came to Edward Lewis, founder and owner of *Essence* magazine. Impressed with her business savvy and vision, he said it was one of the best business plans he had seen in twenty years and especially for someone her age. He saw the potential and invested in her project.

Haubegger's goal was to show the beauty of diversity. She plays up the fact that the magazine might be considered trilingual—with English, Spanish, and Spanglish. It addresses contemporary Latinas, who may or may not speak Spanish, but who still honor their heritage. For once, it seemed Latinas could look in the mirror and at a newsstand and see themselves in a positive light.

Haubegger has gone from *Latina* magazine's CEO and publisher to serving on the board of directors so that she can pursue other ventures. She has been cited as an expert on marketing, brand identity, and the (Latina) female in corporate America.

To provide updated images and a national voice for the approximate 38 million Hispanics in America, she started Latina Media Ventures, which develops vehicles for Latinos in various media, including television and the

Internet. With the young, urban, chic Latina in mind, Haubegger has helped produce a book—*Latina Beauty*—and several movies, including *Chasing Papi*.

Haubegger is the adopted daughter of Anglo parents who encouraged her to retain her Hispanic heritage and reinforced the idea that she could do anything. Their support gave her a vision and strong sense of who she was.

She was named among *Newsweek*'s Women of the Twenty-First Century and as one of *Hispanic Business* magazine's 100 Most Influential Hispanics. She was chosen by Crain's New York Business as one of the most successful young businesswomen in America and by the Ms. Foundation for Women as one of the Top Ten Role Models of the Year. NBC *Nightly News* with Tom Brokaw profiled her as "One of the Most Inspirational Women."

Mary Rodas (United States, 1975–)

One of the youngest executives in the United States, Mary Rodas was vice president of marketing for Catco Toys at age fourteen and by age twenty-three was the youngest president of a toy company.

Perhaps it was being born on Christmas Day that gave Mary Rodas an edge on toys. By the age of nine, she was testing toy products and giving her opinion and analyses of them. By the time she was fourteen she was promoted to vice president of marketing, was earning six figures, and had a 5 percent interest in Catco, Inc., a toy company that brought in annual revenues over $70 million.

One of the youngest executives in the United States, Rodas was known as "the toy wonder." At the age of twenty-three, Rodas became president of Catalyst Toys, the youngest president of a toy company. Analyzing and improving upon toys invented or developed by Donald Specter, the owner of the company, was her job. He was also her mentor and owner of hundreds of patents for toys and other products.

Rodas had first given Specter advice when she was four years old. Rodas made the rounds with her Salvadoran father, the superintendent of an apartment complex. They came across Specter, trying to install floor tiles. She critiqued the way he was installing them and he soon asked her to critique a few of his toy inventions. They formed a bond. Over the years Rodas continued to give her opinions and advice on marketing and design strategies for other products.

> One of the youngest executives in the United States, Rodas was known as "the toy wonder."

Her fame came with the development of the Balzac Balloon Ball, a neon-colored, fabric-covered balloon. The Balzac Balloon became an instant success in the toy industry in almost thirty countries around the world. She grew the Balzac line, which started with two balloons and at its peak developed over thirty.

Rodas had no secret to her keen business eye. She just picked toys she thought kids would want to play with until they wore out. She played with the toys also, asked a lot of questions, observed kids playing with test products, and took parents' reactions into consideration. She visited stores to keep up with customer satisfaction and get their input. Balzac thrived in boutiques at Disneyland, Disney World, Universal Studios, and Bloomingdale's.

Even though Balzac filed for bankruptcy in the late 1990s, Rodas proved her business savvy was not a fluke by venturing into the music and entertainment business. She became vice president of Artists and Repertoire at Deco Disc Industries, another company owned by Specter.

She has worked extensively with toys like die cuts and licensed characters like WWF figures, as well as magic kits with demonstration videos. Wanting to improve family entertainment, she coproduced a Broadway extravaganza with magician Joseph Gabriel Magic. Venturing into the candy industry is a possibility.

She graduated from the Professional Children's School in 1994, and attended New York University where she received her degree in mass communications. Rodas has been featured on *Lifestyles of the Rich and Famous* and in a children's book entitled, *Mary and the Magic Ball*.

Rossana Rosado (United States, 1962–)

First Latina and among the first women to hold a position as editor in chief, publisher, and CEO of a major newspaper, Rossana Rosado is the recipient of numerous awards for her work in print, radio, and television, including an Emmy.

Raised in the Bronx, Rosado loved words ever since she was a little girl and dreamed of writing books. Her stellar career in journalism was different from her intended path.

She expressed a desire to teach for a living but a high school teacher commented that her accent would be a problem. She did not have an accent. The complete lack of support did not stop Rosado.

> The rejections and detours Rosado encountered in her career as a journalist only inspired her to try harder.

Instead, she took the different road. She earned a bachelor's degree in journalism from Pace University and worked at various radio and television stations. In the field however, she once again met with resistance. Even though English was her dominant language, she worked for a variety of Spanish-language newspapers, earned a reputation as an excellent journalist, and had a substantial number of impressive clips when she went to an English-language newspaper to apply for a job she really wanted. She was turned down.

Disappointed and a bit disillusioned, she was still determined to advance in her career in different ways. She worked the public relations field for two New York City mayors, David Dinkins and Rudy Giuliani, which would give her new insight when she returned to print and broadcast journalism.

The rejections and detours only inspired her to try harder and go farther until she landed at *El Diario/La Prensa*, the largest Spanish-language newspaper in the United States. She started as a layout artist but was given a chance to be a reporter—without pay. When she scooped a big story away from a major New York City daily newspaper, *El Diario* hired her, with pay.

She worked her way up the ranks until in 1995 she became editor in chief of the newspaper. In 1999 she became Publisher and CEO. She was the first Latina, and one of just a few women in the United States, to hold these positions at a major newspaper.

At WPIX-TV she was producer of a public affairs program and the producer of *Best Talk in Town*. She won an Emmy Award for her public service campaign "Care for Kids." She also won the New York State Broadcaster's Award and the Folio Award.

As publisher, Rosado, who is of Puerto Rican descent, realizes the responsibility she has to empower the Latino community and that she is in a powerful position to evoke change.

> Rosado, who is of Puerto Rican descent, realizes the responsibility she has to empower the Latino community and that she is in a powerful position to evoke change.

Circulation increased under her leadership. Building an Internet site and producing an English-language edition were major goals. An *El Diario* book club was started to debunk the myth that Hispanics don't read. *Leyendo con Rossana* (Reading with Rossana) was launched in 2002. In the monthly column Rosado recommends fiction, poetry, nonfiction, and children's literature written in Spanish or by Latinos in English. The only criterion is that they "tell the story of Hispanics in America."

Rosado also strives to advance women through networking opportunities and the way they are portrayed within the content of the newspaper.

Rosado was honored with a Women of Excellence Award, presented by the governor of New York in 2002. Her community work includes service with Acción New York, the American Red Cross, Caribbean Cultural Center, Partnership for a Drug-Free America, St. Chrisopher's, and the United Way.

Elizabeth Lisboa-Farrow (United States, 1947–)
Founder of Lisboa Associates, a multimillion-dollar firm, and the winner of numerous awards honoring her skill and drive as a businesswoman.

When Elizabeth Lisboa-Farrow turned thirty and her brother asked when she would be getting married, she realized what she really wanted was to buck traditional Puerto Rican expectations and start her own business.

She founded Lisboa Associates in 1979, a full-service public relations and marketing firm, which generates over $13 million annually. She is also chair of the United States Hispanic Chamber of Commerce, which oversees more than 1 million members across the country.

As a spokesperson for the chamber, she promotes Latinos as a major driving force for the United States economy. This is what she has learned from her position: Latinos come from all parts of the world, members vary from mom-and-pop places to multimillion-dollar corporations; the Hispanic population is not a welfare population; and U.S. Hispanic businesses spend about $200 million in goods and services annually. In short, Latinos are a force to be reckoned with. Lisboa-Farrow also became a force to be reckoned with. She was born in the Bronx on Tiffany Street, which to her meant graduating from high school was a big accomplishment. Though her family was poor, they always dressed up, mostly in clothes her mother had painstakingly sewed for them. Her Puerto Rican parents instilled pride and a strong work ethic in her and her three siblings.

Lisboa-Farrow always loved to work. When she was twelve she helped her aunt at the local Catholic rectory. When she went to the New York City Public Library for an interview, she was in awe of the power within the building. Inspiration came from reading autobiographies and biographies of people like Marie Curie and the works of authors like Esmeralda Santiago and Gabriel García Márquez.

Her hunger for knowledge continued into her first job in a bank where she wanted to learn about money and credit issues. When she kept getting passed up for a promotion even though all her bosses seemed pleased with her performance, she asked a supervisor what was wrong. She was told outright that it was because she was Hispanic and would probably get married, leave, and have babies. Lisboa-Farrow was shocked and quit after the blatant racism.

> Lisboa-Farrow's Puerto Rican parents instilled pride and a strong work ethic in her and her three siblings.

Soon after she found office work with a public relations firm, a mentor in Steve Ellman, and a career she loved. When she started Lisboa Associates, it was from her New York studio apartment with one account, Playboy Clubs International, and zero funding, yet her clientele grew through her references.

She met and married Jeffrey Farrow in 1979 and took a big leap of faith in moving to Washington, D.C., where she had to re-establish her company and reputation.

Her targeted clientele included government agencies but they were not impressed with her former clients like Paul Newman and David Susskind. Still, she persisted. In 1989 she secured her first contract with the National Institute of Mental Health. Her client list grew to include the Department of Health and Human Services, the National Institute on Drug Abuse, the Departments of Agriculture, Labor, and Transportation, the Environmental Protection Agency, and the United States Peace Corps.

Lisboa-Farrow has worked with the Hispanic College Fund and as chair for the Inter-American Chamber of Commerce. She received the 1996 Hispanic Business Woman of the Year Award, the 1995 Excellence in Entrepreneurship Award, the AAUW Women of Distinction Award, and the Outstanding Women in Business Award.

8

Writers and Editors: The Power of Words Frees Us

Gabriela Mistral (Chile, 1889–1957)

The first Latin American to win the Nobel Prize in literature, Gabriela Mistral was named Chile's "Teacher of the Nation" and received the country's top prize for poetry. She served as a consul and ambassador to the League of Nations and the United Nations.

A name that flowed like poetry would only be fitting. When Lucila Godoy Alcayaga was just a schoolgirl, she replaced Lucila with "Gabriela" in honor of the archangel Gabriel. Changing her last name proved more poetic. She had heard about the "mistral," a cold dry wind that blows down from the Alps 100 days a year to chill the plains of southern France. That, too, was poetry to her ears and so she adopted it. That is how Gabriela Mistral, poet, was born.

Mistral became the first Latin American to win the Nobel Prize in literature. She became a national treasure in Chile. Known as "the people's poet," her lyrical, passionate, and idealistic verses resonated deeply. They reflected the aspirations of the Latin-American world but her topics were universal.

She believed that poetry was not just for the elite. Over the course of her career, she wanted to make fine literature available to everyone. She became the voice of her people.

> Known as "the people's poet," Mistral believed that poetry was not only for the elite, and she worked to make fine literature available to everyone.

Born in Montegrande, Mistral embraced the beauty of her country from the countryside to the towering Andean mountains. Both her mother, Petronila Alcayaga, and father, Jeronimo Godoy Villanueva, were teachers. Villanueva was also a poet. Her schoolteacher sister, Emelina, taught Gabriela as a teen. Mistral found a passion for teaching, even as her writing blossomed.

Her first love was a hopelessly romantic railroad worker who committed suicide when they ended their relationship. She was able to turn her grief, sadness, and pain into the poetry collection, *Sonetas de la Muerte* (Sonnets of Death). When she published three of the *Sonetas* in 1914, she received Chile's top prize for poetry. When she moved near Santiago to teach, she established herself in literary circles and was published in many periodicals. Her friend, Chile's prime minister of justice and education, Pedro Aguirre Cerda, appointed her director of a secondary school for girls in 1918, located in Puntas Arenas. The rough terrain inspired her series of poems entitled "Patagonian Landscapes."

In 1922 she accepted an invitation to establish educational programs for the poor in Mexico. She started a mobile library system to rural areas there and traveled the world to learn better methods of teaching and resources that could improve Chile's educational system. In 1923, she was named "Teacher of the Nation."

She taught Spanish literature at reputable schools such as Columbia, Barnard, Middlebury, and the University of Puerto Rico. She also served as Chilean consul and ambassador in European and Latin-American posts for twenty years, including at the League of Nations and the United Nations in the 1950s.

When the military seized control of Chile in the 1920s and asked Mistral to serve as an ambassador to all Central American countries, she refused. Her pension was revoked and she fled to live in exile in France while supporting her mother, sister, and herself through her writing.

Mistral is remembered for her compassion. She worked to help victims—mostly women and children—of World War I and II. She accepted the Nobel Prize on behalf of the "poets of my race," which she said included the humble Indians, mestizos, and *campesinos*.

Her collected works include *Desolación* (1922), *Tala* (1938), *Lagar* (1954), and *Ternura* (1924), a children's poetry collection, among others.

Julia de Burgos (Puerto Rico, 1914–1953)

One of the most celebrated and prolific Puerto Rican poets of the twentieth century, Julia de Burgos received the posthumous degree of Doctor Honoris Causa for her contribution to Puerto Rico's literary culture.

The poetess loved the wrong men and in her traumatic relationships found a voice and an outlet in deeply moving poetry. Julia de Burgos was one of the most celebrated and prolific Puerto Rican poets of the twentieth century.

She was ahead of her time but her topics were timeless. She wrote of unrequited love, self-negation, feminism, sexuality, and cultural richness.

De Burgos graduated from the University of Puerto Rico and received a teaching certificate. She began teaching in a small provincial town that brought back nightmares of her own childhood poverty.

She married Ruben Rodriguez Beauchamp in 1934 and stopped teaching, although she did work at a day care center and wrote educational plays and songs for the Puerto Rico Department of Education's *Escuela del Aire*, which played on the radio.

Her first book of poetry, *Poemas Exactos a Mi Misma*, was published in 1937, the same year she was divorced. *Poema en Veinte Surcos* was published in 1938. *Canción de la Verdad Sencilla*, a 1939 publication, won a prize from the Institute of Puerto Rican Literature.

She moved to New York in 1940, worked as a journalist, and fell in love with exiled Dominican Juan Isidro Jimenes Grullón. They later moved to Cuba where she continued her studies in literature at the University of Havana. Grullón deeply inspired her poetry.

In 1942 she returned to New York where she married again, this time a poet, Armando Marín. She found support for her poetry through the Circle of Ibero-American Writers and Poets and was awarded another prize for her editorial "Ser o no ser la Divisa." Her own pain and suffering that dated back to her childhood were brought to life in her poem "Rio Grande de Loiza." She worked for a variety of publications, where many of her essays and other works were also published.

De Burgos became involved with a movement called "Negritude." Caribbean writers protested against European influence and its denigration of African culture. They promoted the idea to look to African heritage for inspiration. She was dedicated to this and other social changes.

> De Burgos became involved with a movement called "Negritude." She was dedicated to this and other social changes.

Her poetry showed great diversification for "every woman" but was deeply personal. Through her lyricism, symbolism, and feminist viewpoint, her poems provided glimpses into her troubled soul and the way she often felt lost and abandoned. By the same token, her sharp words attacked the restrictions imposed on women by society.

Her last years made her a living testimony to her tormented poetry. She fell into depression, alcoholism, and suffered from cirrhosis of the liver. She became a recluse and was in and out of hospitals for treatment.

Toward the end of 1953, she was released from a hospital but disappeared. She was discovered unconscious on a street corner and taken to Harlem, where she died. She was buried in a public cemetery. When she was later identified, her body was transported back to Puerto Rico, given last honors by the Sociedad de Periodistas (Journalist Society), and was given a Christian burial.

In 1987 she was given the posthumous degree of Doctor Honoris Causa for her contribution to the island's literary culture.

Nicholasa Mohr (United States, 1935–)

Artist and author Nicholasa Mohr is the winner of numerous awards for her work, including the Hispanic Heritage Award in literature, the Edgar Allan Poe Award, and the American Library Association Best Book Award.

*N*icholasa Mohr's school counselor advised her to find a school where she could sew since she would not be going to college. Feeling powerless and humiliated, Mohr knew there was no one to fight for her rights or come to her defense at the treatment. Despite the counselor's words, Mohr went on to find acceptance and respect in the art world and as an author.

Mohr attended a high school of fashion and design where she pursued her first love—drawing. From 1953 to 1969, she attended the Art Students' League of New York, the Brooklyn Museum Art School, and the Pratt Center for Contemporary Printmaking. She found success as a printmaker and illustrator. Still, she never forgot the counselor's image of her and the pain associated with it.

In the 1970s her artistic creativity turned to writing. She wrote *Nilda*, a critically acclaimed book about a Puerto Rican child who rises above the crushing humiliations of being poor and a minority. In the fictionalized autobiography aimed at young readers, Nilda's pain comes straight from Mohr's heart. Mohr wanted readers to see the human child underneath the skin.

Nilda won the School Library Journal Best Book Award, the Outstanding Book Award in juvenile fiction from the *New York Times*, and the Jane Addams Peace Association Award. She designed the book cover and won the Society of Illustrators' Certification of Merit.

Born Nicholasa Golpe, Mohr was raised in New York's Spanish Harlem by Puerto Rican–born parents. She was the youngest and only girl of seven children. Her father died when she was eight and her mother was sickly but supportive and independent—Mohr's first feminist role model.

She gave Mohr pencils, paper, and crayons and encouraged her to use her God-given talents to make important contributions to the world. Mohr realized she could create her own worlds, far from the one she lived in, through art.

While studying at the Art Students' League, she worked odd jobs to earn enough money to travel to Mexico to study the great painters and muralists like Diego Rivera and Frida Kahlo. Their use of bold, strong colors and designs inspired her.

Upon returning, she studied at the New School for Social Research. She met and married Irwin Mohr, a clinical psychologist, and had two sons. They moved to New Jersey, where she set up her studio. Her art was getting noticed.

A publisher she had done book covers for asked her to write about her experiences growing up Puerto Rican in New York. She initially said no, but then realized there were no books about Puerto Rican girls like herself.

> Mohr's book *Nilda* won the School Library Journal Best Book Award, the Outstanding Book Award in juvenile fiction from the *New York Times*, and the Jane Addams Peace Association Award.

Her collection of vignettes was rejected but another publisher took a look at her writing. Three weeks later she was offered a contract.

Other books by Mohr include *El Bronx Remembered* (1975), *Rituals of Survival: A Woman's Portfolio* (1985), *Going Home and Other Stories* (1986), *All for the Better: A Story of El Barrio* (1994), and *The Song of El Coquí and Other Tales of Puerto Rico* (1995).

Mohr has also written for public television and radio. She served as head creative writer and coproducer of the television series, *Aquí y Ahora* and other PBS specials.

Mohr won the 1997 Hispanic Heritage Award in literature, the Edgar Allan Poe Award, and the American Library Association Best Book Award. She is a member of the New Jersey State Council for the Arts and the Young Filmmakers Foundation.

Esmeralda Santiago (Puerto Rico, 1940–)
Award-winning author and documentary filmmaker who cofounded Cantomedia.

Esmeralda Santiago wanted to get back her feeling of "Puertoricanness." Like many other immigrants who moved to the United States, acclimated, and returned to their homeland, she was lost.

When she returned to Puerto Rico twelve years after arriving in the United States, people she encountered told her she was no longer Puerto Rican because her Spanish was rusty, she was too assertive, and she refused to eat some traditional foods.

She wondered who had decided that there were degrees of how "Puerto Rican" someone could be. By the same token, being called Latina or Hispanic in the United States frightened her. These American "labels" were terms she had never heard in Puerto Rico. She felt contaminated by Americanisms yet in the United States she was a foreigner, a non-American because of her skin color and accented speech.

When she returned to the United States after her negative reception in Puerto Rico, she questioned who she was. When she had her first baby, she wondered about her mother who at the same age already had nine children and raised them mostly alone. Santiago began to write essays about her identity and the fabric of her life.

She was "discovered" when publisher Merloyd Lawrence saw one of her essays in the *Radcliffe Quarterly*. Lawrence, who had her own imprint, suggested Santiago write a book about her life and offered her a contract. That is how Santiago's touching memoir *When I Was Puerto Rican* came to be. The book is a coming-of-age story of Santiago growing up first in a tiny barrio in Puerto Rico and then in the vivid contrast of New York. It speaks of transitions, losses, and joys.

Her second memoir, *Almost a Woman,* was made into a film of the same name. It is the first film by a Hispanic author to be featured on *Masterpiece Theatre's American Collection.* It aired on PBS in 2002 and won the 2003 George Foster Peabody Award for excellence in electronic media.

> Santiago wondered who had decided that there were degrees of how "Puerto Rican" someone was.

Santiago graduated from the High School of Performing Arts in New York. She attended Harvard University to study film production on full scholarship and graduated in 1976. Her master's degree in fine arts is from Sarah Lawrence University. She and her husband, Frank Cantor, started Cantomedia, a film and media production company, which has won many awards for excellence in documentary filmmaking.

Her first published essay, "Bilingual Dreamer," appeared in the *Christian Science Monitor.* Other written works appeared in literary magazines, in newspapers such as the *New York Times* and the *Boston Globe,* and in magazines such as *House & Garden, Metropolitan Home,* and *Good Housekeeping.*

Santiago also helped cowrite and edit *Las Christmas: Favorite Latino Authors Share Their Holiday Memories* and *Las Mamis: Favorite Latino Authors Remember Their Mothers. America's Dream* was her first novel. Her third memoir is due out in 2004.

Active in her community, Santiago is a spokesperson for public libraries and is involved with programs for teens and shelters for battered women and children.

Isabel Allende (Peru, 1942–)

One of Latin America's most highly esteemed authors, Isabel Allende is a best-selling author who has received worldwide critical acclaim and numerous awards for her work.

"As long as it is written, it will be remembered."
—Isabel Allende, *www.isabelallende.com*

I sabel Allende's love of language and stories came from living with her grandparents. Her connection to her grandfather was fierce. He spoke in proverbs and was a great storyteller of folktales. He read the entire Bible and an encyclopedia set. Her grandmother was a clairvoyant and talked to the souls of the dead during her séances.

Their lives, planted deeply in Chile, centered around family and politics. Her father was a diplomat and secretary at the Chilean embassy. Her uncle, Salvador Allende, founder of the Chilean Socialist Party, became president of Chile in 1970. Her stepfather, also a diplomat, worked abroad in the Middle East and Europe until he was appointed ambassador to Argentina by Salvador.

Allende married Miguel Frias in 1962 and had two children. She wrote for a women's magazine that promoted feminism and for a children's publication. She also hosted a television show. Their world began to unravel in 1973. A military regime took control of the country and murdered President Salvador Allende in a violent, bloody uprising. Outraged, Isabel spoke publicly against the new military government. Her family feared for her safety. She was fired from both magazines and quit the television station.

She began helping people find asylum in foreign embassies, passed along information, and collected food for displaced families. In 1975 her family had to flee Chile and settled in Venezuela. In exile, she missed her family and country. Writing gave her a voice, rescued her memories, and enabled her to create a universe of her own, saving her from despair.

When Allende learned her grandfather was dying in 1981 and she could not return to see him, her heart tore open. She sat down and wrote 185 him a letter nonstop for twelve hours. She continued writing to him daily, even long after his death. The letter turned into her first novel, *The House of the Spirits.*

The fictionalized version of her own family history chronicled four generations of a Chilean family set against the backdrop of a turbulent historical time. The book was published to critical acclaim, sold more than 6 million copies, was translated into twenty-seven languages, and was made into a movie. Love and violence always seemed to fill Allende's life and triggered profound emotion in her writing. She divorced her husband in the mid-1980s. Her first nonfiction work was the tragic story of her twenty-eight-year-old daughter who died due to a hereditary disorder, porphyria. Allende was unable to write fiction for three years following Paula's death, but once she started, she cried healing tears every day she wrote. When *Paula* was finished, she felt it captured the nightmare of her daughter's untimely death and celebrated life in a collage of memories they shared together.

> When Allende learned her grandfather was dying in 1981 and she could not return to see him, her heart tore open. She sat down and wrote him a letter nonstop for twelve hours. She continued writing to him daily, even long after his death. The letter turned into her first novel, *The House of the Spirits.*

Allende believes destiny brought her book tour to Northern California where she eventually married lawyer William Gordon in 1990. They reside in California, where she continues to write and works for women's rights.

Her books include *Eva Luna, The Infinite Plan, Aphrodite: A Memoir of the Senses,* and *Daughter of Fortune. City of the Beasts,* her first young adult novel, is the first in a trilogy. *Kingdom of the Dragon* and *Forest of the Pygmies,* which she is currently working on, follow.

Allende won the Hispanic Heritage Award in Literature (1996), the Gabriela Mistral Award (1990), and the Dorothy & Lillian Gish Award (1998) for "contributing to the beauty of the world."

Dolores Prida (Cuba, 1943–)

One of the most important contemporary Latina playwrights in the United States, Dolores Prida is recipient of the Cintas Fellowship Award for Literature and the Creative Public Service Award for Playwriting.

> "American theatre will be richer because of our Hispanic theatre because it's part of the whole mosaic of what this country is."
> —Dolores Prida, *www.repertorio.org*

Dolores Prida arrived in Florida from Cuba with absolutely nothing. The first thing she did was call her uncle to ask him to lend her $50 to get to New York. She started working at a bakery and within six months had moved into the office where she became editor of the employee newsletter. She found her destiny.

Prida is one of the most important contemporary Latina playwrights in the United States. Many of her works can be laugh-out-loud funny but have serious undertones about issues like racism, feminism, social injustices, feminine stereotypes, and biculturalism—anything that reflects Latino reality. The prevalent focus in her plays is on being a woman who is searching for identity between two cultures.

Her theatrical work started in 1976 with the Teatro Popular where she gained practical training before ever trying to write a play. She was a "techie" first, learning lighting, props, and music cues. The most important thing she learned was that she wanted to produce theater that everyday people could identify with.

In the next decade she wrote nine plays that ranged from musicals to one-acts. Most were performed at the Duo, an experimental theater. Her works were either bilingual, English, or Spanish.

Her debut, *Beautiful Señoritas,* was a bilingual musical comedy with a theme of liberating Latinas from the repression of domineering men and the Catholic Church. A special performance was presented at the National Organization for Women's annual convention.

Other plays soon followed. *Coser y Cantar, The Beggars Soap Opera*

(1979), *Pantallas* (1986), *Botánica* (1991), and *Casa Propia* (1999). *Four Guys Named José and Una Mujer Named María* (2000) is her most commercial, a musical revue built around the best-known Latino songs of the 1940s and 1950s. She is now working on her first novel, *Red Tacones in the Sunset.*

Prida has worked as a writer or editor for various publications such as the Spanish-language daily *El Tiempo*, *Latina* magazine, *Nuestro*, and *AHA!* the Association of Hispanic Arts' publication.

She has written poetry and essays. For Spanish-language television and film she has written sitcoms, series pilots, educational films, and documentaries. She has even been a city commissioner's speech writer.

Her first collection of plays was published by Arte Publico Press (1991). *Botánica* is one of her plays featured in *Puro Teatro: A Latina Anthology*, which showcases women's works in Latina theater. She received the Cintas Fellowship Award for Literature (1976) and the Creative Public Service Award for Playwriting (1979–1980). In 1989 she was awarded an Honoris Causa doctorate by Massachusetts' Mount Holyoke College for her contributions to the American theater.

Prida traveled to Cuba in 1978 with members of *Revista Areito*, a publication of young Cuban intellectuals who sought to understand the revolution. The dialogue revolved around visitation rights by exiles. When she wrote about her trip she received death threats from militant anti-Castro exiles. Her works were banned from heavily populated Cuban-American areas like New Jersey and South Florida. The ban affected her professionally and soon became a national First Amendment issue.

Carolina Garcia-Aguilera (Cuba, 1949–)

The first Latina author to write a mystery series with a Latina heroine, Carolina Garcia-Aguilera worked as a private investigator for ten years, earned a Ph.D., traveled the world, and raised three daughters in addition to establishing a career as an Award-winning author.

_L_upe Solano is a private investigator with a weakness for designer clothes, good colognes, café con leche, brand names, and red wine. She comes from a big, loving, and wealthy Cuban family, and wears the title, Cuban-American Princess (CAP) well. She is "a good daughter, a good sister and the best Catholic she can be" since she is often caught in situations that put her to the test. For that reason, she carries a beretta in her Chanel bag.

"Lupe Solano" is the main character in a successful series of mystery novels created by Carolina Garcia-Aguilera. She is the first Latina author to build such a series around a Latina heroine.

The humorous, fast-paced novels based in Miami are steeped with rich details of Cuban-American family life involving politics, culture, and religion.

Garcia-Aguilera always loved a good mystery. When she decided to write one, she interned with an investigative agency. She initially wanted to see what it was like to conduct surveillance and experience how a woman's mind would operate under those circumstances. She also wanted to find out how she would fit into a traditionally male-dominated field. Besides, she liked the idea of tying up loose ends.

She stumbled on two things: She could not find women in the field and she had a talent for deciphering details and clues herself. Her career took a little detour into the P.I. life. She applied for a private investigator's license and started her own practice, where she worked for ten years.

When she opened up case files, story lines jumped out at her. Her experiences helped her come up with plot lines that would grab readers' attention.

Garcia-Aguilera's rich cultural details come from her deep-rooted Cuban heritage. Her great-great-great grandfather fought for Cuban freedom from the Spanish. Even though his face appears on the Cuban $100 bill, Garcia-Aguilera's family fled to Florida to escape possible political repercussions one year after Fidel Castro came into power.

The Aguilera family moved on to New York. Garcia-Aguilera spent four years at Miss Porter's School in Connecticut, then attended Rollins College in Florida, where she earned degrees in history and political science. She later earned a master's degree in languages and linguistics at Georgetown University, but her first marriage postponed her studies.

Traveling the world was the tradeoff, and another way she learned about various cultures and how to pay attention to details. The couple spent a lot of time in Asia and from 1973 to 1981 lived in Beijing, where their two daughters were born.

Her marriage ended after eleven years. Garcia-Aguilera moved to Miami to be closer to her brother and sister. She worked on a Ph.D. in Latin-American affairs at the University of Miami, remarried, and had another daughter. Many of her books are dedicated to her three daughters.

Garcia-Aguilera's biggest obstacle is not so much being Hispanic as it is being a woman writing the genre. She inserts curse words in Spanish, for example, where a male writer might not need to censor that way.

The Lupe Solano detective series includes *Bloody Waters* (1996), *Bloody Shame* (1997), *Bloody Secrets* (1998), *A Miracle in Paradise* (1999), *Havana Heat* (2000)—winner of the Shamus Award for "best private eye novel" from the Private Eye Writers of America—and *Bitter Sugar* (2001). Mainstream novels include *One Hot Summer* (2002) and *Luck of the Draw* (2003).

Angeles Mastretta (Mexico, 1949–)
Bestselling writer and journalist, and winner of the prestigious Mazatlan Prize for literature.

When her infant daughter lay bedridden and gravely ill, Angeles Mastretta sat by her bedside and brought her comfort by weaving together stories based on their family tree. She wanted her to see that she was a necessary link in their family chain of strong and extraordinary women. What Mastretta created through the soothing cadence of her expressive voice, was a story with a magical cast of colorful women at pivotal moments of their lives.

Mastretta's autobiographical book, *Mujeres de Ojos Grandes* (Women with Big Eyes), was born from that experience. It was published in 1995, firmly establishing her as a fiction writer. The first English translation was published in 2003. Described as a "timeless and memorable tapestry of vibrant women's voices," it falls somewhere between a novel and a collection of short stories.

Much of Mastretta's writing revolves around pivotal moments in Mexican history, mostly during tumultuous times that produce dramatic and emotional elements for a love story. Using a backdrop of revolutionary times also produces strong and independent women who learn that the most important thing is life. Living.

> 🔖 Much of Mastretta's writing revolves around pivotal moments in Mexican history, mostly during tumultuous times that produce dramatic and emotional elements for a love story.

Mastretta was a journalist whose creative freedom was buried underneath everyday time and business commitments. She worked at *Siete*, a magazine published by the Ministry of Public Education, and an afternoon newspaper called *Ovaciones*.

When she won a scholarship in 1974, she attended a conference where she honed her writing skills next to the likes of Juan Rulfo, Salvador Elizondo, and Francisco Monterde. Her book of poetry, *La Pájara Pinta* (Colorful Bird) was published the following year. Based on that success, an editor at a local publishing house offered to pay her salary for six months so that she could work on a novel full time.

Arráncame la Vida (Tear This Heart Out) was the end product. Not only was it published, it won the Mazatlan Prize for literature's "best book of the year." Only 2,000 copies were initially printed, but the novel eventually sold more than 1 million copies in Mexico alone.

It became an international hit and Mastretta made a grand entrance into the fiction-writing world. *Mal de Amores* (Lovesick) was published in 1997 and won the prestigious Rómulo Gallegos literary award.

She wants her literature to be both accessible and exotic. Through her writings, now published in both Spanish and English, she wants to continue to create female characters that symbolize every woman's dreams and visions. Finally, she wants to project the power that females have within families, communities, and society.

Tradition carries on. Mastretta's daughter, who survived the early illness, tells stories through her film studies in New York. Her son is a journalism student in Mexico and her husband is the renowned author Hector Aguilar Camín. Mastretta credits her father, also a journalist, for inspiring her to write, even though he died when she was a teenager. Her mission is to see that more libraries are built in Mexico.

Julia Alvarez (United States, 1950–)

A tenured professor of English at Middlebury College, Julia Alvarez published her first novel at age forty-one to critical acclaim. She has received numerous awards for her fiction and poetry.

> "I am a Dominican, hyphen, American. As a fiction writer, I find that the most exciting things happen in the realm of that hyphen—the place where two worlds collide or blend together."
> —Julia Alvarez, *www.emory.edu/ENGLISH/Bahri/Alvarez.html*

Julia Alvarez had always thought of herself as American while on her island, the Dominican Republic. She attended American schools, wore American clothes, ate American food. Her parents had lived in the United States but moved back to the island when she was three months old. Her uncles had all attended Ivy League colleges and her grandfather was a cultural attaché to the United Nations. Her extended family was wealthy, had prestige, and was affectionate and supportive.

When her father became involved with the underground movement to oust Rafael Trujillo, they had to flee the country to escape persecution. They landed in the United States with nothing. At ten years old, Alvarez was thrust into a new world where she felt isolated. Children taunted her at school and made fun of her accent.

The contrast was a cruel awakening. Torn between two cultures, Alvarez escaped the pain of racism by diving into books to escape reality and explore the English language in relative safety. The experience awakened a muse within her, and she poured the deep emotion it provoked into her own writing. Alvarez continued to write while she earned undergraduate and graduate degrees in literature and writing from Middlebury College in Vermont and Syracuse University in New York.

Her first novel, *How the Garcia Girls Lost Their Accents*, was published in 1991 when she was forty-one years old and a tenured professor at Middlebury College. It portrayed a family much like her own, adjusting to a new life in the United States, with many of the same trials and tribulations she had faced.

> As a child, Alvarez read books to escape the pain of racism. As an adult, she published her first novel at forty-one years old.

As part of a surge of ethnic novels, *Garcia Girls* was a stellar example of this new literary genre. In her works, Alvarez gave a voice to immigrants' pains, made political observations, and evoked emotion.

Alvarez wrote *In the Time of the Butterflies* to remember the real-life murders of the three brave, young Mirabal sisters who were assassinated for their opposition of the dictator Rafael Trujillo. (See the Mirabal Sisters' biographies on page 139.) *Butterflies* was nominated Best Book of 1994 by the National Book Critics Circle and was made into a movie produced by and starring Salma Hayek.

Teaching was another passion for Alvarez. From 1975 to 1978 she considered herself a migrant writer as she traveled throughout Kentucky, Delaware, and North Carolina with the "Poets-in-the-Schools" program.

Alvarez and her husband bought a 280-acre coffee farm and school in the Dominican Republic called Alta Gracia. In a unique cooperative effort, American students can work alongside *campesinos* in the fields daily while attending writing workshops taught by Alvarez in the afternoons. Alvarez believes the cultural exchange serves to enrich the students' writing experiences. Profits from sales of the organic coffee fund a local literary and arts center.

Alvarez won the ALA Award for *How the Garcia Girls Lost Their Accents*, the Américas Book Award for children's and young adult literature for *Before We Were Free*, and the Nebraska Book Award (2002) for Fiction for *A Cafecito Story*. *Child* magazine named *How Tía Lola Came to (Visit) Stay* the Best Children's Book of 2001 and *In the Name of Salomé* was chosen as one of the Top Ten Books of 2000 by Latino.com.

Her poetry collections include *The Housekeeping Book* (1982) and *Homecoming* (1984). Essays in *Something to Declare* (1998) focus on her life as a writer. Future book releases include *A Gift of Thanks: The Legend of Altagracia*, *Keeping Watch*, and *Finding Miracles*.

Alvarez was honored as Woman of the Year 2000 by *Latina* magazine. In 2002, she won the Sor Juana Award and the Hispanic Heritage Award for literature.

Pam Muñoz Ryan (United States, 1950–)

Author of more than twenty-five young adult and children's books, Muñoz Ryan has garnered numerous awards for her writing, including the Young Reader Medal, the Willa Cather Award, and the National Teachers' Choice Book Award.

The girls are princesses who have fallen, heroic girls in disguise, compassionate animal lovers. The women are strong and adventurous, fearing nothing, making positive contributions to society and history in general. They all live life rather than wait for life to happen to them.

Such are the characters that fill the stories written by children's author, Pam Muñoz Ryan. With more than twenty-five books and picture books in print, she has garnered numerous awards for her writing.

Ryan grew up in Southern California. She calls herself "truly American" because of her rich cultural background, which consists of

Spanish, Basque, Mexican, Italian, and "Oklahoman." With one grand-mother she ate enchiladas, rice, and beans; with another she ate black-eyed peas, fried okra, and peach cobblers.

Her Mexican family came to the United States and worked in the fields with the hopes of a better life in America. Ryan's multiple-award-winning book *Esperanza Rising* is a fictionalized account of the riches-to-rags story of her own grandmother. Esperanza means "hope."

Stories were always magical for Ryan. At her Mexican grandma's house, she used to read from an old set of encyclopedias because there were no toys around. Her favorite volume was G because she could read about Greek mythology.

🔖 Stories were always magical for Pam Muñoz Ryan.

Her grandmother told her family stories about life and work on the farm camps in California as she tried to start a new life after losing every-thing—wealth, prestige, and friends—in Mexico. Her mother, Esperanza Muñoz, was born on the campgrounds. Ryan took the sacrifices her grand-parents and parents made to heart.

They survived the many strikes for better working conditions for farm laborers. They survived horrible prejudice. They survived competing for jobs with people from other states or countries who were just as poor. They survived the Mexican Repatriation and the Deportation Act during the Depression when anyone who looked Mexican was deported to Mexico, even if they were U.S. citizens.

When she was young, she discovered the library, which became her refuge and fueled her imagination with thoughts of queens and doctors, explorers and adventurers. She became a bilingual teacher after college, quit to raise her four children, then pursued her master's degree in education. One of her professors was impressed with her writing and suggested she pursue it.

Fate agreed. A friend asked for her help in writing a book and she jumped at the chance. From that moment on, she knew she wanted to write children's books.

She loves the freedom to research remarkable women and bring them to life in a way young readers might relate to them. Charlotte in *Riding Freedom* is strong as the first woman stagecoach rider. *Amelia and Eleanor Go for a Ride* features the adventurous side of Eleanor Roosevelt and Amelia Earhart.

When Marian Sang: The True Recital of Marian Anderson was the School Library Journal Best Book of the Year and the 2003 Orbis Pictus Winner for outstanding nonfiction for children.

Esperanza Rising won the ALA Best Book for Young Adults Award, the Américas Book Award, Jane Addams Children's Book Award, the Pura Belpré Award, *Publishers Weekly*'s Best Book of the Year, and the Smithsonian Institution Notable Book for Children Award. *Riding Freedom* won the California Young Reader Medal, the Willa Cather Award for best young adult novel, and the National Teachers' Choice Book Award.

Laura Esquivel (Mexico, 1951–)

Laura Esquivel is the author of the international bestseller Like Water for Chocolate. *She also wrote the screenplay for the movie, which became the largest-grossing foreign film ever released in the United States.*

*L*ove is a powerful force in the books written by Laura Esquivel. *Like Water for Chocolate* was loaded with love and powerful emotions, recipes handed down to her from her mother and grandmother, and the inspiration of magic realism.

In her grandmother's home when she was growing up, a chapel was built right between the kitchen and dining room. Esquivel began to savor the smells that mingled through her house. The chapel smells mixed with that of the nuts, chilies, and garlic and her grandmother's carnations, liniments, and healing herbs. Magic lived in that kitchen. While Esquivel learned to cook generations-old recipes from her mother and grandmother, the air was punctuated with their laughter and rich smells, and she thought how wonderful it would be to tell a story bringing those elements to life. The experiences in her family's kitchen provided the inspiration for Esquivel's first novel.

   ✥ While Esquivel learned to cook generations-old recipes from her mother and grandmother, the air was punctuated with their laughter and rich smells, and she thought how wonderful it would be to tell a story bringing those elements to life.

Originally published in 1990 as *Como Agua Para Chocolate: Novela de Entregas Mensuales con Recetas, Amores, y Remedios Caseros*, it became a bestseller in Mexico. The translated work, *Like Water for Chocolate*, brought Esquivel international acclaim.

She won the prestigious ABBY Award, which is given annually by the American Booksellers Association to the book the members most enjoyed hand-selling. The novel has been translated into thirty languages with more than 3 million copies in print worldwide.

Esquivel also wrote the screenplay for *Like Water for Chocolate*. Her then-husband Alfonso Arau directed the film, which was released in Mexico in 1989. *Like Water for Chocolate* swept the 1992 Ariel Awards— the equivalent of the Academy Awards—from the Academia Mexicana de Artes y Ciencias Cinematográficas. She won eleven in all. In 1993, the movie went on to become the largest-grossing foreign film ever released in the United States.

The story revolves around Tita de la Garza, who is madly in love but, as the youngest daughter, is doomed to remain single and take care of her mother in her old age. Tita reluctantly, sadly, accepts her fate, and food becomes her scapegoat, her vent, her passion and delight. The recipes and remedies she prepares from that moment on are filled with her tears, spells, and remedies that affect the people she feeds, evoking emotions and passions unlike any other.

Esquivel was a screenwriter before becoming a novelist because as a teacher for elementary school and for children's theater workshops, she saw there was very little material available. She began to write children's plays and for children's public television.

Arau taught her to write film scripts and promoted her in the industry. She was nominated for an Ariel Award in the best screenplay category for her first work, *Chido One* in 1980. Despite her success in the field, she still became frustrated with the medium when producers always tried to change her work.

Like Water for Chocolate was originally a film idea but when Esquivel was told it would be too expensive to produce because it was a period film, she wrote it as a novel. Ironically, when the novel became so overwhelmingly successful, she received many offers to make it into a film. She decided to write the screenplay herself.

Other books by Esquivel include *The Law of Love, Between Two Fires*, and *Swift as Desire*.

Cherrie Moraga (United States, 1952–)

Cofounder of Kitchen Table/Women of Color Press and author of the first published book by an openly lesbian Chicana, Cherrie Moraga has received numerous awards for her work as a poet, playwright, and novelist.

> "Women are crucial for furthering social change."
> —Cherrie Moraga, Voices from the Gap interview
> with Maria Antonia Oliver-Rotger

F eminist. Lesbian. Chicana. Radical. The labels limit the description of Cherrie Moraga.

As one of the leading Chicana/Lesbian writers of our times, she broke silences surrounding taboo topics such as ethnicity, feminism, sexuality, lesbianism, sexism, homophobia, Chicano culture, and racism.

Moraga helped establish the "women of color" concept in writing. As cofounder of Kitchen Table/Women of Color Press, named for cofounder

Barbara Smith's kitchen table where the idea was conceived, the goal was to write, collect, and edit writings of other minority women, giving them a voice in print.

She also discovered a need to bridge the gaps between various minority groups she belonged to: white feminist writers vs. ethnic writers; heterosexual Chicanos vs. gays and lesbians of the same ancestry; women vs. the macho.

> ✎ Moraga used her writing as a way to bridge the gaps between the various minority groups she belonged to.

The conflicts were mirrored in her works, whether they were poems, essays, or stage plays.

In 1983, her book *Loving in the War Years: Lo Que Nunca Pasó por Sus Labios* became the first published book by an openly lesbian Chicana and shed light on her multilabeled identities as a Chicana, lesbian, and feminist.

A work that started as her thesis, *This Bridge Called My Back: Writings by Radical Women of Color* (1981, 1983) ended up as an anthology coedited with writer Gloria Anzaldúa. It was the 1986 winner of the Before Columbus Foundation American Book Award and became critical in women's studies courses.

Moraga's Mexican-American mother and her aunts were great storytellers as they gathered around their own kitchen table. She soaked it up. But their Spanish language was not passed on to Moraga.

Her mother saw Moraga's light skin as a blessing. She believed her children would have more opportunities and privileges if they "passed for white" and had a command of the English language. With her light skin, Moraga did realize the advantage of white privilege as she pursued her education, even if it meant losing her connection to her Chicana roots.

After her college graduation, she started teaching at the high school level, but a writing course she took at the Los Angeles Women's Building opened a new world to her.

A move to San Francisco expanded her vision. She earned a master's degree from San Francisco State University in 1980. She sought links that existed between the issues that interested her: feminism, lesbianism, racial divides, and the treatment of minorities. Moraga's inspiration came from bilingual working-class theater, especially El Teatro Campesino, the poetic sensuality of Federico Garcia Lorca, and the teachings of Maria Irene Fornes in playwriting. Becoming a mother of a son also influenced her work. She needed to teach him how to embrace indigenous history while respecting himself and women in a new world.

Her plays include *Giving Up the Ghost: Teatro in Two Acts* (1986), *Shadow of a Man* (1988), and *Heroes and Saints* (1992). *Watsonville: Some Place Not Here* (1996) was the first play performed at the Brava Theater Center in San Francisco. *Watsonville* won the Fund for New American Plays Award from the Kennedy Center for the Performing Arts.

Her other writings include *Cuentos: Stories by Latinos* (1983), *The Last Generation* (1986), and *Waiting in the Wings: Portrait of a Queer Motherhood* (1997).

Moraga is a recipient of the National Endowment for the Arts Theater Playwriting Fellowship Award. She also organizes women-of-color groups against violence.

Sandra Cisneros (United States, 1954–)

The first Latina to receive a major publishing contract and a leading writer in Latino literature, Sandra Cisneros is a recipient of the MacArthur Foundation "genius prize" and the National Endowment for the Arts fellowship in fiction.

"I am determined to fill a literary void."
—Sandra Cisneros, Profile by Andres Chavez

She has called herself "a macha hell on wheels." As the first Chicana to receive a major publishing contract, Sandra Cisneros is one of the leading writers in the growing field of Latino literature.

Cisnero's work has power, eloquence, lyrical beauty. It is vigorous, playful, and filled with compassion. It serves as a catalyst for internal and social change.

Her first novel, *The House on Mango Street* (1983), gives a vivid portrayal of life in a poor Hispanic neighborhood although it was sometimes criticized for reinforcing Latino stereotypes. It reflects one poor girl's childhood in a cramped house, longing for her own room, and longing to fit in.

The book won the Before Columbus Foundation American Book Award. It is required reading in many classrooms across the country, has been translated into twenty-seven different languages, and has sold more than 2 million copies. It was a long way from where she started.

Born in the barrios of Chicago, Illinois, she lived in a succession of low-income housing. The family moved often from the States to Mexico to visit her grandmother, so she was never able to establish real roots.

Her parents stressed education, however, and made sure each of their children had library cards. Well protected as the only daughter with six brothers, Cisneros's father allowed her to attend Loyola University only because he thought she would meet a potential husband. He never dreamed she would graduate, remain single, and become a professional writer.

School was painful because she did not fit in. Nothing she said or did garnered attention. Cisneros retreated into her own world, becoming an astute observer of people and things around her, while writing secretly at home. She found comfort in books, and in the library, a surrogate mother.

Cisnero found comfort in books, and in the library, a surrogate mother.

One lone high school teacher saw Cisneros's talent and urged her to read her poetry aloud in class and to work on a literary magazine, which she did. She eventually became editor of the magazine. At the University of Iowa Writers' Workshop, Cisneros earned a master's of fine arts degree in creative writing in 1978. Once, given an assignment to describe their childhood homes, Cisneros finally looked deep into herself. Once she saw herself as truly "distinct" from the privileged Anglo students in her class, her true writing voice emerged. Race, gender, class, and cultural divides that had caused an imbalance in her life instead added depth to her work. She decided to write about something her classmates couldn't, and *The House on Mango Street* was born.

Even after the book was published by Random House, Cisneros went through periods of depression and self-doubt. She surfaced every time, stronger than before. One of her poems was selected to appear in public buses in Chicago. She did public readings, had poems published in literary magazines, and was an artist-in-residence at a foundation in France.

Her long-awaited second novel, *Caramelo* (2002), took ten years to write, and earned rave reviews. *Vintage Cisneros*, a "best of" collection of her works, is a 2004 release.

Cisneros taught creative writing in Chicago's Latino Youth Alternative High School and at California State University. She received the MacArthur Foundation "genius prize" in 1995 and won the National Endowment for the Arts fellowship in fiction. *Woman Hollering Creek and other Stories* (1991) was selected Noteworthy Book of 1991 by the *New York Times* and as one of the Best Books of 1991 by the *Library Journal*.

Liza Gross (Argentina, 1957–)
Journalist and managing editor of the Miami Herald.

"I love journalism . . . I want to spend the remainder of my career in journalism, maybe till I die."
—Liza Gross in "A Latina Lois Lane Who Made It Without Superman" by David Everett, *Latino Leaders* magazine (August/September 2001)

Liza Gross had no career plan when she first started out in the journalism business. Her aim was only to get the greatest "scoop" on earth. Her journalism career exceeded even her own expectations.

As a managing editor at the *Miami Herald*, she is responsible for the newspaper's visual appearance, daily production, and weekend news sections. Determined to transcend gender, race, and stereotypical roadblocks in her career path, she has always tried to practice what her history professor and mentor once advised—to identify her strengths, to avoid superficial thinking, and to have a professional approach in whatever she does.

> Determined to transcend gender, race, and stereotypical roadblocks, Gross practices what her history professor and mentor advised—to identify her strengths, to avoid superficial thinking, and to have a professional approach in whatever she does.

Gross studied art history at National University in Buenos Aires, but many schools were shut down there in the 1970s and her studies were constantly disrupted. Against her parents' wishes and fears, she packed up her bags and moved to New York where her aunt and uncle lived so that she could pursue her studies. She majored in history with a minor in journalism, always thinking she would return to her homeland.

But she was offered her first real journalism job right out of school, with the Associated Press in New York, on the Latin-American Desk. It was there that she met her husband, Michael Gross, also a journalist, and started a family.

She won a Kiplinger Fellowship to attend Ohio State University for a master's degree in public affairs reporting. It gave her a framework of focus when her husband died unexpectedly. The kindness of strangers who supported her and her son helped her get through the tragedy and set her on her way again.

When she moved to Washington, D.C., she became editor of *Hispanic Magazine*. She then moved on to a position as executive editor of *Times of the Americas*, the only English-language magazine that covered Latin America.

When that publication folded, she returned to school to earn a doctorate in journalism with a specialty in women journalists in Latin America. She worked with the Latin-American journalism program at Florida

International University and taught throughout Latin America.

In the middle of her studies, the *Chicago Tribune* called and made her an offer she could not refuse. They were launching a new weekly called *!Exito!* and she could mold it as she saw fit as its publisher.

It was an incredible milestone—not only for her personally, but for the entire all-Hispanic staff. Most were under thirty and launching their own careers. Gross also saw the newspaper's commitment to addressing the needs of the Hispanic community. Circulation reached 100,000 copies weekly. In 2001 Gross was recruited yet again. She moved to Puerto Rico to become executive managing editor of *El Nuevo Día*, the island's leading newspaper with almost 200 on staff. In 2002, she moved to the *Miami Herald.*

Through her experiences as an immigrant and a journalist, Gross sees acculturation rather than assimilation as an important goal for all Latinos living in the United States. Embracing roots and visiting homelands while becoming truly bilingual would help citizens develop their full potential and allow them to mentor other Latinos.

Gross belongs to the National Association of Minority Executives, the International Women's Media Foundation, and is on the board of the National Association of Hispanic Journalists.

Cristina Garcia (Cuba, 1958–)

Garcia's writing straddles the two rich cultures of America and Cuba. Her work was nominated for a National Book Award.

When she visited Cuba for the first time in 1984 since leaving there twenty-odd years before, images came to Cristina Garcia with great clarity. Meeting relatives for the first time, they welcomed her with open arms and she finally felt she had the missing link to her identity as a Cuban American. There was a definite connection. She had another home.

Her family had moved to New York when she was a baby. Garcia had always heard stories about Cuba, but had not engaged in anti-Castro sentiments, which at times made her feel estranged from other Cubans. She spoke Spanish at home and English at school while growing up. She liked her life in the United States. But, like she emphasized in her novels, there are different types of Cuban exiles and each deals with American life in his own ways, with his own demons and yearnings. And she came to her own revelations.

The visit to Cuba haunted Garcia for a few years. Eventually with such strong images and emotional ties, she began writing *Dreaming in Cuban*. The debut novel would establish Garcia as an important new voice in Latin-American literature.

> ✒ Her debut novel, *Dreaming in Cuban*, would establish Garcia as an important new voice in Latin-American literature.

Nominated for a National Book Award, *Dreaming in Cuban* shows the effects of the Cuban revolution on the del Pino family from the 1930s to the early 1980s, in three very different viewpoints. Garcia's style swings between time frames, places, and points of view. From grandmother matriarch Celia, to dramatic daughter Felicia, and impatient granddaughter twins, *Dreaming in Cuban* tells a personal family story, yet tells the story of every immigrant.

Garcia showed how difficult a transition it was for some, more than others, to leave Cuba and start afresh in a new country. Economic opportunities were bountiful but so was the discrimination Cubans faced. Feelings of being uprooted and disconnected mixed with a yearning for a sense of identity and a connection with their families of old. The struggles of their ancestors had to be appreciated, respected, and kept alive.

Garcia's writings invite readers into that world that straddles two cultures. *The Aguero Sisters* (1997) and *Monkey Hunting* (2003) explore identity struggles and the quest for what constitutes "Cuban-ness."

Garcia fell in love with literature through an English course at Barnard College. With a political science background, however, Garcia earned her master's degree in international relations from Johns Hopkins

University. She was a Guggenheim Fellow, a Hodder Fellow at Princeton University, and received a Whiting Writers Award. She traveled throughout Italy and Europe and worked in Germany for a short time.

She had worked as a copy girl at the *New York Times*. When she returned to the United States from her travels, she remembered that taste of journalism which prompted her to intern at the *Boston Globe*. She took on various reporting jobs until she landed at *Time* magazine in New York. As a correspondent, she traveled to major cities including Los Angeles, San Francisco, and Miami, where she became bureau chief. After a few years, she wanted to write more than factual stories, and her fiction storytelling took root.

She constantly shares stories and traditions with her only daughter to keep the link to their heritage alive.

Sandra Guzmán (Puerto Rico, 1964–)

A successful reporter, editor, and Emmy Award–winning television producer, Sandra Guzmán is the first Latina to write a self-help book for a major publisher.

"I knew that in order for me to know where I was going in life, I needed to know where I came from first."

—Sandra Guzmán in "Magazine Editor Discusses Latino Life," *The Review*, by April R. Smith

There's a new Latina on the block and she walks a fine line. She may speak Spanish; she may not. She may be torn between doing daughterly duties and striking out on her own. She may wonder at the importance of tradition when she is looking toward the future.

She embraces Spanglish, the variety of skin colors and body shapes under the "Hispanic" umbrella, and dating non-Latinos. Plopped in the middle of two worlds, she deals with confusion, guilt, and uncertainties as she tries to make a name for herself.

Sandra Guzmán has been there, done that. She poured her journalistic knowledge and resources into a book that finally addressed the contemporary Latina's needs. *The Latina's Bible: The Nueva Latina's Guide to Love, Spirituality, Family, and la Vida* (2002) is a groundbreaking contemporary self-help book for young Latinas seeking direction in a bicultural world.

Guzmán is the first Latina to write a self-help book for a major publisher. She was paid a six-figure sum by Random House.

With humor, wisdom, and a community-oriented feminism, she points out ways to meld the best of Latin culture with American values. Writing like a girlfriend, Guzmán's style lends itself to the "sisterly love" type of advice on family, health, spiritual, relationship, and career issues. *The Latina's Bible* also features sidebars with statistics and short capsule biographies of inspirational, "fierce" Latinas.

> Guzmán is the first Latina to write a self-help book for a major publisher. She was paid a six-figure sum by Random House.

Guzmán wants young Latinas to be armed with knowledge. She wants to see them empowered—to have a voice, resources, and to be assertive. She wants them to see the importance of taking on the responsibility to mentor other young women.

Coming from a poor Puerto Rican family that moved to New Jersey, Guzmán withstood the pains of prejudice. She tried changing her name and appearance for a while to avoid the racial epithets directed at her. The stability of her family love pulled her through, pushed her forward, and made her appreciate her roots. Then she took charge of her life.

Guzmán earned a degree in philosophy and history from Rutgers University and went straight to work as a reporter for *El Diario/LaPrensa,* where she covered education and city politics.

As a producer for Fox Television's morning program, *Good Day New York,* she covered diverse communities and cultural events. As an assignment manager and public affairs producer for the evening news at Telemundo's local affiliate in New York, Guzmán won an Emmy Award.

Her award-winning piece, "Embargo Contra Cuba," analyzed the controversial U.S. embargo against Cuba.

She served as editor in chief of *Latina*, the first national, glossy, bilingual lifestyle magazine targeting Hispanic-American women. Circulation doubled during Guzmán's tenure.

Her career branched out into other areas. She helped launch SOLOELLA.com, a bilingual interactive Web site in 1999, and served as its first content director and editor in chief. She also served as spokeswoman to former New York City Controller, Elizabeth Holtzman.

Rutgers University honored Guzmán as one of seven alumni for her outstanding leadership and contribution to the arts. She mentors Latino youth organizations and is a board member of the Smithsonian Institution's National Board on Latino Initiatives.

Yasmin Davidds-Garrido (United States, 1971–)

Yasmin Davidds-Garrido started a movement to empower Latinas with her book Empowering Latinas. *She is founder of the Latina Youth Leadership Institute for HOPE and the Latina Empowerment Institute.*

> "When traditionalists try to tell me 'that's just the way it is for us Latinos' I answer: 'Not for me. I chose to live my life on my terms, so could you.'"
>
> —Yasmin Davidds-Garrido

Tradition is a double-edged sword. Latinas sacrifice their lives, wants, and needs for everyone else. It can lead to a cycle of despair and dead ends for generations.

Making wrong choices, bending to machismo or traditional beliefs, or not knowing about available resources can make them powerless victims who lose their sense of identity. They may try to fill that void with men, martyr-ism, and guilt, and in so doing, might live in a constant state of depression. But Latinas need to know there are options in how they live their lives and that they can create their own destiny. They have power through the choices they make.

That is the message in the book *Empowering Latinas: Breaking Boundaries, Freeing Lives*. Yasmin Davidds-Garrido started a movement from her one book and her life's mission became clear: to help empower Latinas all over the world.

According to Davidds-Garrido's statistics, one out of every five women in the United States will be Latina in 2005—and this group will have the least amount of personal, political, and economic power.

Empowering Latinas centers around concepts that are basic to empowerment: education, developing realistic hopes and goals, faith, embracing culture, and incorporating powerful affirmation skills into daily life. She believes that if women improve their sense of worth, they can improve the quality of life for themselves and those they love.

> Davidds-Garrido believes that if women improve their sense of worth, they can improve the quality of life for themselves and those they love.

She travels the world over to share how to overcome personal and cultural obstacles. For example, going away to college does not mean a Latina is abandoning her parents or being a bad daughter. The cycle of repression and self-denial repeats itself unless the young Latina sheds guilt and chooses education and a chance at the life she deserves.

Davidds-Garrido experienced her own personal tragedies and harsh realities from choices she made. After a stay at a rehab facility, she turned tragedy into triumph.

By talking about her experiences she seemed to inspire others to share their stories and motivate them to make positive changes. In the process, she empowered them and herself. From this, the seed for her book was planted.

Education was at the core of her comeback. She returned to school to earn a business degree from the University of Southern California in 1995.

At the University of Cambridge in England she studied gender roles in a variety of ethnic groups. In 1999, she earned a master's degree in women's studies from San Diego State University.

Davidds-Garrido took her empowerment premise to the next level when she co-chaired Latina Action Day in Washington, D.C. More than 600 Latinas met with legislators, putting their concerns on the table. She was also appointed spokesperson for Latino Scholastic Achievement Corporation's "Prove It" campaign, which urges Latino high school students to stay in school.

She established the Latina Youth Leadership Institute for HOPE (Hispanas Organized for Political Equality), the Latina Empowerment Institute in Southern California, and serves on the board of the University of Southern California's Mexican-American Alumni Association.

Davidds-Garrido developed *The Latinas' Seven Principles to Self-Love and Personal Freedom*, an audio program to further her message of empowerment.

Nancy de los Santos (United States)

Producer, writer, and director of television and film, Nancy de los Santos has won numerous awards for her work. Her documentary The Bronze Screen, *which chronicles the history of Latinos in cinema, is a pioneering work that has earned critical acclaim.*

Nancy de los Santos shines in the Hollywood spotlight. She has made a name for herself writing scripts for movies, television shows, documentaries, and plays.

She came up with her own documentary, *The Bronze Screen: The History of Latinos in Hollywood*, because she wanted to chronicle how much Latino actors, directors, producers, and writers have contributed to U.S. cinema and Hollywood moviemaking over the years.

De los Santos was the writer, director, and producer of the film. She spent five years in production with the project. She hoped it would increase awareness of how Latinos have been portrayed in film throughout the years, where they are today, and perhaps inspire more meaningful participation of Latinos in the industry in the future.

The award-winning documentary aired on HBO and Cinemax to critical acclaim. *The Bronze Screen* was a 2002 ALMA award nominee for outstanding television documentary, among other awards.

De los Santos has contributed to Hispanic and Latino publications, and for over twenty years, she has worked in the Hollywood film industry as a producer, writer, and director.

She is the associate producer of such motion pictures as *Mi Familia* and *Selena*.

She began her career as a producer for the Roger Ebert and Gene Siskel television series, *At the Movies*. She has written scripts for a variety of television shows including Showtime's drama series *Resurrection Boulevard*, the PBS series *American Family*, and the PBS music special *Vikki Carr: Memories, Memorias*.

> De los Santos began her career as a producer for the Roger Ebert and Gene Siskel television series, *At the Movies*.

Breaking Pan with Sol, a short film she wrote and produced, won the Best Short Film Award from the Chicago International Latino Film Festival. Her work, *Lalo Guerrero: The Original Chicano*, cowritten with Dan Guerrero, was one of fourteen projects that won funding from Latino Public Broadcasting's open call competition. The award was presented at the LPB's Fifth Annual Awards in 2003.

De los Santos was named one of the top Ten To Watch by *Hispanic Magazine*. She received an Achievement Award from the University of Southern California's Latina/o Cinema Society during the Third Annual Film Festival. It recognizes individuals who have made "exemplary contributions to the entertainment industry and the community."

She has taught courses on Chicano cinema at various film schools throughout the United States. She helps students develop an awareness of the cultural influences behind key Latino stereotypes and invites guest speakers like Edward James Olmos, Raquel Welch, and Cheech Marin to cover various aspects of the business.

Other scripts she developed include a documentary of Chicano rocker Chris Montez and a Disney project about a Latina girls' dance team. She signed on with CBS and Mel Gibson's Icon Productions to write a script with Tomas Benitez for a new television series called *Chi-Town*. Her teleplay about the Mexican-American woman who founded Mothers Against Gangs was developed with Olmos Productions.

9

Doctors: Healing Us Spiritually, Mentally, and Physically

Jane Arminda Delano (United States, 1862–1919)
Founder of the American Red Cross Nursing Corps and posthumous recipient of the Red Cross Distinguished Service Medal.

She was compassionate and willing to serve. Jane Arminda Delano was the founder of the American Red Cross Nursing Corps in 1909.

Thousands of nurses would benefit from her efforts as Delano changed the role and image of nurses worldwide. Her strong and uplifting spirit gave nurses dignity and purpose, standards and ideals.

She graduated from the Bellevue Hospital of Nursing in 1886 and went to work, determined to tend to war victims after her father had died in the Civil War. For twenty years, Delano worked as a nurse, starting with the Spanish-American War. The shortage of nurses greatly affected the type of aid they provided. She saw the need for more trained nurses, especially in isolated areas and in emergencies and suggested a national plan to prepare nurses. She also thought it important to have a ready reserve of nurses in case another military conflict arose.

From 1890 to 1895, Delano was assistant superintendent of nurses and an instructor at the University of Pennsylvania Hospital School of Civics and Philanthropy. She directed the girls' department of the New York City House of Refuge and was superintendent of the Bellevue nursing schools.

Delano's strong and uplifting spirit gave nurses dignity and purpose, standards and ideals.

While supervising nurses in Florida, she insisted on using mosquito netting to prevent the spread of yellow fever even though it was not yet known that mosquitos carried the disease. In Arizona, she established a hospital for miners suffering from scarlet fever.

From 1906 to 1908, she took care of her most treasured patient, her mother, who was in the last years of her illness before dying.

In 1909 Delano was appointed superintendent of the Army Nurse Corps and was named chairman of the National Committee on Red Cross Nursing Service. She worked simultaneously as president of the American Nurses' Association and as chairman of the board of directors of the *American Journal of Nursing.*

To provide health care to rural areas and training courses for nurses, she established the Red Cross Town and Country Nursing Service. By 1918, more than 20,000 Red Cross nurses volunteered to serve at home and overseas. When World War I started, there were more than 8,000 fully trained nurses ready to report to duty. She became director of the wartime organization, the Department of Nursing, which supplied nurses to the Army, Navy, and Red Cross.

Delano also oversaw and developed Red Cross courses and coauthored the book, *The American Red Cross Textbook on Elementary Hygiene and Home Care of the Sick* in 1913. She helped nurses become recognized as full members of the medical profession.

While on a trip to France where she had gone to inspect hospitals and train nurses, she became ill and died. Her body was brought back to the

United States and her wish to be buried in the Arlington National Cemetery was granted. A monument in her honor was constructed in the nurses' corner, a tribute to the nurses who lost their lives in war service. A gold star was added to her Service Flag and she was awarded the Red Cross Distinguished Service Medal posthumously.

Today, there is a Jane Delano Society, which encourages active nursing and preserves artifacts that document the history of Red Cross nursing. The society was formed in 1990 by the National Nursing Committee of the American Red Cross.

Sor (Sister) Maria Isolina Ferre (Puerto Rico, 1914–2000)

Known as "the Mother Teresa of Puerto Rico," Maria Isolina Ferre received the United States Medal of Freedom for her humanitarian efforts throughout her life.

A missionary with a gentle healing hand, endless hope, and encouraging words, Sor Maria Isolina Ferre became known as "the Mother Teresa of Puerto Rico." Her mission took her beyond the island and her message of hope touched thousands as she worked to overcome poverty, violence, and despair.

Sor Isolina wanted to make people self-sufficient and nondependent on government programs. She spread the word of hope and opportunities, and tried to transform ravaged neighborhoods by helping residents to advocate for themselves.

A Roman Catholic nun from a wealthy Puerto Rican family, Sister Maria Isolina Ferre devoted her life to suppressing violence and helping the desperately poor. She took her vows with the Missionary Servants of the Most Blessed Trinity in 1935 and her work began in Philadelphia, Pennsylvania.

Educated in the United States, she earned sociology degrees from Fordham University and the St. Joseph College for Women in New York.   215

When she was twenty-one, a trip through Havana, Cuba, made her realize her mission. She wanted to devote her life to service through her Catholic faith.

Working with Appalachian coal miners, Portuguese immigrants, Hispanic communities in New York, and rural youths in Puerto Rico, Sor Isolina instilled hope. She taught leadership skills and ways to build self-confidence through educational opportunities where once there were none.

> Isolina spread the word of hope and opportunities, and tried to transform ravaged neighborhoods by helping residents to advocate for themselves.

She used her family wealth and influence to establish schools, community centers, and clinics throughout the island and in the United States.

Her brother, Luis Ferre, was the former governor of Puerto Rico and founder of the New Progressive Party. Their family owned two newspapers on the island and there were more family ties in Miami politics.

Still, her destiny had been set. Her work with inner-city gangs in the 1950s and 1960s, especially at the Doctor White Community Center in New York, put her in the spotlight. As the director of a Catholic Charities Center in Brooklyn where violence escalated between warring African-American and Puerto Rican gangs, she intervened as a mediator. Teaching them to resolve disputes without violence brought an end to neighborhood violence in the community.

When she returned to Puerto Rico in 1969, she had intended to retire in her hometown of Ponce. But the poverty and hopelessness that greeted her needed to be addressed. She founded several multiservice youth and community centers now known as Centros Sor Isolina Ferre, Inc., in the poorest areas of the island. They provide youth workshops, career training, and a living area for runaways and families in turmoil.

She promoted education and cultural richness and founded the Ponce Trinity College, a vocational school in 1988. With the help of her brother, they founded the Ponce Art Museum.

For her work in organizing support and assistance for the unemployed, under-skilled, illiterate, ill, and handicapped, as well as establishing community centers and outreach programs, she earned many awards like the Hispanic Heritage Award for education (1993) and the Rockefeller Public Service Award. She was presented the United States Medal of Freedom, the highest of civilian honors, for more than sixty years of service to humanity.

Upon her death from respiratory illness in 2000, American and Puerto Rican flags were lowered to half-mast throughout Puerto Rico and at the United States Capitol Building in Washington, D.C. President Clinton said at the time: "Her lifetime of selfless commitment to others will remain her greatest legacy."

Dr. Helen Rodriguez-Trias
(United States, 1937–2002)

The first Latina president of the American Public Health Association, Dr. Helen Rodriguez-Trias received the Presidential Citizen's Award for her humanitarian work.

> "No one is going to have quality of life unless we support everyone's quality of life. We still have a system that excludes, underserves and even misserves all too many people . . . there are over 44 million Americans without health insurance. That's inexcusable."
>
> —Dr. Helen Rodriguez-Trias, *American Journal of Public Health*

The tragedies Dr. Helen Rodriguez-Trias saw included back-alley abortions, women being sterilized without being fully informed of the consequences, and children walking into medical clinics infected with HIV and AIDS or with respiratory diseases related to lead paint.

The critical link she saw was that patients' health was directly related to the degree of poverty and inequality they suffered.

Rodriguez-Trias married and had three children in New York before returning to the University of Puerto Rico to study medicine in 1960. During her residency, she established the first center in Puerto Rico for the care of newborn babies, and the hospital death rate for newborns decreased by 50 percent within three years.

When she returned to work in the Bronx in the 1970s, her patients were women, the poorest of the poor, people of color, or the physically disabled. Her mission as a pediatrician and educator became clear: She wanted to ensure full and equal access to health care for all. With unwavering conviction, she challenged discriminatory practices in health care while becoming an advocate for women's and children's rights.

As assistant professor in pediatrics at various medical schools, she urged students to practice medicine on a human scale. She wanted them to be aware of the real conditions in the neighborhoods they served and stressed the need to learn cross-cultural skills and respect diversity. She promoted activism and practiced what she taught.

Rodriguez-Trias was named the first Latina president of the American Public Health Association (APHA) in 1993, the largest and oldest organization of public health professionals. She also chaired the Association's Committee on Women's Rights. She served as medical director of the New York State AIDS Institute from 1988 to 1989, and on the boards of the National Women's Health Network and the Boston Women's Health Book Collective.

As a founding member of the Committee to End Sterilization Abuse in the early 1970s, she joined a women's right to choice advocate group. She felt that Puerto Rico had been an experimentation lab for birth control technology. A government-sponsored population control project had sterilized one-third of the women of child-bearing age over a thirty-year span.

She testified before the Department of Health, Education, and Welfare for the passage of federal sterilization guidelines, which she helped draft. A woman's consent to sterilization had to be offered in a language she could understand and a waiting period between the consent and the operation had to be honored. The New York City Health and Hospitals

Corporation adopted the guidelines and a law was passed to protect women against related abuses.

She cofounded the nonprofit Pacific Institute for Women's Health in California. She served on the Women's Health Commission, the Latino Coalition for a Healthy California Council, Community Anti-Drug Coalitions of America, the Reproductive Health Technologies Project, and the Society of Physicians for Reproductive Choice and Health.

In 1991, she was presented with the Presidential Citizen's Award by President Bill Clinton for her work on behalf of women, children, people with HIV and AIDS, and the poor. The award recognizes individuals who have performed exemplary deeds of service for the United States.

Up until her death in 2002, children and women were foremost on her mind. A last request for her funeral was that in lieu of flowers, donations be sent to "the Hospice Project in northern California or a children's charity of choice."

Clarissa Pinkola Estés (United States, 1943–)

Award-winning psychologist and author of the book Women Who Run with the Wolves, *which holds a record for being on the* New York Times' *bestseller list for 145 weeks.*

"There must be a little spilled blood in every story if it is to carry medicine."

—Clarissa Pinkola Estés in
The Rhythm of Compassion by Gail Straub

As a *cantadora*—a keeper of the old stories in Mexican tradition—Clarissa Pinkola Estés knew the powerful magic of stories. They could soothe a troubled soul, give hope, and connect generations.

When she applied such stories to her Jungian psychotherapy practice, she gave birth to a book that would speak to women like never before.

Women Who Run with the Wolves was hailed as a feminine manifesto for all women, urging them to return to their wild roots.

> As a *cantadora*—a keeper of the old stories in Mexican tradition—Clarissa Pinkola Estés knew the powerful magic of stories.

Her groundbreaking work used myths, fairy tales, folklore, poetics, and psychoanalytic commentary to explore the nature of a woman's psyche. For twenty years Estés wrote stories. As she wrote each one, she gave commentary and psychological insight to their meaning and how they related to women and healing powers.

In *Wolves*, the story "Bluebeard," talked about wounds that would not heal, while "Skeleton Woman" gave the reader a glimpse of the mystical power of relationships and how dead feelings could be revived.

Born to Mexican migrant workers, Clarissa was adopted by loving Hungarian parents who also valued oral storytelling since they could neither read or write. She grew up in the northern woodlands where wolves did roam—and she felt a connection to them as she saw how they lived, nurtured their young, played, and adapted to their environment. They were brave, stalwart, and strong. Her assessment set up the concept of the wild woman archetype, celebrating the fact that all women are born gifted and that they should trust their instincts.

Pinkola Estés has taught and practiced privately for more than thirty-five years. She earned her Ph.D. in intercultural studies and clinical psychology from the Union Institute in Cincinnati, Ohio. In 1984, she earned a diploma in Jungian analysis, which is based on the philosophy that all people have the same images in their minds and can relate to common experiences and symbols that help them understand themselves better. She specialized in intercultural mythology, cultural groups, and the psychology of women and creative and gifted individuals.

She entered the publishing world through through the back door. She stepped into a cancellation spot on a radio show and was interviewed
about Jungian analysis by Tami Simon, who was president of Sounds True,

a company that produces audiotapes. She offered Pinkola Estés a chance to tape her stories. Pinkola Estés recorded a new tape every few months and they were a big hit. Before long, publishers asked her to write the book based on the tapes. *Wolves* has since been published in thirty languages and holds a record for being on the *New York Times'* bestseller list for 145 weeks over a three-year span.

To promote the art of storytelling in everyday lives, she teamed up with a paperback club to start the Clarissa Pinkola Estés International Storytelling contest. The top prize includes a book club contract and monetary award.

In 2000, Dr. Estés appeared at Carnegie Hall with Maya Angelou, Toni Morrison, and Jessye Norman. Together they gave the world premiere of a commissioned work called *Woman.Life.Song.*

She won the Las Primeras Award from MANA, the Colorado Governor's Award for Excellence in the Arts, the Gradiva Award from the National Association for the Advancement of Psychoanalysis, and the Spirit of Women Award from the National Consortium of Health and Hospitals. Pinkola Estés is the first recipient of the Joseph Campbell Keeper of the Lore Award.

Dr. Antonia Novello (Puerto Rico, 1944–)

The first woman and first Latin American to serve as Surgeon General of the United States, Dr. Antonia Novello was inducted into the National Women's Hall of Fame in 1994.

Watching patients fall through the cracks of the health care system tore at the heart of Dr. Antonia Coello Novello. When she was appointed by President George H. Bush in 1989 as the fourteenth Surgeon General of the United States and was later sworn in by Justice Sandra Day O'Connor, her mission became clear. She wanted to make a difference in health care services for children and women.

The Surgeon General acts as the president's chief medical advisor and serves as a member of his cabinet. Promoting health and wellness across the nation, the Surgeon General also oversees the U.S. Public Health Service, an organization associated with the U.S. Navy. Novello oversaw 6,000 commissioned corps health professionals who hold military rank. They work in poverty-stricken areas where there is no access to doctors, assist in national emergencies, and conduct research on multiple diseases.

Wearing the gold braid on her arm that designates her as a vice admiral in the Public Health Service, Novello finally had her chance to focus on health issues pertinent to children and women that were not often discussed. Some of her main concerns were AIDS-infected children, heterosexual AIDS, teenage drinking and smoking, breast cancer, battered women, and mental illness.

As the first woman and first Latina to hold the position of Surgeon General, she helped create the National Hispanic/Latino Health Initiative in 1992, a forum that addressed Latinos' health needs. It provided better access to insurance and health care at community levels, and found ways to inspire Hispanics to pursue science and health careers.

> Novello helped create the National Hispanic/Latino Health Initiative in 1992, a forum that addressed Latinos' health needs.

Her interest in medicine started during her childhood in Puerto Rico. As a child, Novello suffered from a congenital colon condition. The painful ailment was finally corrected when she was eighteen. By then she had undergone annual treatments by numerous doctors. Their care had a great impact on her decision to enter the medical field. She hoped to ease the suffering of others, as her doctors had helped her.

She earned a bachelor's degree and medical degree from the University of Puerto Rico. In 1970, she married Navy flight surgeon Joseph Novello, who later became a psychiatrist. They both pursued their studies in Ann Arbor, Michigan.

She completed her internship and residency at the University of Michigan Medical Center. Focusing on pediatrics and later on pediatric nephrology, specializing in kidney problems, she became the first woman to earn the UM Pediatrics Department's Intern of the Year award in 1971.

She remained there until 1973 when she began her own practice in Virginia while teaching pediatrics at Georgetown University. In 1978 she joined the U.S. Public Health Service in the active reserve and as a project leader at the National Institutes of Health.

Novello decided to pursue public health to help her see a more global picture of health issues. She enrolled at Johns Hopkins University and earned a master's degree in public health in 1982. Ultimately she worked her way to the National Institute of Child Health and Human Development, coordinating research on AIDS and how it affected women and babies. She became Deputy Director of the Institute in 1988.

After her term as Surgeon General ended in 1993, Novello began work for UNICEF, addressing women's and children's health issues on a worldwide level. In 2000, she became Health Commissioner of New York.

Novello earned the Simon Bolivar National Award in 1991, the Outstanding Achievement Award from Cuban American Women USA, and the Hispanic Heritage Leadership Award. She was inducted into the National Women's Hall of Fame in 1994.

Dr. Jane Delgado (Cuba, 1953–)

A clinical psychologist and author of the first health book written by a Latina, for Latinas, Dr. Jane Delgado is president and CEO of the National Alliance for Hispanic Health.

Those who did not speak English were not getting the medical treatment they needed. Dr. Jane Delgado has made it her life work to correct that injustice.

She has served as president and chief executive officer of the original national Coalition of Hispanic Health and Human Services Organizations (COSSMHO) since 1985. Now known as the National Alliance for Hispanic   223

Health, the organization is the oldest and largest network of health and human service providers. It services more than 10 million Hispanic consumers throughout the United States and serves as a liaison for community-based clinics and health service providers that target Hispanics.

Delgado oversees training and technical assistance, policy and research, and public affairs in the areas of the environment, AIDS and other chronic diseases, alcohol and substance abuse, maternal and childrens' health, and mental health.

In all areas, what she wants to get across is the importance for health providers to understand the language and culture of their patients.

> ✂ In all areas, what Delgado wants to get across is the importance for health providers to understand the language and culture of their patients.

Delgado has dedicated her life to improving the health and well-being of Hispanics and underserved communities through quality outreach programs. The alliance connects them to communities by offering translators, a family hotline, and information on available health insurance so that they can get the competent and appropriate treatment they deserve.

She served in the Immediate Office of the Secretary of the U.S. Department of Health and Human Services where she worked on a landmark project and task force on minority health. She has since worked with the Food and Drug Administration to expand consumer access to Spanish-language resources on the FDA Web site.

Delgado is a clinical psychologist, with a master's degree in psychology from New York University and a master's degree in urban and policy sciences from W. Averell Harriman School of Urban and Policy Sciences. Delgado also has a doctorate from State University of New York at Stony Brook.

Delgado is the author of *¡Salud! A Latina's Guide to Total Health—Body, Mind, and Spirit*, the first health book written by a Latina, for Latinas. Delgado wants Latinas to be empowered by knowing what resources are available for them and by taking control of their and their families' health issues.

She touches on subjects that have been taboo in the past, like mental health, AIDS, breast cancer, and suicide and urges Latinos to become educated on the topics, to speak up and get over any stereotypical stigmas a health issue might have. She emphasizes how building a strong home environment for children can strengthen family bonds and give them positive direction.

Voted as the 2003 Community Builder of the Year, Delgado has also been on the National Health Council, the Patient Safety Institute, and the Advisory Panel on Medicare Education. She is on the National Advisory Council for the Carter Center's Task Force on Mental Health.

In 2003, Delgado was presented the Florence Kelley Consumer Leadership Award by the National Consumers League. The award exemplifies a commitment to social justice for consumers and workers and "a willingness to give time, energy, and leadership to important causes that may not be popular."

Dr. Nora Volkow (Mexico, 1956–)

One of the United States' leading experts on the science of brain imaging and drug addiction, Dr. Nora Volkow is director of the National Institute on Drug Abuse.

What fascinated Dr. Nora Volkow most was the way a drug could take over the process of free will. She had seen individuals give up their family, profession, and money because of a drug addiction they could not control.

Volkow's research focuses on studying the brain patterns of drug-addicted individuals. She is a recognized expert on the brain's dopamine system. She has also studied how alcohol, cocaine, methamphetamine, heroin, marijuana, schizophrenia, obesity, and aging affect the brain.

Today she is director of the National Institute on Drug Abuse, which falls under the umbrella of the National Institutes of Health in Washington, D.C. She is one of the United States' leading experts on the science of drug addiction.

225

Because Volkow is multilingual, she believes she can educate twice as many people about the crisis of drug abuse in society and in the Hispanic community.

Her groundbreaking discoveries on brain imaging and addiction showed the long-term negative effects of cocaine addiction and the use of therapeutic drugs for schizophrenia. She was the first to suggest that prolonged treatment with therapeutic drugs blunted normal thought patterns and emotions in schizophrenics.

She completed her bachelor's degree at the Modern American School in Mexico City, her Ph.D. at the National University of Mexico, and her postdoctoral work in psychiatry at New York University. Her father was a chemical engineer, the grandson of the Russian revolutionary Leon Trotsky. Her mother was a Spanish fashion designer.

🖑 Because Volkow is multilingual, she believes she can educate twice as many people about the crisis of drug abuse in society and in the Hispanic community.

Volkow was always fascinated with people's behavior and interactions. Her investigative spirit led her to study biomedicine at the Modern American School in Mexico City, where she graduated best student and "outstanding medical student" from a class of 2,000 students.

Scientific research is her passion. She spent a year studying behavioral medicine at the Sainte Anne Psychiatric Hospital in Paris, France, before she received her postdoctoral training.

She was ready to head to the Massachusetts Institute of Technology but was sidetracked when she read a copy of *Scientific American* highlighting brain imaging, which is the study of the human brain in three dimensions by using scanners to detect radioactive tracers injected into a patient. She went wild when she thought about actually imaging the human brain "live."

Without knowing anyone in New York, she hopped on a plane and flew to New York University to see if she could volunteer with the study. It was the start of her research career and her numerous contributions to the study of drug addiction and its effect on the brain.

Her research has been recorded in books, professional medical journals, and research papers. She served as the director of nuclear medicine, the director of the NIDA Department of Energy Regional Neuroimaging Center, and as an associate director for life sciences at Brookhaven National Laboratory. She was also a professor in the department of psychiatry and associate dean of the medical school at the State University New York (SUNY)-Stony Brook.

Volkow was elected to membership in the Institute of Medicine in the National Academy of Sciences and was named Innovator of the Year in 2000 by *U.S. News and World Report*.

Dr. Ana Nogales (Argentina, 1951–)

Founder of Nogales Psychological Counseling and Casa de la Familia, Dr. Ana Nogales is a trained psychologist and successful author, columnist, and radio and television personality who has earned fame in the Latino community as a relationship counselor.

Dr. Ana Nogales is the relationship doctor. She helps women and men in the Latino community with their unique concerns of living between two cultures while dealing with family, marriage, and intimacy concerns.

Nogales sees the needs of Latino couples as unique to other cultures. Other variables affect a Latino couple's success. There is extended family, traditions, machismo, and Latinas' changing roles and self-image.

Nogales knows Latinos relate to families differently than other cultures. Family is top priority. Couples may either look for help within the family structure at times of conflict or be unable to share secrets that could be detrimental to an individual.

Many women endure domestic violence rather than tell relatives. Nogales adds that Latinos do not regard infidelity as betrayal. Many men stay in the family and feel loyal even when they are unfaithful. Adding to marital conflicts is the role reversal that many Latinas experience, because they work and sometimes earn more than their husbands. Second- and third-generation couples might find new roles easier to accept, but might still have trouble telling their families to stay out of their lives.

As a trained psychologist, columnist, and television personality, Nogales speaks with compassion and professional expertise to Latino couples who need answers and guidance. She helps Latinas draw on their inherent strengths.

Her books give practical advice. *Latina Power!: Using 7 Strengths You Already Have to Create the Success You Deserve* and *Dr. Ana Nogales's Book of Love, Sex, and Relationships* are published in English and Spanish.

Dr. Nogales's books, *Latina Power!: Using 7 Strengths You Already Have to Create the Success You Deserve* and *Dr. Ana Nogales's Book of Love, Sex, and Relationships*, are published in English and Spanish.

Nogales is a clinical psychologist and founder of Nogales Psychological Counseling and the nonprofit organization Casa de la Familia. Casa was established for victims of such crimes as rape, assault, child sexual and physical abuse, and domestic violence.

Beyond her private practice, she shares professional advice through her newspaper and magazine columns, books, television, and radio call-in shows. The overwhelming response to her show *Aquí Entre Nos* (Just Between Us) inspired her to produce a series of self-help audiocassettes called *Auto-Ayuda Psicológica*. The tapes address many of the topics that are discussed during Nogales's television appearances such as combating depression, managing anxiety, and understanding the opposite sex.

She completed her master's degree in psychology in Argentina, and was instructor and director at the nonprofit Instituto Uriburu in Buenos Aires. She moved to the United States in 1979 and completed her doctorate at the United States International University in California. She started her private practice in Southern California, supervising a clinical program for professionals in mental health.

Her media career started in 1980 well after she had established herself with her practice. Nogales keeps a pulse on the community by writing a weekly column in *La Opinión*, the country's number one Spanish-language newspaper, and in the national magazine *Para Todos*. She had a regular segment on Telemundo-LA's evening news and is a frequent guest on various television shows, including *The Cristina Show, Padre Albert,* and *Despierta America,* the top-rated national talk show on Spanish television.

At Univision, Nogales hosted a weekly segment called *Ella y El.* Her own show, *Aquí Entre Nos*, established her as a household name throughout the Latino community.

10

Educators: Paving the Way for Our Future

Evelina Lopez Antonetty (Puerto Rico, 1922–1984)
Founder of United Bronx Parents, the organization that reflects Evelina Lopez Antonetty's lifelong dedication to civil rights, community service, and achieving equal education for minorities.

Evelina Lopez Antonetty had had enough with the New York public school system's lack of responsiveness toward the needs of Puerto Rican and other minority children.

She wanted to unite parents to have a say in their children's education and thus, their future. Their very real concerns prompted her to found United Bronx Parents, Inc. As the driving force behind the organization, she became known as "the Hell Lady of the Bronx," a hard-earned and well-deserved title.

The organization's mission was to demand educational reform and to address the needs of every child within the school system. The Bronx Parents grew in numbers and in strength as a united front.

Prompted by the momentum of the civil rights movement, she was determined to make the organization an advocate on the parents' behalf. She knew that educational reform had to start with the parents.

Her goal was to train parents to take on leadership roles so that they could effectively voice their concerns. They had to know their rights and have access to resources that could assist them. The organization provided them with bilingual instructional materials to keep them informed. As the organization's reputation and grass-roots activism sprouted, students, teachers, educational workers, and parochial school parents joined in the movement for educational rights.

> Antonetty wanted to unite parents to have a say in their children's education and thus, their future.

Within a few years, the organization branched out and started addressing other needs. In 1970 it established bilingual and bicultural day care centers, a citywide summer lunch program, a youth leadership program, and adult education programs such as GED preparation and literacy training. Today the mission statement of United Bronx Parents covers basic human services in addition to education reform.

The community-based organization influenced changes in politics, education, community improvements, empowerment, and leadership opportunities. Activism was visible and ongoing. The United Bronx Parents worked with other community groups and issues of concern such as the Committee Against *Fort Apache: The Bronx*, a movie that negatively portrayed Puerto Ricans in the neighborhood.

Antonetty's daughter, Lorraine Montenegro, took over the reins as executive director shortly after Antonetty died in 1984. Schools and facilities have been named after Antonetty, such as the Evelina Lopez Antonetty Children's Literacy Center (1999), reiterating her aspirations— to support and nurture children and serve the community. The United Bronx Parents has also served as a model for and provided parent training to other community groups across the nation.

The Evelina Lopez Antonetty Award was established in 2000 and is presented to an individual demonstrating distinguished public and community service.

Mari-Luci Jaramillo (United States, 1928–)

First woman U.S. ambassador to Honduras and the winner of numerous awards for her work as an educator and a humanitarian.

> "I remember how my knees knocked and that I held onto the podium until my knuckles were white. At those moments I had to remind myself that what I was doing was for a greater cause, not for myself."
>
> —Mari Luci-Jaramillo, Latino Scholastic Achievement
> Corporation interview, *www.lsac.net*

The scariest moment of Mari-Luci Jaramillo's life was standing before the Senate Foreign Relations Committee, which had the power to confirm her as ambassador to Honduras. She had come a long way from teaching in a second-grade classroom to standing before government officials to represent the president of the United States.

Jaramillo was the first woman to be named a U.S. ambassador to Honduras. During the Carter administration, she passed Senate background scrutiny, worked on an international level, and made speeches to presidents, military officials, and other national leaders. She was in a position to suggest and implement change for Latinos and educational rights.

Known as "the shoemaker's daughter" because of her humble upbringing and her dedication to increasing the level of education in the Latino community, she saw in her hometown, Las Vegas, New Mexico, that education was the answer for breaking the cycle of poverty.

When she left the town, the realization hit hard—there was a lack of educational and professional opportunities for Latinos everywhere.

In the 1960s, she started lecturing at the University of New Mexico, teaching English as a second language and offering classes in Spanish for Latin-American students. She joined the Department of Elementary Education, which she eventually chaired.

She held the promise of the civil rights movement to heart and worked on larger projects so that she could reach more people. She worked at the university's Cultural Awareness Center, promoting biculturalism. With the U.S. Agency for International Development and the University's Latin-American educational programs, she traveled to Argentina, Colombia, Ecuador, Venezuela, and Central America to train teachers and give educational development workshops.

She saw similar needs of the poor across the world and wanted to be part of the solution. When she got "the call" from President Carter, it was a chance of a lifetime to work on education on a global scale.

As ambassador, she lived in Honduras between 1977 and 1980 and served as chief of mission for six government agencies, 500 Peace Corps volunteers, and as liaison for 2,000 Americans living there. She believed the two countries could improve relations and benefit from positive cultural differences.

After her term, she returned to the University of New Mexico and served as vice president of student affairs. Her career took another detour when she began working with Educational Testing Services, which develops and administers tests for universities, departments of education, and professional organizations worldwide. As assistant vice president of all United States field offices, she saw the power of education at work at a different level.

Jaramillo continued to promote education for Latinos. Her book, *Madame Ambassador: The Shoemaker's Daughter* is her life story, reiterating the power of education, especially when aligned with a noble purpose and service to others.

Jaramillo received the Harvard Graduate School of Education's Anne Roe Award, which honors leading educators who contribute to women's professional growth. She was recognized as one of the 100 Most Influential Hispanics in the United States by *Hispanic Business* magazine. She won the Primera Award for being the first Hispanic woman to be appointed U.S. ambassador to Honduras. The American Association for Higher Education honored her with an award for Outstanding Leadership in Education in the Hispanic Community.

Graciela Olivarez (United States, 1928–1987)

The first woman to graduate from the Notre Dame School of Law. As director of the Community Service Administration, activist Graciela Olivarez was the highest-ranking Latina in President Jimmy Carter's administration.

She was the student of all students even though she had to drop out of high school to help her family survive. Helping her family was the only motivation Graciela Olivarez needed to quit school and get a job. She immediately took business courses and found a job in radio as director of women's programming. She became the first Latina disc jockey in the Phoenix, Arizona, area.

Olivarez was fueled by the civil rights movement and upon seeing the plight of the many poor people in her community, was determined to help in any way she could.

She would become known as "Washington's Top Advocate for the Poor." She built her varied career working on behalf of the underprivileged. She could not forget that is where she came from.

Her compassion and determination to help the impoverished won her an influential position with Arizona's Office of Economic Opportunity. As director, she saw the sad situation of poor children in the community and started her life of activism. She helped implement programs like Head Start, Legal Services, Job Corps, and VISTA volunteers. She helped migrant workers and their families.

As an avid feminist and pro-choice advocate, she wanted women to take responsibility for their lives, to develop their full potential, and overcome social injustices. Olivarez, along with twenty-six other women, were charter members of the National Organization for Women (NOW), which was established in 1966.

At the height of her activism, Olivarez was introduced to the president of the University of Notre Dame. Her dedication to community service and innate intelligence impressed him. He invited her to apply to the School of Law.

Olivarez was in her late thirties when she accepted his invitation. In 1970 she became the first woman to graduate from the Notre Dame School of Law. She was forty-two years old. She taught law at the University of New Mexico, ran the Institute for Social Research and Development, and resumed community work.

Tapped by President Jimmy Carter to serve as director of the Community Service Administration, she moved to Washington, D.C., and became the highest-ranking Latina in his administration. As the director of the Community Services Administration, she was able to continue her mission to fight poverty on a larger scale.

When she returned to the Southwest United States in 1980, she started a television company and later, a management consulting and public relations firm. It was at this time that she also became senior consultant with the United Way of America, where she continued to lobby for the poor and equal education. She urged the public, especially women, to work together with the contributions and compassion of private companies in their quest to keep poverty at bay.

> Olivarez built her varied career working on behalf of the underprivileged. She could not forget that is where she came from.

Olivarez believed that taking an active role showed a concern for the future of all Americans. When she died, she left a legacy of hope for thousands of women in education, business, and politics, and in the fight against poverty. The Graciela Olivarez Award was established by the Notre Dame Hispanic Law Students Association (HLSA). It "honors an outstanding judge or lawyer who made a significant contribution to the Hispanic legal community."

Amalia Betanzos (United States, 1938–)

Founder, president, and CEO of the Wildcat Academy, one of the most successful alternative high schools in America and a model for similar schools in Latin America, Amalia Betanzos has served in numerous positions dedicated to the education and rehabilitation of the "forgotten" in society.

235

They were the forgotten. There were ex-offenders, public assistance recipients, former alcohol and substance abusers, high school dropouts, the unemployed, and people who spoke limited English.

Amalia Betanzos saw they simply needed a second chance and someone to give them a break. If she could get them on their feet as contributing members to society, they could break their cycle of poverty and dependency. They needed to become proficient in English and learn basic skills so that they could become a part of the regular work force. But they needed more than traditional resources to achieve that.

Betanzos founded the John V. Lindsay Wildcat Academy, an alternative high school funded by the New York City Board of Education. As president and CEO of the multimillion-dollar nonprofit facility, she runs one of the most successful alternative high schools in America. The graduation rate, college enrollment, and SAT test scores exceed those from other alternative high schools.

> Betanzos runs one of the most successful alternative high schools in America.

Based in a downtown office building, several hundred students are enrolled in the high school at one time. The high school helps divert troubled or at-risk students before they have the chance to get into deeper trouble. Classes have no more than ten students.

Students alternate between one week of classes and one week of paid internships. They attend classes from nine to five, twelve months a year to make up for lost time. According to academy statistics, there is only an 8 percent dropout rate versus the 20 percent for the city and even higher percentages for minorities.

The school's location links them directly to the community. Betanzos worked with various companies to employ graduates from the school. Her goal was to train them to get jobs, but then find "real" jobs with salaries that could support families and would not disappear after a year.

The Manhattan Institute's Inter-American Policy Exchange used Wildcat Academy as a prototype to establish similar schools for troubled teens in Chile. They helped design the facility, train teachers, and develop a governance structure for the school. In 1997, El Colegio La Puerta opened its doors for teens that the Chilean school system had previously given up on. There are plans to establish similar schools in other Latin-American countries such as Venezuela and Argentina.

Betanzo was appointed chair of the New York Commission on the Status of Women by Mayor Rudolph Giuliani in 1995. She has served on the New York City Board of Education and the National Puerto Rican Coalition. She was appointed commissioner of the Youth Services Agency, where she oversaw the needs of more than 1.5 million New York youths.

When she was executive secretary to Mayor John Lindsey, she was in charge of programs for the poor, the physically handicapped, and the mentally challenged, and subsequently became president of NYS Industries for the Disabled. She is currently director for the Citizen's Union.

She was awarded the 1997 Hispanic Heritage Award in education and was recognized as a Senate Woman of Distinction in 2003, which credited her with bringing thousands of ex-offenders into the world of self-sustaining productive employment.

Maxine Baca Zinn (United States, 1942–)

The first Latina educator to be elected to the governing council of the American Sociological Society, Maxine Baca Zinn is considered a pioneer in the study of family, race, and gender issues.

While studying sociology at California State University at Long Beach, Maxine Baca Zinn listened to her professors discuss minorities. Their perceptions about minorities were wrong and were nothing like her; she could not relate to what they were saying.

She decided to set the record straight and went on to her earn her degree in sociology so that she could dispel the myths surrounding Mexican Americans, women, and other minorities. She was the first Latina educator to be elected to the governing council of the American Sociological Society in 1992.

> Baca Zinn wanted to set the record straight so that she could dispel the myths surrounding Mexican Americans, women, and other minorities.

Since those days, Baca Zinn has become a prominent sociologist, redefining the roles and perceptions of minorities, especially Latinas and African Americans. Considered a specialist and pioneer in the study of family, race, and gender issues, Baca Zinn examines and challenges what it is like to be a stereotype in real life and in the way others perceive those stereotypes. She is one of the first to conduct sociological work on Latino families and Mexican-American women.

Baca Zinn has worked as a professor of sociology and of women's studies at many universities in the United States while conducting her research and writing corresponding books. Referred to by colleagues as "the foremother of Chicana feminism," she served as a senior researcher associate at the Julian Samoria Research Institute while researching her topics.

At the Henry A. Murray Research Center of Radcliffe College, Baca Zinn's research centered around the lives of women from different racial and ethnic families. She spent two decades studying the impact of social and economic change on the family, particularly Latino and African-American families and the diversity that occurs within family structures and between cultures.

She has reassessed what it means to be a Chicana feminist as compared to a black feminist, how the ideals of feminine liberation differ between racial groups, and how minority women deal with oppression and the limited opportunities that result. Her books, such as *Women of Color in U.S. Society* and *Diversity in Families,* validate her research.

As a result, a new "women of color feminism" has emerged. More and more scholars are revising past data and are accepting new interpretations of the sociological framework of minorities, Latinas, and their families.

Baca Zinn has been recognized for her research efforts. She has won the Outstanding Alumnus Award from the College of Social and Behavioral Sciences (1990) and the 1989 Cheryl Miller Lecturer Award on Women and Social Change. She was awarded a dissertation fellowship from the Ford Foundation and one from the University of Oregon, where she earned her Ph.D. As a professor at the University of Michigan, she was presented the Distinguished Faculty Award.

Sara Martinez Tucker (United States, 1955–)
CEO of the Hispanic Scholarship Fund and one of the top foundation fundraisers in the nation, Sara Martinez Tucker is the first Latina to hold an executive position with AT&T.

When her brother graduated from college at the age of thirty-seven, emotion overcame Sara Martinez Tucker. Her parents believed in the power of education and sacrificed to send their children to Catholic schools. All her father had wanted was for his three children to earn their college degrees.

Tucker has continued to embrace the importance of education. As chief executive officer of the Hispanic Scholarship Fund, her goal is simple: to double the rate of Hispanics earning college degrees by 2010.

She is well on the way. Since her tenure started with the organization, scholarship awards have jumped from $3.5 million a year to $26 million per year. She is one of the top foundation fundraisers in the nation.

In 2000, she handed out a record $20 million from the scholarship fund to a record 6,000 kids. The average scholarship grew from approximately $1,400 to $4,000 per scholar.

Founded in 1975, the Hispanic Scholarship Fund is the nation's leading organization supporting Hispanic higher education. It has awarded more than 60,000 scholarships to outstanding Hispanic-American scholars throughout the United States.

Tucker takes her job personally. Cringing at the statistics of Hispanic youths struggling to pursue higher education, the Laredo, Texas, native became an advocate for students. Cultural expectations, old-fashioned traditions, financial hardships, and an ambivalence about the value of a college degree have been setbacks for many students. Many parents still think Latinas do not need an education beyond high school; yet Latinas are still told to be financially independent.

> Tucker takes her job personally. Cringing at the statistics of Hispanic youths struggling to pursue higher education, the Laredo, Texas, native became an advocate for students.

When Tucker wanted to pursue college, her father, who worked at a state employment agency, and her mother, who ran a small grocery store, were reluctant for her to leave home. She held her ground and went on to the University of Texas, where she earned a journalism degree and an MBA and graduated with honors.

She started out as a features writer for the *San Antonio Express* newspaper, with hopes to start a regional Texas magazine. Her plans were waylaid when she applied to AT&T, the telecommunications giant, and quickly worked her way up the ladder. She was the first Latina to reach an executive level at AT&T.

When she took a sabbatical in 1996, she remained involved with civic organizations, including the Hispanic Scholarship Fund. When the founder retired, her husband urged her to take on the position herself. She did.

Tucker began approaching companies to help them see Hispanics as the fastest-growing community in the United States that, if given the chance, would offer a wealth of talent as educated workers. In other words—they would make a good investment.

From her connections, she was able to negotiate the largest direct gift
to Hispanic higher education ever—a $50 million grant from the Lilly

Endowment (funded by the Lilly pharmaceutical company). The donation put the HSF in the Chronicle of Philanthropy's annual survey of the most successful foundations. Later Tucker secured a deal with the $1 billion Gates Millennium Scholars program.

She continues to expand the foundation's mission. It will focus on working with community college transfers, community outreach programs for graduating high school seniors, and developing a program where foundation graduates mentor other students.

Tucker served on the Council for Aid to Education and on the White House Commission with the Initiative on Educational Excellence for Hispanic Americans. She won the 2003 National Mujer Award, has been named one of the 100 Most Influential Hispanics three times by *Hispanic Business* magazine, and won the Heritage Achievement Award for Education in 1998.

Dr. Vicki Ruiz (United States, 1955–)

One of the most renowned historians in the field of Latin-American history, Ruiz is the fourth Mexican-American woman in the United States to receive a doctorate in history.

> "As a historian I have had the privilege of interviewing people whose quiet courage made a difference in their lives and in their communities."
>
> —Dr. Vicki Ruiz

Vicki Ruiz tells stories, weaving in the rich contributions of women— the unsung heroes who have been left out of history books for far too long.

She is among the first generation of scholars dedicated to documenting the historical experiences of Latinas in the United States. She also created her own subfield—twentieth-century Mexican-American women in the western United States.

As one of the most renowned historians in this field Ruiz's research has contributed to a fuller understanding of the labor movement, women's roles, immigration, and the American West. She is a professor of humanities, Chicano/Latino studies, and history who enriches her research by using a variety of archival resources.

Uncovering a treasury of letters, diaries, court transcripts, memoirs, newspapers, and family experiences provides images and voices of women hidden from public view. She personalizes her work so that readers see triumphs as well as tragedies, and can connect the past to contemporary issues. She makes history personal, interesting, and accessible.

Born in Atlanta, Georgia, Ruiz was the daughter of Ermina Pablita Ruiz and Robert Mercer. His parents disowned him for marrying a Hispanic woman, so the children used Ermina's surname. She was proud of her heritage and enjoyed sharing it with her children through rich storytelling.

They lived a nomadic life, moving from place to place via a sport fishing boat manned by her father. But when they anchored in Panama City where Ruiz had to attend high school, discrimination was still rampant. Education was her way out. She attended Florida State University and applied to Stanford University for graduate school.

Her sponsor, professor Al Camarillo, introduced her to the history of women's cannery unions in California. After interviewing union activist Luisa Moreno personally, Ruiz had a new role model and knew what she would study.

Ruiz earned a history doctorate from Stanford—the first to be given in this field—and became the fourth Mexican-American woman in the United States to receive a doctorate in history. Her dissertation, inspired by Moreno, turned into her first book—*Cannery Women, Cannery Lives: Mexican Women, Unionization, and the California Food Processing Industry, 1930–1950*. It was immediately hailed as an outstanding addition to historical literature on labor, women's studies, and Chicano history.

She taught at various universities and at the University of California, Irvine, was director for the outreach program Humanities Out There (HOT), which serves area schools by teaching oral history techniques to a new generation of students. For example, while studying Homer's *Odyssey*, middle school students trace the journeys their own families made to the United States. High school students read *The Grapes of Wrath* and interview local elders about the Great Depression.

Her works continue to give a glimpse into the rich tapestry of American history. Other books include: *Unequal Sisters: A Multicultural Reader in U.S. Women's History, Women on the U.S.–Mexico Border,* and *From Out of the Shadows: Mexican Women in Twentieth-Century America.* She is working on books featuring nineteenth-century Latina history, school desegregation in the West, and a biography of Luisa Moreno. Her groundbreaking history book *Latinas in the United States: A Historical Encyclopedia,* coedited with Virginia Sanchez-Korrol, chair of the Department of Puerto Rican and Latino Studies at Brooklyn College, is due out in 2004.

Ruiz has served as a consultant to the National Women's History Project, is an executive board member of the Immigration of American Historians, the Committee for Minority History and Minority Historians, and the American Studies Association. Her efforts earned her a presidential nomination to the National Council on the Humanities. She was *Latina* magazine's Woman of the Year in 2000.

Irene Martinez (United States, 1942–)

Founder and executive director of the Fiesta Educativa, one of the few advocacy groups in the United States dedicated to empowering Latino families with special-needs children.

Irene Martinez had been working on behalf of developmentally disabled children for quite some time. With a background in social work, she worked for the East Los Angeles Regional Center for the Developmentally Disabled. In 1979, her office was inundated with Spanish-speaking parents with questions.

They did not know what their rights were, where there might be resources, how they could find someone to talk to who could relate to what they were going through.

The bottom line was they were not receiving the level or quality of services that their Anglo counterparts were. They were not being treated fairly. Parents were frustrated. Martinez was frustrated. She finally offered to give a workshop to answer their questions and provide experts in the field to do the same. It was a start to help educate them to their rights and resources while providing a networking and support system.

Martinez was flabbergasted at the overflowing room of concerned parents, friends, teachers, and relatives that came to the workshop. The need for Spanish resources for special-needs children and their families was very real.

Within a few months, Martinez founded the Fiesta Educativa, an advocacy group for Spanish-speaking families with special-needs children. It is one of the few organizations in the United States that is dedicated to empowering the Latino families of persons with special needs through education, training, referral, and information. Because Martinez wanted parents to have the power in their own hands, Fiesta Educativa became a home-based program with small groups of parents at the helm of each. Their access to resources and education empower them to secure the best treatment available for their children.

> Martinez was flabbergasted at the overflowing room of concerned parents, friends, teachers, and relatives that came to the workshop. The need for Spanish resources for special-needs children and their families was very real.

In twenty-five years the organization has grown to include many regional offices in the western United States. Thousands of participants including parents, professionals, educators, psychologists, and service providers attend the annual Fiesta Educativa conference, held at the University of Southern California in Los Angeles. Martinez remains executive director of the organization.

11

Entertainers:
Stage, Screen, and Song

Luisa Espinel Ronstadt (United States, 1892–1963)
Singer, dancer, and actress of international fame, Ronstadt's collection of songs,
Canciónes de mi Padre, *is a significant historical document of Mexican music of*
the mid-nineteenth century.

Luisa Espinel grew up surrounded by music in the tiny town of Tucson, Arizona, but her musical passion took her into the international spotlight.

Espinel, who was born Louisa Ronstadt, carried on the family tradition of sharing music. She was deeply connected to the Mexican folk songs she heard as a child, and as she became famous, she incorporated much of her musical background into her performances.

She starred in a local performance of the opera *Il Trovatore*, directed by Professor Jose Servin in 1917. In the 1920s and 1930s, she became a famous singer, actress, and dancer, performing Hispanic folk music in Los Angeles, New York, San Francisco, Paris, Madrid, and other European cities. While traveling, she gathered songs from over twenty different

245

Spanish cities. Her work was touted for the way she wove music, acting, and dance into vignettes that captured the soul of Spanish people.

Her United States debut was at the Edith Totten Theatre in New York City in 1927 and received rave reviews. Her songs were mostly Spanish rather than Mexican and the three-act performance featured dancing and singing from three different regions of Spain.

In 1928, Espinel was invited by First Lady Coolidge to participate in the chamber music festival at the Congressional Library in Washington, D.C. It was one of many of her musical highlights.

Ronstadt was deeply connected to the Mexican folk songs she heard as a child, and she incorporated her musical background into her performances as she became famous.

She appeared in films in the 1930s. During one movie, she and Marlene Dietrich had a "free-for-all fight" in one of the scenes. Espinel lost her footing. The director tried to break her fall and was injured when his hand crashed through a glass window. The news made the Arizona newspapers, where she still had her biggest fan base.

Espinel's father, Federico Ronstadt, was a carriage maker by trade, but music was his life. He started the first orchestra in the area, the Club Filharmonica Tucsonense, which toured throughout the Southwest.

Espinel was trained in classical music. While growing up in the Tucson area, she performed regularly at the Saturday Morning Musical Club, which sponsored classical recitals.

She married artist Charles Kassler, who painted the fresco mural *Pastoral California* at Plummer Auditorium in Fullerton, California, in 1934 (restored in 1997). It is said that he used Espinel as a model for the singer he featured in the mural—Laura Moya—a singer of the 1800s, in the times when the last Mexican governor, Pio Pico, oversaw California. They divorced after several years.

Espinel wrote *Canciónes de mi Padre* (My Father's Songs), which was published in 1946 by the University of Arizona. Many of the songs she had learned from her father she transcribed and included in the labor of love.

Canciónes became a relevant historical document that showed what people were singing in Ronstadt's hometown of Sonora, Mexico, in the mid-nineteenth century. Scrapbooks and handwritten music highlighting her own career between 1915 and 1933 were also preserved and are archived in the Arizona Historical Society.

Espinel's niece is Linda Ronstadt, folk and pop star icon of the 1970s, whose work spanned decades. Ronstadt revived some of her grandfather's songs from Espinel's records and released an album with the same name, *Canciónes de mi Padre,* in 1987.

The Ronstadt family was awarded the Copper Letter Award from the city of Tucson in 1994, for "keeping the town beautiful with song for well over a hundred years."

Dolores del Río (Mexico, 1905–1983)

Legendary film actress who at one time was one of the ten biggest movie box-office attractions in the United States, del Río was the first internationally famous Mexican movie star and won the Mexican Ariel Award three times.

*D*escribed as a female Rudolph Valentino, Dolores del Río was one of the legendary beauties of the silver screen in the 1920s. Regarded as highly romantic for her exotic allure, she was able to avoid typecasting and at one point, she was one of the ten biggest movie box-office attractions in the United States. Her fifty-year career spanned the transition from silent films to talkies, and she captivated audiences in both.

Born Lolita Dolores Martínez Ansúnsolo López Negrette, she came from a wealthy Mexican family. Schooled in a French convent, she also learned Spanish dancing there. She married socialite Jaime Martínez del Río in 1921 and they took a two-year honeymoon to Europe.

When Hollywood director-producer Edwin Carewe met the del Ríos in the early 1920s, he urged her to pursue a career in silent films. She accepted but her husband could not deal with her success. The relationship ended in divorce, but she kept his name.

Del Río appeared in Carewe's movie *Joanna* (1925). Others followed in quick succession—*The Whole Town's Talking, Resurrection, What Price Glory,* and *The Loves of Carmen.* Her most famous role came in the movie *Ramona* (1928), where she played an Indian maiden in old California. She learned English by the time her first talkie was released—*The Bad One* (1930).

> *Del Río became known as "the First Lady of the Mexican Theater."*

In 1930 she married MGM art director Cedric Gibbons, who designed the Academy Award statuette. He also designed their home in Santa Monica, California, where they lived extravagantly.

She suffered a nervous breakdown but returned to film *Girl of the Rio* (1932) and *Flying Down to Rio* (1933). The movies were banned in some Latin-American countries because of the insulting portrayal of Hispanics. When she danced her tango to "Orchids in the Moonlight" with Fred Astaire, however, her image changed. She was not in a stereotypical role. Her introduction of the two-piece bathing suit in the film also put her in a new light.

By 1934, right in the middle of the Depression, del Río signed a three-picture deal with Warner Bros. to the tune of $100,000. Her marriage to Gibbons dissolved in 1941. She then dated Orson Welles, who directed her in *Journey into Fear* (1942).

After her father died, she realized how much she missed her homeland. After twenty-five films in Hollywood, she returned to Mexico. She starred in several movies there, including *María Candelaria* and *La Malquerida.* She often worked with Mexican filmmaker Emilio Fernández and starred opposite Pedro Armendáriz. Director John Ford filmed *The Fugitive* (1947) in Mexico and cast her in it.

Her stage career was launched in Mexico, as well. Del Río became known as "the First Lady of the Mexican Theater." She won the Ariel—the Mexican Academy Award—three times.

She attempted a return to Hollywood in the 1950s but because she had allegedly aided people fleeing the Spanish civil war and was labeled a communist sympathizer, her visa was not issued. She returned in the 1960s to play a mother to both Elvis Presley, in *Flaming Star* (1961), and Omar Sharif, in the Italian movie *More Than a Miracle* (1967), which also starred Sophia Loren.

Del Río's last movie, *The Children of Sanchez* (1978), also had the most valuable social content of her career. The U.S.–Mexico coproduction featured a poor Mexican family and included Hispanic actors like Anthony Quinn and Katy Jurado.

In 1971 she founded Estancia Infantil, a government-sponsored day care center for children of Mexican performers and took great pleasure in teaching fine arts to the children.

Imogene Coca (United States, 1908–2001)
One of the greatest comediennes of her day, her career onstage and in film and television spanned eight decades. Imogene Coca received the 1951 Emmy Award for Best Actress.

With her parents' blessing, Imogene Fernandez y Coca left home when she was only fifteen and headed straight for New York. They had given her the choice to pursue high school or professional stage studies. The choice was easy.

Coca had taken piano, voice, and dance lessons since she was five years old. She knew exactly what she wanted: the stage.

Before too long, her career took a detour. Instead, she became one of the greatest comediennes of her day, preceding Lucille Ball and Carol Burnett. At the top of her career, she cohosted the famous television variety show *Your Show of Shows*, with Sid Caesar.

Imogene's Spanish father, Joseph Fernandez y Coca, conducted Philadelphia's Chestnut Street Opera House. Her mother, Sadie Brady, was a vaudeville actress and dancer who had run away from home to join a magic show.

Groomed in show business early on, Coca made a stage debut at age nine and by age thirteen was tap-dancing, doing acrobatics, and dancing ballet regularly onstage. At fifteen, she started dancing at Jimmy Durante's Silver Slipper Nightclub.

> Coca knew exactly what she wanted: the stage.

Innovative, creative, and spontaneous, she performed in nightclubs, plays, and vaudeville shows. Her Broadway debut came as a chorus dancer in *When You Smile* (1923). She adopted a comedic slant to give her an edge over the many performers vying for parts.

Her enthusiasm, charm, and rapport with audiences were genuine, especially with comedy routines. She became known as the comedienne with the flexible face.

In a 1934 stage show, *New Faces*, the heat went out during one performance. She was sent out onstage in an oversized coat alongside Henry Ford to distract the audience. She started miming, making fun of a striptease number she had invented during rehearsals. The producer enjoyed it so much, he made it a permanent part of the show.

After World War II and the introduction of television, she and Sid Caesar were chosen to host the NBC comedy show the *Admiral Broadway Revue* in 1949, which was later changed to *Your Show of Shows*. They shared the spotlight with Carl Reiner and Howard Morris, and performed skits and numbers in the vaudeville style.

The show's success came from the way they played off each other and the incredible stable of writers who wrote for them—Neil Simon, Mel Brooks, Woody Allen—all of whom became famous comedians, writers, and directors.

The show ran until 1954. Coca was offered her own show, *The Imogene Coca Show*, while she and Caesar continued to make guest appearances on television variety shows. They teamed up for a fortieth anniversary reunion of *Your Show of Shows* in 1990 in New York, Chicago, and California.

Coca continued to act in Broadway musicals such as *On the Twentieth Century,* for which she won rave reviews. Movies she worked on include *Under the Yum Yum Tree* with Jack Lemmon, *Ball, Coca and Other Funny Females, The Beverly Hillbillies* (1982), *National Lampoon's Vacation* (1983), and *Nothing Lasts Forever* (1985). Her television guest spots included appearances on *Bewitched, Moonlighting, Playhouse 90,* and *One Life to Live.* She earned the 1951 Emmy Award for best actress.

Featured in a variety of magazines in the 1950s, including *Life* (1951), *Dance* (1952), and *Colliers* (1954), her comedy genius spanned eight decades. Contemporary comediennes Lily Tomlin, Whoopie Goldberg, and Tracey Ullman credit her for inspiring their work.

Coca formed the Imogene Coca Charitable Foundation, which donates proceeds to the humane society and human and civil rights groups.

Carmen Miranda (Portugal, 1909–1955)
At one time the most popular female performer in all of South America, Carmen Miranda was also once one of the highest-paid actresses in the United States.

Fruit-topped headdresses, colorful skirts, and platform shoes were Carmen Miranda's trademark as "the Brazilian Bombshell." With a radiant smile and personality, bare midriffs, and hips gyrating to a samba rhythm, she became one of the most popular and best-remembered personalities of the 1940s.

Her exaggerated, flamboyant Brazilian character was an instant hit in Hollywood. As the inspiration for "Chiquita Banana," she was often imitated and spoofed. But her performing talent was genuine and her singing ability, sense of humor, and comedic skills endeared her to the public. She could laugh at a good joke but she also brought American wartime audiences a taste of the eroticism and sensuality of South America through her character and outlandish costumes.

Maria do Carmo Miranda da Cunha was born in Portugal but raised in Brazil, where she was extremely successful as a recording and film star before she came to the United States. She was a pioneer for the music known as samba. From 1932 to 1939, she was the most popular female performer in all of South America, where she sang on the radio, performed in nightclubs, and went on concert tours.

> As the inspiration for "Chiquita Banana," Miranda was often imitated and spoofed. But her performing talent was genuine and her singing ability, sense of humor, and comedic skills endeared her to the public.

Brought to the United States by movie producer Lee Shubert, Miranda made her Broadway debut in 1939 in *The Streets of Paris* with Abbott and Costello. Her first American film was *Down Argentine Way* in 1940.

Miranda appeared in several Hollywood films, which were made to encourage the Good Neighbor Policy between the United States and Latin America. To help boost that image, she often appeared on television shows and was a top attraction at nightclubs. Her extreme South-of-the-Border persona came complete with mangled English and accent and flashy costumes.

Even though she was the highest-paid actress in the United States in 1945, she was trapped in the stereotyped image. The tradeoffs did not pay and her personal life took a destructive tone.

When she returned home to Brazil, she was attacked as being "Americanized"—ridiculing her country for the sake of American audiences. It broke her heart. She embraced a song written for her called "Disseram que en Voltei Americanizada" (They Said I Came Back Americanized), which was aimed at her detractors.

She returned to the United States and was cast in *That Night in Rio* (1941), *The Gang's All Here* (1943), *Doll Face* (1945), *Copacabana* (1947), *A Date with Judy* (1948), *Nancy Goes to Rio* (1950), and *Scared Stiff* (1953).

Hollywood often twisted her upbeat personality, unique style, and sense of humor, and spit out a gaudy likeness of her. Her phrase "Bananas is my business" turned into a protest song about the perception of being stereotyped.

Miranda died from a heart attack in 1955 while preparing for an appearance on the *Jimmy Durante Show.* The documentary *Carmen Miranda: Bananas Is My Business,* written and directed by Helena Solberg, gives a glimpse of the sad, sweet, talented artist Miranda was behind the fabulous facade.

Lydia Mendoza (Mexico, 1916–)

The first recording star of Tejano music and a Mexican-American musical legend, Lydia Mendoza sang professionally for more than sixty years. President Bill Clinton presented her with the prestigious National Medal of the Arts for her cultural contributions to the country.

Celebrated as "La Alondra de la Frontera"—the Lark of the Border—Lydia Mendoza was the first recording star of Tejano music. She has become a Mexican-American musical legend, recording more than 1,000 titles with various labels. She went from playing for pennies in the streets of Texas border towns to singing at the 1977 inauguration of President Jimmy Carter.

Also known as "La Canciónera de los Pobres" (Songstress of the Poor), she became the voice of immigrant labor in Texas during the first half of the twentieth century. She was praised for her mezzo-soprano and the way her rich vocal style captured the longing, desire, sadness, and joy of the workers she sang about.

Recognized as one of America's great "roots" music singers, she sang professionally for over sixty years.

Born in Houston, Texas, Mendoza was the daughter of Mexican immigrants. Her father did not believe in educating women, so her mother,

Leonor, taught her at home. Her grandmother was her musical influence, teaching her how to play the twelve-string guitar, the mandolin, and fiddle and how to sing by the age of seven.

When her father lost his job as a railroad mechanic, the family performed to earn a living. In 1928 La Familia Mendoza signed with the Columbia subsidiary, Okeh, for what would be the first recordings of the popular regional music. They hit the vaudeville circuit and were successful until World War II started. Mendoza also toured with her sisters Francisca, Juanita, and Maria as Las Hermanas Mendoza, but the group split up when their mother died in 1952.

Despite their success, they had to deal with racism and poverty as they toured the frontera, especially during the Depression. La Familia Mendoza played for pennies in market squares, traveled like gypsies, and worked as field hands while having to deal with restaurants and other locales that hung signs that read: "No Dogs or Mexicans Allowed."

Still, they persevered. Mendoza entered a singing contest sponsored by a radio station and went solo in the mid-1930s, signing on with the RCA Victor-Bluebird label. Her release "Mal Hombre" became a hit, as well as "Pero Hay Que Triste." She performed Tejano, Latin, and Southwestern music on a weekly segment on a San Antonio radio station.

🎵 Mendoza went from playing for pennies in the streets of Texas border towns to singing at the 1977 inauguration of President Jimmy Carter.

An awareness of regional folk music in the United States emerged in the 1970s and Mendoza went from being a local treasure to a national phenomenon. She sang and recorded for such organizations as the Library of Congress and the Smithsonian Institution, representing Mexico in the Smithsonian Festival of American Folk Life. She also appeared at the Library of Congress in 1977 for the conference on Ethnic Recordings in America.

She stopped recording in the 1980s after suffering a stroke. She was inducted into the Tejano Music Hall of Fame (1984), the Texas

Women's Hall of Fame (1985), and the Conjunto Music Hall of Fame (1991), and was awarded the National Heritage Award. President Bill Clinton presented her with the National Medal of the Arts in 1999. He said of the recipients that they "defined who we are and what we are as a nation."

Mendoza is featured in the Tex-Mex music documentary *Chulas Fronteras* by Les Blank and Chris Strachwitz.

Violeta Parra (Chile, 1917–1967)

Folklorist, songwriter, and singer whose work inspired the New Chilean Song movement of the late 1960s. A successful poet and artist as well, Violeta Parra was the first Latin American to have a one-person exhibit at the Louvre.

> "Don't cry when the sun is gone because the tears won't let you see the stars."
>
> —Violeta Parra, *www.brainyquote.com*

Much like the troubadours in days of old, Violeta Parra was a wandering soul, looking for places to sing and share her love of music and art. Known as "the Mother of La Nueva Canción Chilena," Parra revived almost-forgotten traditional Chilean songs by adding her own poetic and rhythmic touch. The result was a new dimension of musical landscapes. As a folklorist, songwriter, and singer, her work inspired the New Chilean Song movement of the late 1960s.

Born in San Carlos, Chile, Parra and her brother Eduardo helped their seamstress mother by singing and acting in trains, restaurants, and circuses when their teacher father lost his job. Parra taught herself guitar, piano, the Venezuelan cuatro, and the charango. By age twelve, she was composing her own songs. At her brother's invitation, she moved to Santiago to return to school. Instead, she fell in love with the city and the musical opportunities it offered. In 1937, she married Luis Cereceda, a railroad worker and had two children, Isabel and Angel. They divorced in 1948, but her children would carry on her legacy in music and art.

In the early 1950s, she recorded a few singles of traditional songs with her sister, Hilda. "Casamiento Entre Negros" and "Que Pena Siente el Alma" flamed Parra's creativity.

When she was in her forties and recuperating from a lengthy illness, she began painting and weaving tapestries known as *arpilleras*, a decorative form of Latin-American folk art. She displayed her pieces during her performances.

Parra won the 1954 Caupolican Prize, honoring her as a folklorist. She was invited to the Festival de Juventudes in Poland that same year and traveled throughout Russia before settling in France, where she recorded her first album, *Violeta Parra, Guitare et Chant: Chants ed Danses du Chili* (1956).

In 1956 she returned to Chile where she was hired by the Universidad de Concepción to manage the Museum of Popular Art, record new albums, continue compiling music, and perform recitals. Her poem "Gracias a la Vida" was praised and has since been translated into many languages.

In 1960, she married Gilbert Favre, a Swiss musician who was studying folklore in Chile. Her music became more complex, political, and philosophical. She performed at La Candelaria, La Scala Theatre, at the United Nations, and for UNESCO, and with Angel and Isabel in El Festival de la Juventud in Finland.

They traveled throughout Argentina and Europe before settling in Paris for three years. Parra recorded more albums and prepared art expositions. Her creative force extended from music to poetry and art. She was the first Latina—the first Latin American—to have a one-person exhibit at the Louvre in Paris. In 1964, her paintings, oleos, *arpilleras,* and wire sculptures were exhibited there.

When she returned to Chile in 1965, she founded La Carpa de La Reina (The Queen's Tent), an exhibition center for the arts, especially cultural and folkloric. She committed suicide there in 1967. A museum was built in her honor in Santiago to promote the arts and the cultural diversity of Latin America.

Rita Hayworth (Mexico, 1918–1987)
One of the most famous Hollywood pinup girls and a premier leading lady.

"Men went to bed with Gilda and woke up with me."
—Rita Hayworth

Called "the Great American Love Goddess," this legendary actress with Spanish roots became a famed Hollywood pinup girl and premier leading lady. As one of the most glamorous actresses of the 1940s, she replaced 1930s sex symbol Jean Harlow and preceded Marilyn Monroe.

Shy and unassuming offstage, she warmed the sets of her many movies, especially with her dancing. She performed opposite Hollywood leading men like Tyrone Power, Fred Astaire, Gene Kelly, Orson Welles, Cary Grant, Glenn Ford, and James Cagney. Astaire called her his favorite dance partner.

She was told she could be the next Dolores del Río, and was actually slated to do a movie remake of *Ramona* but her contract was dropped when Fox merged with Twentieth Century.

Her debut screen performance was *Dante's Inferno* (1935), followed with *Under the Pampas Moon*, and *Charlie Chan in Egypt*. When she appeared opposite Tyrone Power as temptress Doña Sol in *Blood and Sand* (1941), it launched her career. She floated across the screen dancing with Fred Astaire in *You'll Never Get Rich* (1941) and *You Were Never Lovelier* (1942). Her striptease—where she only took off long black gloves—in *Gilda* (1946), was the peak of her career.

By 1942, she was earning more than $6,000 a week and a quarter of the profits of each of her movies.

257

Her 1947 movie *Down to Earth* was included in a historical twentieth-century time capsule. Her popularity soared with five glamorous photo spreads in *Life* magazine. In one famous shot by Bob Landry, she is in a black lace negligee. It became one of the most popular pinup posters of World War II. Her picture was pasted to a test atomic bomb that was dropped in the Pacific in 1946. She performed in USO halls and served meals to military men. They became her heroes; she became theirs.

Born Margarita Cansino, her career started when she performed with her father, a Spanish Andalusian dancer, as the Dancing Cansinos. She saw her strength onscreen as a dancer because it was in her blood. All her singing was dubbed.

Her first ten movies were made under the name Rita Cansino, but a complete remake of her image started by adopting her mother's maiden name, Haworth (later respelled Hayworth). She lost weight, withstood electrolysis to broaden her forehead, and dyed her hair strawberry blonde and various shades of red over the years to produce the glamorous Rita Hayworth.

She married and divorced five times, including Orson Welles and Prince Aly Kahn. She was the first actress to marry a prince and become a princess. A documentary, *Champagne Safari*, was made about their honeymoon trip to Africa. She had two daughters, Rebecca Welles and Princess Yasmin Aga Kahn.

During the 1960s she struggled to memorize lines and her health deteriorated dramatically. Princess Yasmin cared for her until her death in 1987. It was discovered she had been a victim of the little-known disease, Alzheimer's. Princess Yasmin became a great advocate for fundraising for and education about Alzheimer's.

Hayworth was ranked in *Empire* magazine's Top 100 Movie Stars of All Time and as One of the Sexiest Stars in Film History. The movie *The Barefoot Contessa* (1954) is loosely based on her life.

Celia Cruz (Cuba, 1924–2003)

A five-time Grammy winner with twenty gold albums to her credit, singer Celia Cruz is the first Latino pop singer to earn a presidential National Medal for the Arts.

> "As a performer, I want people to feel their hearts sing and their spirits soar."
>
> —Celia Cruz, Hispanic Heritage Awards

The legend goes that when a young Celia Cruz sang lullabies to the little ones in her Cuban household, her voice enchanted neighbors to come in and listen.

As "the Queen of Salsa," Cruz mesmerized audiences with her powerful voice for over fifty years. Shouting out "Azucar!" in between songs, her dynamic performances were highlighted by her bigger than life personality, flamboyant costumes, and passion for her music.

Influencing multiple generations and crossing cultural boundaries made her an ambassador of Latino culture. Cruz initially wanted to be a teacher, but her yearning to sing pulled her into a performing career. Her family supported her career choice under the condition that chaperones—mostly older women in the family—accompany her to all her performances. Cruz agreed.

After studying at Havana's Conservatory of Music from 1947 to 1950, she sang on Cuban radio programs. She became lead singer for the island's top dance band, La Sonora Matancera in 1950. They left Cuba shortly after Fidel Castro came into power and settled in the United States in 1961. Castro refused to let her return to Cuba, even when her parents were dying years later.

In 1962, Cruz married the band's trumpet player, Pedro Knight. He later became her manager and the inspiration for many of her songs. He was at her bedside when she died in 2003.

Pursuing a singing career in the United States was difficult not only because of cultural differences but because she was up against the newest rage, rock 'n' roll. She persisted. By the 1970s, a resurgence of traditional

Latin music found a mainstream crowd. Joining Tito Puente's band in 1966 revived the salsa sensation and incorporated use of strong, metallic African rhythms. Cruz became an "overnight" success.

Performing in international tours regularly with "the King of Salsa" gave them worldwide recognition and expanded their influence to younger generations of Latino entertainers. She appeared with many talents including Johnny Pacheco, Willie Colon, Pete Conde, Ray Barretto, Gloria Estefan, Patti Labelle, David Byrne, and Dionne Warwick over the years, even reuniting with La Sonora Matancera in 1982.

She released more than seventy-five albums including the bestselling *Grandes Exitos de Celia Cruz*, and *Feliz Encuentro*. Twenty albums turned gold. She won five Grammys and two Latin Grammy awards.

Cruz appeared in movies and theater, including the film *The Mambo Kings* (1992) and performed in *Hommy—A Latin Opera* at Carnegie Hall in 1973. She has been honored with a star on the Hollywood Walk of Fame and a statue of her likeness stands in the Hollywood Wax Museum.

In 1995, she was awarded the National Medal for the Arts by President Bill Clinton, making her the first Latino pop singer to earn that distinction. She earned the Hispanic Heritage Award, the Lifetime Achievement Award from the Smithsonian Institution, and the Presidential Medal of Arts award from the Republic of Colombia.

Beyond music she touched lives through fundraising for AIDS, cancer awareness, orphans in Honduras, and the handicapped in Costa Rica.

Rita Moreno (Puerto Rico, 1931–)
The only performer ever to win an Oscar, a Tony, a Grammy, and an Emmy.

". . . never, not for one minute, have I forgotten where I came from or who I am."

—Rita Moreno, *Hispanic Magazine*

*R*ita Moreno followed her passion for singing, dancing, and acting—and landed a Guinness World Record for being the only performer ever to win all four major entertainment awards—an Oscar, a Tony, a Grammy, and an Emmy.

Born Rosita Dolores Alverio in Humacao, Puerto Rico, she was raised in New York in poverty by her divorced mother. She never saw her father or brother after leaving the island.

Unable to speak English when she started school, the transition was painful and humiliating. She felt like an outcast but eventually learned to speak English perfectly and found happiness in Spanish flamenco and ballet dance classes.

When she was only twelve, she performed in nightclubs, at Macy's department store and in children's theater. As she grew older, opportunities arose in film, theater, radio, nightclubs, and television.

Her biggest source of frustration was having to settle for the stereotypical roles of "Latin spitfires," even though it got her jobs. She did a mean imitation of Carmen Miranda, complete with fruit headdresses and exaggerated dance moves.

Before long, however, Moreno wanted to be appreciated for her talent and not her look. This conflict would prove a curse throughout her career.

Until her film break, one of her favorite lines of work was voiceovers in movies. She dubbed dialogues into Spanish for Elizabeth Taylor, Margaret O'Brien, and Judy Garland.

At fourteen, Moreno appeared in her first film, *A Medal for Benny* (1945). MGM's Louis B. Mayer, who thought she looked like a Latina Elizabeth Taylor, offered her a seven-year contract in 1949. She appeared in over twenty-five movies.

She changed her name to Rita Moreno (her stepfather's last name). Her breakthrough came in *Singin' in the Rain* (1952) and for her role as Tuptim in *The King and I* (1956).

Her 1961 film role as Anita in *West Side Story* brought her international fame and an Oscar for best supporting actress. Instead of launching her as a serious actress, however, she was offered stereotypical "Anita" roles.

Proud of her heritage, but frustrated with racial discrimination and being typecast, she headed back to New York. She found work in stage productions such as *Wally's Café, Last of the Red Hot Lovers* (1970), and *The Odd Couple* (1985).

In 1964 she took time to work with a Dr. Martin Luther King leadership conference supporting the civil rights movement.

In 1965, at the age of thirty-three, she married Lenny Gordon, whom she met on a blind date. In 1967 her only child, Fernanda Luisa, was born.

She returned to Hollywood in 1969. Her friend and one-time lover, Marlon Brando, helped her back into film when he persuaded his producer to give her a role in *The Night of the Following Day*. She was also featured on the cover of *Life* magazine at this time.

She earned Emmys on *The Muppet Show* (1978) and *The Rockford Files* (1979). Her Grammy was for the soundtrack of her children's television series, *The Electric Company*.

After earning a Tony for her performance as "Googie Gomez" in *The Ritz* (1975), Moreno learned that playwright Terrence McNally had written the Broadway comedy specifically for her. He had seen Moreno at a party, where she was poking fun at Hollywood's image of the fiery Latin Woman, and was inspired.

In 2000, she appeared in *Blue Moon*, on the cable series *Oz*, and in summer stock and regional theater. She worked with her daughter in *Steel Magnolias* and *The Taming of the Shrew*.

In 1990 she earned the Hispanic Heritage Award in the Arts. She works with Third World Cinema, the National Foundation of the Arts, and the Hispanic Heritage Awards Foundation.

Lola Beltran (Mexico, 1932–1996)

Singer Lola Beltran brought ranchera—or mariachi—music to the forefront on stages all around the world. She performed for presidents, kings, queens, and emperors worldwide.

"The composer writes the words and music. I simply put in the passion and feeling."

—Lola Beltran

With a restless spirit and a voice too large to remain in her little church, Lola Beltran belted out music that reached the masses. With deep-felt emotion, she sang of the hardships of the country's migrant working class, of life, love, and hope. She sang to the spirit of her people.

Known as "La Reina de la Música Ranchera" (the Queen of Ranchera Music) and "Lola, La Grande," Beltran gained the love of all Mexico. Her voice brought ranchera—or mariachi—music to the forefront on stages all around the world, from the Palacio de Bellas Artes in Mexico City to Madison Square Garden in New York City, the Olympia in Paris, and Tchaikovsky Hall in Moscow.

She performed for President John F. Kennedy, and in fact, for all United States presidents from Eisenhower to Nixon, as well as President Charles de Gaulle of France, the Ethiopian emperor Haile Selassie, and the king and queen of Spain.

Born Maria Lucila Beltran Ruiz in El Rosario, Sinaloa, near Mazatlan, she started singing at her church. Her teacher, Maestro Gallardo, saw her potential and taught her ballads and romances from composers like Pedro Infante and Agustin Lara, where her emotional range could take flight.

She married famous bullfighter Alfredo Leal. They had a daughter, Maria Elena Leal, and a son, Jose Quintín Enriquez.

While working as a secretary for radio station XEW, she was discovered by musicians Matilade Sanchez, "La Torcacita," and Miguel Aceves Mejia. Beltran's beautiful, strong voice awed them. Her career was launched when she signed with Peerless Records, making her debut in 1954. The famous Ignacio Fernandez Esperón, or "Tata Nacho" as he was better known, knighted her with her stage name, Lola Beltran.

Recording more than 100 albums and appearing in more than fifty movies, she reached many corners of the world. She starred in *Cucurucucu Paloma*, based on a popular song by Tomas Mendez. She performed with

263

Pedro Vargas and Miguel Aceves. She coproduced many films with Julio Aldam, through their production company, Conacine.

Great hits included "Paloma Negra," "La Cigarra," and "Huapango Torero." More than seventy albums were recorded with great mariachi bands including Vargas de Tecalitlan, Mariachi de America de Jesus Rodriguez de Hijar, Los Camperos de Nati Cano, Sol de Mexico, and Charros de Ameca de Roman Palomar. She also sang with other greats such as Jose Alfredo Jimenez, Cuco Sanchez, and Ignacio Jaime.

In 1994, a celebration of her forty years in the music business was held at the Palacio de Bellas Artes in Mexico City. The title of the tribute was "One Voice, One Woman . . . Lola Beltran."

Her influence reached colleagues as well as fans. Contemporary singer Linda Ronstadt said Beltran "was the greatest voice to come out of Mexico."

Beltran earned the Medalla Artistica del Extranjero in 1982, an award that praised her for her efforts as Mexico's ambassador, while she represented her country abroad. Her greatest fans were at home. When Beltran died from a stroke in 1966, her body was carried from Mexico City back to her hometown, El Rosario, where she was buried. Thousands of mourning fans paid their last respects in both cities.

Chita Rivera (United States, 1933–)

Actress, dancer, and singer Chita Rivera is the recipient of two Tony Awards and is the first Hispanic recipient of the prestigious Kennedy Center Honor, presented by the president of the United States. She was inducted into the Television Academy Hall of Fame.

er stage name underwent a few changes. Dolores Conchita Figueroa del Rivero was also known as Conchita del Rivero and Chita O'Hara. In the mid-1950s "Chita Rivera" stuck.

The name is timeless—synonymous with a dynamo stage presence.

As a stage actress and dancer, Rivera has proved that talent transcends time, age, and stereotypes.

When she was sixty, Rivera starred in *Kiss of the Spider Woman*. At age seventy, she starred opposite Antonio Banderas in the award-winning Broadway revival of *Nine,* which they performed in through 2003.

Rivera earned many Tony nominations for roles such as Velma in *Chicago* and Anita in the original stage production of *West Side Story.* Her two Tony Awards were for her performances in *The Rink* (1984) and *Kiss of the Spider Woman* (1993).

As a stage actress and dancer, Rivera has proved that talent transcends time, age, and stereotypes.

In television, Rivera played the secretary in *The Dick Van Dyke Show* (1971–1974), based on her character, Rosie, in *Bye Bye Birdie.* She appeared in several television shows including *The Imogene Coca Show, The Ed Sullivan Show,* and *The London Palladium Show.* In 1964 she appeared in a British show with the Beatles. Her PBS television specials include *Broadway Plays Washington: Kennedy Center Tonight* and *Night of 100 Stars.*

Rivera was born in Washington, D.C., to Puerto Rican parents. Her father, a clarinet and saxophone player for the Navy Band, died when she was only seven. Her mother returned to work as a government clerk at the Pentagon.

Enrolled in the Jones-Hayward School of Ballet when she was eleven, Rivera was one of two students picked to audition at the legendary George Balanchine School of American Ballet in New York. When she was fifteen, she won a scholarship to attend.

Intending to support a friend auditioning for the Broadway play *Call Me Madam*, Rivera tried out and landed a part herself. She was only seventeen. It launched her career. She performed in such productions as *Chicago, Bye Bye Birdie, Guys and Dolls, Can-Can, Seventh Heaven,* and *Mr. Wonderful* with Sammy Davis, Jr.

She married *West Side Story* dancer Anthony Mordente in 1957. Because her performance propelled the play, in 1961 the London production was postponed until she gave birth to her daughter, Lisa Mordente.

The lyricist-composer team Fred Ebb and John Kander collaborated in creating a cabaret act for her, which she took on the road in 1966. Rivera toured the United States, Europe, and Canada through the 1980s.

She was in a car accident in 1986 when she was in her fifties, which resulted in a broken leg that needed twelve pins to set it. She made a comeback to critically acclaimed performances in *Kiss of the Spider Woman* (1992) and *Nine* (2003).

She is the first Hispanic recipient of the prestigious Kennedy Center Honor, presented by the president of the United States, which recognizes lifetime contributions to American culture through the performing arts. She won Best Variety Performance in 1980, presented by the National Academy of Concert and Cabaret Arts. In 1985 she was inducted into the Television Academy Hall of Fame and won Entertainer of the Decade from the National Hispanic Academy of Media Arts and Sciences in 1993.

Astrud Gilberto (Brazil, 1940–)

Recipient of the Latin Jazz U.S.A. Award for Lifetime Achievement for her outstanding contribution to Latin Jazz music, singer-songwriter Astrud Gilberto was inducted into the International Latin Music Hall of Fame in 2002.

The sensual sounds of bossa nova music blended Brazilian rhythms of samba with the sophisticated harmony of jazz, a bit of American pop, and lots of melody. Gilberto became "the Queen of Bossa Nova" in the 1960s for her rich renditions of Brazilian classics and ballads.

Drawing in easy-listening audiences worldwide, Gilberto started her musical career quite by accident. In 1964, saxophonist Stan Getz was to record a new album with the best musicians from Brazil, which included Gilberto's husband, guitarist João Gilberto.

To appeal to a wider audience, producer Creed Taylor suggested a few English vocals mixed into the album to increase crossover potential. Gilberto was the only Brazilian with a grasp of the English language at the recording session. As a favor, she added vocals to "The Girl from Ipanema." The work was so spontaneous and supposedly inconsequential, she was not even mentioned on the record sleeve.

Her voice and rendition of the song, however, became instant hits. "The Girl from Ipanema" was a Grammy-winning recording, reaching the top five on the *Billboard* charts in the United States and becoming the best-selling jazz album of the time. Gilberto's career was launched.

> "The Girl from Ipanema" was a Grammy-winning recording, reaching the top five on the *Billboard* charts in the United States and becoming the best-selling jazz album of the time.

Born Astrud Weinert to Dr. Fritz Weinert, a German linguistics professor, and Evangelina, a primary schoolteacher, the family settled in Rio de Janeiro. Gilberto immigrated to the United States in the early 1960s.

As her career flourished, she added her style to a variety of contemporary songs from Tim Hardin, Jimmy Webb, and the Doors. Her renditions of American songs "Windy," "Fly Me to the Moon," "I Haven't Got Anything Better to Do," "Love Story," and "The Shadow of Your Smile" were hits.

For many years she was the voice of Eastern Airlines, for which she recorded award-winning commercials. In the 1970s her songwriting blossomed and was featured in the albums *Astrud Gilberto Now*, *That Girl From Ipanema*, and *Astrud Gilberto Plus the James Last Orchestra*. She toured throughout Europe, Asia, Canada, and the United States. She attended an acting school for two years to help her get over her stage fright.

In 1990, she and her sons, Marcelo Gilberto and Gregory Lasorsa formed Gregmar Productions, Inc., to take on even more projects.

In 1996, she was the first "jazz" artist to sing at the House of Blues, which until then had featured blues and rock acts exclusively. She broke attendance records there, selling out as she had at the Jazz Café club in London and other venues.

Her music has spanned generations and genres. Recording with legendary musicians like her idols Chet Baker and Gil Evans have been the most rewarding highlights of her musical career. Her performance with French singer Etienne Daho in "Les Bordes de Seine," seduced hip-hop fans, while "Desafinado," performed with George Michael for *Red Hot & Rio*, a record benefiting AIDS charities, gained international attention in 1996, and a whole new slew of pop fans.

She was awarded the Latin Jazz U.S.A. Award for Lifetime Achievement for her outstanding contribution to Latin Jazz music in 1992 and was inducted into the International Latin Music Hall of Fame in 2002. Her 2002 release, *Jungle*, is a showcase of her songwriting. In recent years she has recorded music for movies, including *Down with Love*.

Raquel Welch (United States, 1940–)

Actress of television, stage, and film, Raquel Welch is one of the best-known pinup girls in the history of Hollywood. She has maintained a successful career for decades and is the winner of a Golden Globe.

Being a sex symbol was "rather like being a convict." So spoke Raquel Welch, the timeless bombshell of Hollywood. "Sexy" might have been synonymous with Welch, but there was more to her than her measurements.

She did not remain locked into the stereotype, even though she has made heads turn for decades. Whether in animal-skin bikinis or in sequined evening gowns with plunging necklines and bold cuts that enhanced her hourglass figure, Welch was a sight to behold on the silver screen.

Immortalized on "the Poster," she posed in revealing caveman-wear, her long hair flowing, to promote the movie *One Million Years B.C.* The film brought her international prominence in the 1960s and made her a pinup sensation. The sex symbol image also helped launch her acting career.

Born Raquel Tejada, Welch waited tables while winning beauty pageants, including the Fairest of the Fair in her hometown of San Diego, California. She was a teenager, but she already knew that acting would be her life. Not many Latinas had successfully ventured into this realm in the late 1950s.

As she became seasoned and gained more and more years of experience, her true acting abilities surfaced. Even though she is one of the 100 Sexiest Stars in Film History according to *Empire* magazine, she is also a Golden Globe–winning actress. She earned the award as best actress for her role in *The Three Musketeers*. Working alongside leading men such as Elvis Presley, Frank Sinatra, Burt Reynolds, Hector Elizondo, and James Olmos gave her confidence to try her hand in television movies, specials, and sitcoms.

She wowed audiences in a one-woman cabaret show that traveled the country. She stepped in for Lauren Bacall in Broadway's *Woman of the Year* production and made the lead role her own.

Her greatest work, she believes, comes from being part of ensemble casts because it allows her to experiment with characters and develop them in-depth. She had the greatest joy and fulfillment working on *American Family*, a PBS show with an all-star cast. Produced by fellow San Diegan Gregory Nava, it aired in 2002, the first prime-time drama series featuring a Latino cast.

Projects like *American Family* made Raquel yearn for answers about her roots. Deeply buried were the treasures and traditions of her Latino culture. When she was a girl, her parents had wanted what was best for her. At that time, being bilingual and bicultural might have been detrimental to advancement in any career, so her Bolivian-born father refused to talk about her roots.

> ⸎ In the late 1950s, not many Latinas had successfully ventured into the acting realm, but even as a teenager, Welch knew that acting would be her life.

He wanted her to be the all-American girl. They focused on excelling in English. She was on the honor roll, was a cheerleader, performed in the drama department, and later with San Diego's Old Globe Theatre.

Raquel always knew the proverbial puzzle piece was missing from her life. Filming *American Family* and *Tortilla Soup* helped her self-journey. When she filmed in the Canary Islands, France, Spain, and Italy, she immersed herself in the cultures, wanting to speak Spanish and finding what had been missing for so long. As publicity increased for the projects, she emphasized her pride in being Latina. It had taken a long time to reach this point.

Perseverance and dedication to her art has allowed for comeback after comeback in different venues as she celebrates life in her sixties. Comedic roles have been added to her repertoire. She has a bestselling book and video on fitness and a new line of beauty products.

The constant spotlight has taken its toll on a personal level. She has been married four times, but her children are her joys. Tahnee is following in her mother's footsteps with her own acting career.

Joan Baez (United States, 1941–)

Singer Joan Baez, known as "the Queen of Folk Music," earned eight gold records. A dedicated activist, she received the American Civil Liberties Union's Earl Warren Award for her work in human rights, among other honors.

Known as "the Queen of Folk Music," Joan Baez earned eight gold records, but it was her commitment to civil and human rights that made her one of the greatest performers and activists of the twentieth century.

By the mid-1960s, her voice became the voice of young Americans, stirring them with consciousness about the Vietnam War and the civil rights movement. Songs like "Blowing in the Wind," "We Shall Overcome," and "The Night They Drove Old Dixie Down," a top *Billboard* hit, spoke to them.

Her father, Mexican-born physicist Albert Baez, and her mother, Joan, a Scottish immigrant teacher, raised her with nonviolent Quaker beliefs, which inspired her active crusade for peace and justice.

A victim of racism, Baez never quite fit in with Anglos because of her name and skin, and never fit in with Hispanic children because she did not speak Spanish. Her pacifist beliefs also set her apart. In her loneliness, she expressed herself creatively.

A high school essay she wrote became her life guide. In "What I Believe" she realized she was only a speck in the grand scheme of things so her time would be better invested in helping "the less fortunate specks in the world."

While her father taught at Harvard, folksinger friends taught Baez to play the guitar. She embraced folk songs, blues, ballads, and spirituals and began playing coffeehouses and folk festivals in the Boston area by the late 1950s.

Her first record, *Joan Baez,* featured traditional folk songs, including a Scottish ballad and a Spanish song and was produced by Vanguard, a small label known for its quality classical music recordings.

> A high school essay she wrote became her life guide. In "What I Believe" she realized she was only a speck in the grand scheme of things so her time would be better invested in helping "the less fortunate specks in the world."

A highlight of her singing career was performing at the Woodstock Music Festival, which drew more than 500,000 people. It's theme was "five days of peace, love, and music."

Performing with legendary entertainer Bob Dylan and other influential musicians put her in the spotlight and resurrected the mission set forth in her essay: She was in a position to do more with her life than sing.

She became involved with the antiwar movement. In 1965 she founded the Institute for Nonviolence in Palo Alto, California. She married

David Harris, a leader in the draft resistance movement in 1967, and was arrested and jailed the same year for her active opposition. When the Daughters of the American Revolution refused to let her play at Constitution Hall in Washington, D.C., because of her political stance, Secretary of Interior Mo Udall gave her permission to sing at the Washington Monument. More than 30,000 people attended.

She appeared at demonstrations and sang at concerts benefiting causes she believed in. Baez became a liberal icon for racial equality, the hungry, and the oppressed, like the Hispanic farm workers in California or the "boat people" fleeing Communist Vietnam. She sang at the Lincoln Memorial for Dr. Martin Luther King's "I Have a Dream" speech.

She dedicated the 1974 *Gracias a la Vida,* a Spanish-language album, to her father for nurturing her optimism about life and acknowledging his decency as his legacy to her. Her autobiography, *And a Voice to Sing With,* was published in 1987 to critical acclaim.

Never compromising her art or political beliefs, she has survived what she calls "the ashes and silence of the 1980s," a generation she fears lacks ethical and humanitarian values.

She continues her mission, serving on the board for Amnesty International. She also founded Humanitas International, which promotes human rights and nonviolence. In 1987, she joined Sting, U2, and others in Conspiracy of Hope, a concert tour celebrating Amnesty International's twenty-fifth anniversary. She appeared on the 1962 cover of *Time* magazine for her efforts to desegregate colleges. In 1979 she earned the American Civil Liberties Union's Earl Warren Award for her human rights causes.

Vikki Carr (United States, 1941–)

Grammy Award–winning singer Vikki Carr was the first Latina invited to sing for Queen Elizabeth of England. She performed for five U.S. presidents, received a star on the Hollywood Walk of fame, and produced seventeen gold albums.

ikki Carr was the first Latina invited to sing for Queen Elizabeth of England at a Royal Command Performance. It was 1967 and Carr's singing and performing worldwide made her one of the first Latina entertainers to bridge the cultures of the United States and Latin America.

Her career took off abroad in 1961 with her hit song "He's a Rebel," and gave her an opportunity to be a regular on *The Ray Anthony Show.* The 1966 hit "It Must Be Him" was one of three Top 40 hits. She recorded over fifty albums. Seventeen went gold.

Raised in El Paso, Texas, Carr was the eldest of seven children. Her construction engineer father instilled in her a pride in their Mexican-American heritage. She clung to this pride when they moved just outside of Los Angeles and was punished in school for her faulty English.

She started singing when she was four years old. Her first solo was in a church singing "Adeste Fideles" in Latin. After high school, her first gig was with the Pepe Callahan Mexican-Irish Band in Palm Springs. She went by the name "Carlita" but wanting to sound more All-American, took on her saint's name, Bisenta. The shortened English version was Vikki. She also shortened her father's name, Cardona, to Carr. Even with the name change, she makes it a point to remind audiences of her full Hispanic name.

⁙ Carr recorded over fifty albums. Seventeen went gold.

Her first recording contact came in 1961. She performed in radio, television, film, and theater. One of her most fulfilling experiences was touring military bases in Vietnam.

A regular stand-in host for Johnny Carson on *The Tonight Show,* she appeared on many television shows with celebrities such as Bob Hope, Carol Burnett, Dean Martin, the Smothers Brothers, Ed Sullivan, Jackie Gleason, and Red Skelton. She performed in nightclubs in Las Vegas, Hawaii, Atlantic City, and New York, as well as throughout Europe, Mexico, and Central America.

A sweetheart of the U.S. White House, she performed for five U.S. presidents. Her colleagues respected her as well. Dean Martin called her 273 "the best girl singer in the business," while Bing Crosby and Ella Fitzgerald named her among their favorite three female singers of all time.

Carr sang in Broadway musicals such as *The Unsinkable Molly Brown* and *South Pacific*. She appeared in several PBS specials including *The Mexican-Americans* and *Vikki Carr: Memories, Memorias*, where she salutes English hits of the 1940s and 1950s originally composed by Latinos.

Her Grammy Awards were for best Mexican-American performance for *Simplemente Mujer* (1985), best Latin pop album for *Cosas del Amor* (1992), and best Mexican-American performance, vocal or instrumental for *Recuerdo a Javier Solis* (1994).

She runs her own corporation and is a big advocate of humanitarian work. She was voted Woman of the Year by the *Los Angeles Times* for her efforts on behalf of young Mexican Americans. For them, she established the Vikki Carr Scholarship Foundation in 1971.

Carr's awards include Singer of the Year by the American Guild of Variety Artists (1972), Mexico's Visiting Entertainer of the Year, the Latino Spirit Award (2003), the Hispanic Heritage Award (1996), and the Imagen Foundation Humanitarian Award (1998). She was named Woman of the World by the International Orphans Fund and was given a star on the Hollywood Walk of Fame in 1981.

Flora Purim (Brazil, 1942–)

Grammy Award–winning singer-songwriter and recipient of Brazil's 2002 Ordem de Rio Branco for Lifetime Achievement, Flora Purim is legendary in the world of jazz.

> "If we can lift people with rhythm and sound, we will do it."
> —Flora Purim

Known as "the Queen of Brazilian Jazz," Flora Purim was only twenty-two years old when she had the jazz experience of a lifetime. She wanted to learn more about jazz musicians, their styles, and what made them choose that style of music to express themselves. As a new immigrant from Brazil, she spoke broken English, but was determined to find her way in New York City.

Attempting to get into the Club Baron in Harlem to see Thelonius Monk, the doorman gave her a hard time. Monk himself came to her rescue. Taking her hand, he invited her to his table. Not until he sat at the piano and start playing did she realize who he was and what had just happened.

All the musicians she had ever admired were in the club, including Wayne Shorter, Art Blake, Carmen McRae, Miles Davis, and Chick Corea. When they invited her to go on to Walter Booker's house to jam for the night, it was one of the greatest moments of her life.

Purim came to the United States in 1967 to escape political unrest, just on the heels of the bossa nova craze, with her longtime partner in music and marriage, master percussionist Airto Moreira. He has inspired her songwriting, and jazz singers Billie Holiday and Dinah Washington influenced her love of jazz.

Born in Rio de Janeiro, Purim was raised by a Ukrainian father who was the leading violinist with the Rio Symphony Orchestra. Her Brazilian mother was a classical pianist who started Purim with lessons at age eight. Guitar and voice lessons followed. Under the direction of musician Hermeto Pascoal, she raised her vocal range to six octaves, a feat that would set her apart from many other jazz vocalists.

Her first successful group was the legendary Quarteto Novo, which mixed jazz with radical protest songs defying the repressive government of the time.

Purim and Moreira were some of the first to produce commercially successful "electric" jazz groups of the 1970s. Purim toured with Stan Getz, Gil Evans, Chick Corea, Stanley Clarke, and Joe Farrell along with Airto. She jammed with Carlos Santana and Janis Joplin at outdoor festivals in California.

In her first solo album, *Butterfly Dreams* (1973), she offered a twist. She added vocal sounds such as squeaks and squeals, laughs and sobs that enhanced the rhythm.

The Magicians (1986) was nominated for a Grammy. In 1992, she performed on two Grammy-winning albums: Planet Drum, with Grateful Dead drummer Mickey Hart, which won best world music album; and The Dizzy Gillespie United Nations Orchestra, which won best jazz album.

Speed of Light was rereleased as a labor of love, and relaunched her solo career in the mid-1990s. Flutes, electric sounds, and stunning percussion brought life to the rhythms of ritualistic chants and salsa that enhanced her singing.

Musicians such as Giovanni Hidalgo, Changuito, and Billy Cobham pay her tribute as a stunning jazz diva. Her daughter, Diana Purim Moreira, also contributed to the album.

Four years in a row she was voted Down Beat magazine's Best Female Jazz Vocalist. She won two Grammy awards for best female jazz performance. She received Brazil's 2002 Ordem de Rio Branco for Lifetime Achievement.

Linda Ronstadt (United States, 1946–)

Singer Linda Ronstadt is one of America's greatest performers of the twentieth century and is the recipient of nine Grammy Awards.

In the 1800s, Federico Ronstadt made his way to Tucson, Arizona, from Mexico. Though his livelihood was as a carriage maker, his passion was music. He started the Club Filharmonica, one of the city's earliest orchestral groups that toured the Southwest.

Playing with the band established a family tradition. The Hispanic musical lore that filled their home would influence generations, including his granddaughter, Linda Marie Ronstadt.

Ronstadt became one of three Latinas whose singing careers were launched into the mainstream in the 1960s. Alongside Vikki Carr and Joan Baez, she became one of America's greatest performers of the twentieth century. In four decades, she earned nine Grammy awards.

When she was just eighteen, Linda Ronstadt and the Stone Poneys signed a recording contract their first year in California (1964). In 1969, she went solo, becoming part of the sound known as southern California rock.

She wanted to belt out tunes like Lola Beltran but saw herself more as a folksinger. Influenced by opera singer Maria Callas, Joan Baez, and Dolly Parton, her need to experiment with different types of music ranged from folk, pop, country, rock, big band, mariachi, romantic ballads, Spanish, to light opera.

In 1972, her work found cohesion in the selected song material and in the backup group assembled for her—with drummer Don Henley and guitarist, Glenn Frey. Both would later form the core for the Eagles.

 In four decades, Ronstadt earned nine Grammy awards.

Her first hit, *Different Drum*, went platinum. After changing to a country rock recording company, *Heart Like a Wheel* was released in 1974. Ronstadt's versions of "Desperado," Roy Orbison's "Blue Bayou," and Buddy Holly's "It's So Easy" launched her career as America's greatest female pop star of the 1970s.

As one of the first solo female performers who could draw large audiences, she also earned power and control to work on projects of the heart like *Trio* and *Canciónes de mi Padre*, a Spanish-language album embracing her Mexican-American roots and musical influence. *Canciónes* led to a television special and book, both entitled *Mas Canciónes* (1991).

Canciónes revived the musical style she thought was on the brink of extinction, and also tapped the music she had heard as a child growing up on the last ten acres of her grandfather's ranch. Born Linda Marie Ronstadt in Tucson, roots went deep, traditions, deeper. Her father, Gilberto, used to sing at the top of his voice. Her aunt, Luisa Espinel Ronstadt, was a famous singer, dancer, and actress in the 1930s (see her biography on page 245), specializing in Hispanic folk music.

Ronstadt's four siblings were also musical. Pete, the oldest, was a member of the Tucson Boy's Choir. He, sister Suzi, and Linda formed the

Three Ronstadts, a singing trio later renamed the New Union Ramblers. They disbanded when Ronstadt left home for Los Angeles.

In four decades she produced over thirty albums, from her debut, *Evergreen*, to her collection of children's lullabies, *Dedicated to the One I Love*.

She made five platinum records in a row between 1974 and 1977. Her Grammy awards included best female pop performance, best country performance, best Mexican-American performance, and best pop vocal performance. She also received other awards in pop, rock, country, and Latin between 1975 and 2000. She performed at President Jimmy Carter's inauguration in 1977 and appeared in the Broadway musical *The Pirates of Penzance*.

Linked with high-profile celebrities including Jerry Brown (the former governor of California), director George Lucas, and comedian Steve Martin, she settled in the Tucson area alone and adopted two children in the mid-1990s. The Ronstadt family was awarded a Copper Letter from the city of Tucson in 1994 for "keeping the town beautiful with song for well over a hundred years."

Liz Torres (United States, 1947–)

Actress of stage, television, and film who has earned multiple Emmy and Golden Globe nominations, Torres has been honored with a Bravo Award, and received two American Comedy Award nominations for her work.

Liz Torres's career started in small New York City clubs where she and Bette Midler shared Barry Manilow as a musical conductor. The comedienne, actor, and singer did a variety of stage and television work. In Las Vegas, she was the opening act for Liza Minnelli, Tony Bennett, and Helen Reddy, among others.

She credits her big television break to her standup comedy on *The Tonight Show* with Johnny Carson. It opened the door to other roles—

mostly comedic—in television shows including series such as *Gilmore Girls, All in the Family, Over the Top, Ally McBeal, The Nanny, Starsky & Hutch, L.A. Law, Quantum Leap, Murder She Wrote, The Wonder Years, Wise Guys,* and *American Family.*

Her films included *A Million to Juan; Kate's Secret; Silent Storms; Concrete Jungle; The Wonderful Christmas Suit,* which starred Elizabeth Taylor; *Sunset,* with Bruce Willis; *Permanent Midnight,* with Ben Stiller; and *Just Cause,* with Sean Connery.

> Torres credits her big television break to her standup comedy on *The Tonight Show* with Johnny Carson.

On television she worked on the *John Larroquette Show,* which ran from 1993 to 1996. Torres earned multiple Emmy and Golden Globe nominations for her role as Mahalia.

Torres also shone on Broadway. She starred as Googie Gomez in *The Ritz,* as Aldonza in *Man of La Mancha,* as Bunny in *House of Blue Leaves,* and with Tab Hunter in *Bye Bye Birdie.*

She gave a command performance for Morocco's King Hassan III and President Carter invited her to the White House for America's First National Hispanic Week Celebration. All of this in addition to her nightclub performances and one-woman shows.

Torres received an Emmy nomination and received a Bravo Award for outstanding individual performance in a comedy series, for her role in *The Famous Teddy Z.* She has also received two American Comedy Awards nominations for best female television performer.

She is on the Hispanic Heritage Awards Foundation board, works for AIDS awareness, education for minorities, and funding for public television. She is also a member of Women in Film.

Iris Chacon (Puerto Rico, 1950–)

Internationally famous dancer and actress who hosted her own television variety show in Puerto Rico, where she is a sex symbol and national treasure.

K nown as "the Latin Bombshell" and the "Vedette de America" in the 1970s and early 1980s, Iris Chacon sang and danced her way into the lusty hearts of television viewers. Wearing erotic, revealing sequined costumes and with dancers placed strategically around her, she wore a huge red wig that looked like a lion's mane and danced suggestively in her opening act.

She became a national treasure and an ultimate sex symbol of the tropics with measurements of 36-24-42. Dressed like a Vegas showgirl, Chacon drove Puerto Rican audiences wild with her sensual, unhinged, and high-powered outrageousness.

Her dancing became legendary all across Latin America, the United States, Japan, and Europe. Chacon could merengue, salsa, disco, and samba—any lively beat put her in her element. She appeared on her island's national television in her own variety show, *El Show de Iris Chacon*, which ran for over fifteen years on WAPA-TV. She not only performed, but also interviewed her guests. With her dances and skimpy bathing suits, she was a sex bomb on television.

> Chacon could merengue, salsa, disco, and samba—any lively beat put her in her element.

Chacon acted in movies and soap operas, including *Yo Se Que Mentia* and *Desperately Seeking Susan*, which starred Madonna and Rosanna Arquette. David Letterman proposed to her when she was a guest on his talk show.

She released dramatic ballads such as "Yo Te Nombro" and "Libre Como Gaviota," but lively tunes like "Tu Boquita," "Caramelo y Chocolate," and "El Manicero" were her hits.

She has been married to musician Junno Faria for more than thirty years, and they have one daughter. They settled in Florida, where she has a fitness and nutrition radio program. Chacon returned to Puerto Rico with her dance troupe in 2003 to perform in the celebration of the fifty-sixth anniversary of the legendary Cesar Concepción Orchestra at the Teatro Tapia in San Juan.

Charo (Spain, 1951–)

Singer, dancer, actress, comedienne, and award-winning classical guitarist of worldwide fame, Charo's album Guitar Passion *won the 1995 Pop Album of the Year (female artist) at the* Billboard *International Latin Music Conference.*

> "I was born in Murcia, Spain, where the beautiful sound of the guitars flows with the winds all the time. At night, these breathtaking melodies serenade everybody and the babies go to sleep listening to these sounds like lullabies. And that is why, all my life, I felt passion for the guitar."
>
> —Charo, A Letter from Charo,
> *www.aloha.net/~mahalo/charo/letter.html*

When Charo was three years old, she had a puppy named Cuchillo that wiggled when he was happy. She copied him and would say "como cuchi, como cuchi." People would give her cookies and candies because they thought she was cute.

She became a singer, dancer, actress, comedienne, and award-winning classical guitarist who trained under Andres Segovia. As an adult, saying "cuchi, cuchi" and adding her infamous wiggle became her trademark as she performed throughout the world.

It was her sense of humor and use of "Spanglish" that brought Charo international fame. She became a darling of variety shows and appeared in situation comedies as well. A favorite of Johnny Carson on *The Tonight Show,* she performed there often.

Born María Rosario Pilar Martínez Molina Baeza in Murcia, Spain, she was nicknamed Charo when she was just a child. The name 281 and persona stuck throughout her professional career. Discovered by bandleader and musician Xavier Cugat, they married and moved to the United States to launch her career.

Taking her passion for Latin music on the road, she sang in both Spanish and English and had a comedic flair performing live at casinos, fairs, and nightclubs around the country, especially in Las Vegas. Celebrating the beauty of classical Spanish guitar music and dance, she delighted audiences for decades onstage, in television, and in movies.

She was also lauded for her serious dramatic roles when she appeared on the television show *Fantasy Island* from 1978 to 1984, which starred Ricardo Montalban. Other television appearances include *The Carol Burnett Show, The Bob Hope Special, Chico and the Man, The Jeffersons, The Love Boat, The Sonny and Cher Show, Rowan and Martin's Laugh-In, Hollywood Squares, That '70s Show, The Wayne Brady Show,* and *The Today Show.*

She appeared in the movies *Airport '79* (1979) and *Moon Over Parador* (1988). Alongside Elvis, she appeared in the docu-film *Elvis: That's the Way It Is* in 1970.

Her CD release *Guitar Passion* won the 1995 Pop Album of the Year (female artist) at the *Billboard* International Latin Music Conference. Other releases include *Gusto, Cuchi-Cuchi* (Charo with the Salsoul Orchestra), and *Olé, Olé.*

After her second marriage with Hollywood producer Kjell Rasten, they moved to Hawaii where she performed regularly at the Outrigger Hotel and opened a restaurant while raising her son. She is a winner of *Billboard* magazine's Female Latin Performer of the Year.

Gloria Estefan (Cuba, 1958–)

An international superstar, singer Gloria Estefan has sold more than 50 million records and has twenty Top Ten hits. She is the recipient of two Grammy Awards and has a star on the Hollywood Walk of Fame.

The all-male Miami Latin Boys band needed a woman to set it apart from other Cuban bands. When Emilio Estefan, the band's organizer and percussionist, asked Gloria Maria Fajardo to join them in 1975, he made the choice of a lifetime—both professionally and personally. The band became the Miami Sound Machine.

She became Gloria Estefan, famed bilingual singer and songwriter, "the Queen of Caribbean Soul." Her music, especially her ballads, had universal appeal. Estefan and the band fit together effortlessly. They blended their Latin music with pop and rhythm and blues and added Cuban, African, and Spanish beats for a unique sound.

The international superstar has sold more than 50 million records and has twenty Top Ten hits. She has completed five world tours and earned over $45 million in one year.

> Estefan is known as "the Queen of Caribbean Soul."

Estefan was eighteen months old when her family fled Cuba after her father was captured in the Bay of Pigs battle and imprisoned. When he was released and joined them in Florida almost two years later, he joined the U.S. Army. When he returned from Vietnam, he grew ill and was diagnosed with multiple sclerosis, complicated by Agent Orange exposure.

From the time she was eleven until she was sixteen, Estefan cared for her father as his condition deteriorated, as well as her younger sister, Rebecca, while her mother worked days and attended night school to become recertified as a teacher.

The only escape she had was music. Estefan listened to her mother's records, like Agustín Lara and Celia Cruz, Johnny Mathis and Barbara Streisand. She took classical Spanish guitar lessons and soon strummed out her own tunes while giving lessons to earn extra money. She poured her heart into writing emotionally charged poetry, the start of her songwriting career. In 1989 she earned the BMI Songwriter of the Year Award.

Estefan excelled in her all-girl Catholic school. She went on to study French and communications in college. She worked as a translator at

Miami International Airport while singing with the band when she could. She and Emilio kept their relationship professional until 1976 when they started dating. In 1978, they married. They had two children, Nayib and Emily Marie.

The more Estefan performed, the more her transformation from lonely, shy, and responsibility-laden young woman to a dazzling superstar became apparent. Emilio quit his management job at Bacardi to promote the band and develop his production company full-time.

In 1978, they signed with CBS Records. After a string of successful Spanish-language albums, they moved to Epic Records. *Primitive Love* propelled them into the international spotlight. "Conga" became their first English hit to crack *Billboard*'s pop, dance, black, and Latin charts simultaneously. A Guinness World Record was set in 1998 when almost 120,000 people did the conga to Estefan's song in Miami.

The next album, *Let It Loose*, featured Estefan's ballad "Anything for You"—written hastily while she ate in a diner. Record executives reluctantly added it to the album at Emilio's insistence. The song remained on the hit charts for over a year.

In a horrific accident involving the tour bus they traveled in, Estefan's back was broken. With iron will and the support of her family, friends, and fans, she worked through a year of painful rehabilitation and was able to appear at the American Music Awards in 1991. Her 1992 *Into the Light* tour featured songs she wrote as she emerged from the darkness of her accident.

She has performed at the Super Bowl and the World Series. Her song "Reach," from the *Destiny* album, was the official theme song of the 1996 Summer Olympics. She appeared in several films, including *Music of the Heart* with Meryl Streep and *For Love or Country: The Arturo Sandoval Story*, with Andy Garcia.

Estefan was named *Musician*'s Person of the Year in 1994 for her charitable and community efforts. She and Emilio won the 1993 Hispanic Heritage Award in the Arts. She received the American Music Award (1989), was named Crossover Artist of the Year at the Latin Music Awards

(1991), and Best New Pop Artist at the *Billboard* Music Awards (1986). In 1993 she was honored with a star on the Hollywood Walk of Fame. She received Grammys for *Mi Tierra* (1993) and *Abriendo Puertas* (1995). She hosted the first Latin Grammy Awards in 2000.

Estefan also established the Gloria Estefan Foundation, which promotes good health, education, and cultural development. Because of her deep interest in paralysis research, she supports the Miami Project to Cure Paralysis.

Salma Hayek (Mexico, 1966–)

Producer, director, and actress Salma Hayek is honored as the first Mexican Latina to obtain leading roles in Hollywood since Dolores del Río. She has received numerous awards for her work, including a best actress Oscar nomination.

Nadia Comaneci was Salma Hayek's hero when she was a young girl. Hayek believed she could accomplish anything if she put her mind and hard hours into it, including becoming a world class gymnast. At the age of eight, she was chosen to train for the Olympics. Her father refused to let her go, citing that she needed family, friends, and a normal childhood.

The experience saddened Hayek but at the same time it fueled her determination to leave her small town. The road from home eventually led to Hollywood. Her passion and talent transferred to the stage and silver screen.

Hayek is honored as the first Mexican Latina to obtain leading roles in Hollywood since Dolores del Río in the 1940s. Named one of the fifty most beautiful people in the world by *People* magazine, her smoldering and sexy persona gave her stage and soap opera fame in Mexico before she even ventured to Los Angeles in 1990 to pursue her acting career. She has since become a producer and director.

Born in Coatzacoalcos, Mexico, to a Lebanese businessman father and a Mexican opera-singer mother, she was sent to a Catholic boarding school in Louisiana. Because of the incessant pranks she pulled, her parents were asked to take her back after two years. She finished high school early and entered Universidad Iberoamericano in Mexico City, where she studied drama and international relations. She dropped out to pursue acting.

Discovered by a television producer while in a stage production, she was cast in her first television series, *Nuevo Amanecer*, and won the 1989 TV Novela Award for best newcomer. It catapulted her to a new series, *Teresa*, an instant hit in Mexico. It was syndicated to over thirty countries and thrust her into the international spotlight.

Her first starring role in the United States came opposite Antonio Banderas, in Robert Rodriguez's *Desperado* (1995). Her film credits include *From Dusk Until Dawn* (1996), *Fools Rush In* (1997), *The Hunchback* (1997), *54* (1998), *Breaking Up* (1998), *Wild Wild West* (1999), *Traffic* (2000), and *Once Upon a Time in Mexico* (2003).

Returning to Mexico in 1995 she starred in *El Callejon de los Milagros* (Midaq Alley), which landed her a nomination for an Ariel, the Mexican version of an Oscar. At this time, she also appeared in television series, including *Sinbad* (1993), *Nurses* (1991–1994), and HBO's *Dream On* (1990–1996).

She produced and starred in the film *Frida* (2001), about famed Mexican artist Frida Kahlo (see her biography on page 48). She fought for seven years to make the film, battling interest from Jennifer Lopez and Madonna and going through hundreds of scripts with producer Nancy Hardin. The wait paid off. Hayek received critical acclaim and her first best actress Oscar nomination for her role as Frida.

   🎞 Hayek received critical acclaim and her first best actress Oscar nomination for her role as Frida.

Hayek was also the working producer of *In the Time of the Butterflies*, a Showtime movie about the Mirabal sisters of the Dominican Republic who led resistance against dictator Rafael Trujillo (see their biographies on page 139). Hayek received a standing ovation for her directorial debut at the Sundance Film Festival (2003) for *The Maldonado Miracle*, another Showtime movie.

She and Antonio Banderas earned a joint nomination for an MTV Movie Award for Best Kiss. She won the Blockbuster Entertainment Award for favorite supporting actress in an action movie for *Wild Wild West*. *Frida* was named best picture and Hayek won both the best actress and the Creative Achievement Award for the film at the 2003 Imagen Awards.

Jennifer Lopez (United States, 1970–)

Dancer, singer, and actress who in 1997 became the highest-paid Latina actress ever, Jennifer Lopez was nominated for a Golden Globe and was awarded best actress from the American Latino Media Arts Awards (ALMAs). Her debut album sold 8 million copies.

> "Is ambition like a bad thing with women?"
> —Jennifer Lopez

Jennifer Lopez watched *West Side Story* more than 100 times. Like her role model Rita Moreno, she wanted to do it all—sing, dance, act—and be successful in all three.

She started out as a dancer but in 1997 became the highest-paid Latina actress ever, earning $1 million for her part in the movie *Selena*, the story about the famed and murdered Tejano singer Selena Quintanilla Perez. Lopez earned a Golden Globe best actress nomination for her portrayal.

It started an avalanche of movie roles. Her commanding price sky-rocketed to $12.5 million per film by 2002.

Also known as J. Lo and La Lopez, the multitalented superstar of Puerto Rican descent was born in the Bronx, New York. Lopez credits her father, David, a computer technician, for her work ethic. She credits her mother, Guadalupe, a teacher, for her love of life and music. Attending Catholic schools with her two sisters, education was an important priority, as was a deep sense of faith, a firm belief in God, and family.

Her first stage break was a five-month gig dancing in the *Golden Musicals of Broadway*, a European tour in 1985. A Japanese tour of the theater production *Synchronicity* followed. She also appeared in several music videos.

Lopez decided the timing was right to try acting. She was twenty years old when she was selected from more than 2,000 contestants to dance as a "Fly Girl" on the television comedy show *In Living Color* (1990). Though it wasn't acting, producer Keenan Ivory Wayans advised her to take the job to earn more experience and steady money.

It was her true launching pad, and she made many contacts while on the show. Eric Gold, the coproducer, later became her manager. Soon after, she received parts in a few television series that were short-lived, but added to her repertoire. Her big break came when she was cast by director Gregory Nava in the movie *Mi Familia* (1995).

She started getting bigger roles that weren't initially intended for a Latina actress, including *Money Train* and *Jack*. Pretty soon, it didn't matter whether she was Latina or not, only that she was a convincing actress and a believable character, playing opposite celebrities such as Jack Nicholson, Robin Williams, and George Clooney.

Immersing herself in her characters, she vowed to try and research every role. Her hard work and dedication paid off. For *Selena* auditions, she was the only one of seven finalists who performed on four different levels—acting comedically, dramatically, singing (lip synching), and dancing.

Selena, she noted, was important for several reasons: It was a tribute to Selena, a stepping-stone for Lopez's career, and a major breakthrough for Latinos. The big-budget movie featuring a Latino family and Latino cast was awarded best film and Lopez was awarded best actress at the 1998 American Latino Media Arts Awards (ALMAs). In addition, Gregory Nava was awarded best director and Edward James Olmos was awarded best actor at the awards.

It was while playing Selena onstage that Lopez was inspired to reach for her other dream—singing professionally. In 1999, her debut album, *On the 6*, hit the charts. With a mix of music she calls "Latin Soul," it sold 8 million copies.

Lopez has since appeared in many other movies, including *Out of Sight, Anaconda, The Cell, The Wedding Planner*, and *Maid in Manhattan*. More CDs and music videos have been released.

Listed as one of *People* magazine's 50 Most Beautiful People, Lopez has also started a clothing line, a fragrance line, and opened her own restaurant, Madres, in Pasadena, California.

La India (Puerto Rico, 1970–)

The world's top-selling female salsa singer who won a Billboard Latin Music Award for best female tropical album.

La India could feel her fans' love as she inched her way along New York's Fifth Avenue on the top of a float for the Puerto Rican Day Parade in 2000. Honored as one of the grand marshals of the day, all the challenges, setbacks, and triumphs that had rocked her professionally and personally during her singing career disappeared as she looked out over the 2 million people attending.

La India is also known as "the Princess of Salsa"—the world's top-selling female salsa singer. She started as a disco diva but found her home in salsa. Often compared to "La Lupe," the legendary Cuban grand dame of salsa from the 1960s, La India has a powerful, sultry voice, sings unrequited love lyrics, and adds sway to her music. Her style blends some Latin jazz with Latin and a little bit of rhythm and blues.

Criticized for her cigar-smoking, her weight, and her risk-taking, India withstood the tempestuous spotlight. In 1992, she teamed up with pianist Eddie Palmieri to become one of the leading Latina voices of her generation. Cross-over success from her years in hip-hop came quickly with

289

Llegó—La India (India has Arrived), an album she worked on with Palmieri, Little Louis Vega, and Jellie Bean Benitez.

Born Linda Caballero in New York, her father was abusive to her mother and deserted the family when she was only seven. Evictions from their apartments came regularly after that, so India began singing professionally at fifteen to help out. Within several years, she went from doing backup vocals in a hip-hop group to a solo career in salsa. Her earliest albums were produced by Little Louis Vega, whom she married but later divorced.

> La India started as a disco diva but found her home in salsa.

She has forgiven her father and credits her grandmother, who raised her for several years, for the nickname "India." Darker skinned than her sisters, the name fit Caballero's exotic look. To set her apart in the music industry, she adopted it for her professional image.

In 1996, she recorded *Jazzin* with her idol Tito Puente and the Count Basie Orchestra. Puente wanted to produce an album in tribute to the Basie sound. His first choice for vocalist was India for her vocal versatility, depth, and interpretation.

Puente became India's musical mentor and frequent collaborator, but she continues to work in styles as diverse as hip-hop, blues, funk, Afro-Cuban, and gospel. Her hits have included "Seduceme," "Love and Happiness," "Dancing in the Fire," "Hielo," and "Mi Mayor Venganza."

"Seduceme" reached number one on the *Billboard* charts. India moved to the Sony label under Tommy Mottola and won a *Billboard* Latin Music Award for best female tropical album for *Sola*. Her album *Latin Song Bird: Mi alma y Corazon* featured renowned producers like Emilio Estefan, K.C. Porter, Isidoro Infante, and Jose Gazmey. Her dream is to expand her work by collaborating with other artists and to try her hand at rock, opera, and gospel music.

Selena (Selena Quintanilla Perez)
(United States, 1971–1995)

The first female Tejano artist to earn a gold record and the first singer to have five Spanish-language singles simultaneously on the Billboard 200, *Selena received a Grammy Award for best Mexican-American album and at one time was the number one Latina singer in the United States and Mexico.*

More than 50,000 people showed up for Selena Quintanilla Perez's funeral in Corpus Christi, Texas, on April 2, 1995. Selena—"the Queen of Tejano Music" and the number one Latina singing sensation in the United States and Mexico at the time of her death—was only twenty-three when she was shot and killed by the president of her fan club.

Selena's appeal had obviously gone deeper than her music. She created a legacy as she stole the hearts of Mexican Americans, gave them a voice, and brought them worldwide recognition through culture, language, and music.

Born in Lake Jackson, Texas, Selena started performing in the family-owned restaurant that later went defunct when she was eight years old. Her father, a former musician, organized Selena y Los Dinos, which included Selena's brother Abraham (A.B)., who played guitar, wrote songs, and would later produce her records. Her sister, Suzette, played drums. Her mother worked lighting. Other musicians joined the band, including bass player Chris Perez, who would become Selena's husband in 1992.

Los Dinos started playing gigs with traditional ranchera classics of the Texas-Mexican borderlands. A.B. also wrote songs incorporating rhythms from Mexico and South America, embracing cumbias, salsa, rock, pop, and other musical styles. Selena took his songs, gave them her own twist, then adapted them to fit the instrumental preferences of the cities they performed in.

Raised speaking only English, Selena's parents taught her Spanish on the road so they could target a Mexican market. When she was just fifteen, Selena won the Tejano Music Award for performer of the year and female vocalist in 1987. She won this award every single year until her death.

In 1989, Selena signed with the newly launched EMI Latin label. They wanted her to be "the next Gloria Estefan." She gained national recognition with her 1991 album *Ven Conmigo*. It made her the first female Tejano artist to earn a gold record.

In 1994, a banner year of achievements for Selena, she signed an international recording contract with SBK Records, which produced English works. *Amor Prohibido* knocked Estefan's *Mi Tierra* out of the number one spot, went platinum, and featured four number one singles.

Selena earned best female artist, best female vocalist, and best "grupo" album of the year at the 1988 Tejano Music Awards. *Selena Live* won the Grammy Award for best Mexican-American album. She became the first singer to have five Spanish-language singles simultaneously on the *Billboard* 200. She also appeared in the movie *Don Juan de Marco,* starring Marlon Brando and Johnny Depp.

She performed to sellout crowds like the 60,000 who filled the Houston Astrodome in 1993. Dressing in skin-tight pants, short skirts, and low-cut bustiers—many of which she designed herself—Selena was the Mexican-American Madonna—without the controversy.

Earning $5 million annually, she was listed by *Hispanic Business* magazine as one of the top twenty wealthiest Latino entertainers—and the first Tejano artist—to ever make that list.

> Selena created a legacy as she stole the hearts of Mexican Americans, gave them a voice, and brought them worldwide recognition through culture, language, and music.

Selena ventured into designing her own clothing line. When she opened two boutiques, she hired Yolanda Saldivar, the president of her fan club, to run them. The Quintanilla family confronted Saldivar for embezzlement. At a private meeting on the eve of Selena's third wedding anniversary, Saldivar murdered Selena and was later sentenced to life imprisonment.

After her death, Selena's popularity soared. Her debut crossover album, *Dreaming of You,* sold nearly 350,000 copies the first week and hit triple platinum. Featured on the cover of *People*, the magazine sold more than 900,000 copies. A commemorative issue followed—only the third in the magazine's history at the time. The reaction to Selena helped launch *People en Español*. *Billboard* magazine later declared Selena "Latin Artist of the Decade." The Selena Lifetime Achievement Award is now presented at the Tejano Music Awards ceremony annually. The first recipient was Selena's brother, A.B. Quintanilla.

Bibliography

Amdur, Melissa. *Hispanics of Achievement: Linda Ronstadt*. Chelsea House Publishers, Philadelphia, 1993, 1999.

Ashby, Ruth and Deborah Gore Ohrn, eds. *HERSTORY: Women Who Changed the World*. Byron Preiss Book, Viking, New York, 1995.

Bernikow, Louise. *The American Women's Almanac: An Inspiring and Irreverent Women's History*. Berkley Books, New York, 1997.

Bernstein, Leonard and Alan Winkler, Linda Zierdt-Warshaw. *Latino Women of Science*. Peoples Publishing Group, Inc., Saddlebrook, NJ, 1998.

Edmonson, Catherine M., ed. *Extraordinary Women*. Adams Media, Avon, Massachusetts. 1999.

Garza, Hedda. *Hispanics of Achievement: Frida Kahlo*. Chelsea House Publishers, New York, 1994.

Globe Fearon Educational Publisher. *Latino Biographies—Multicultural Biographies Collection*. New Jersey: Globe Fearon Educational Publisher, a division of Paramount Publishing, 1995.

Gourse, Leslie. *Gloria Estefan, Pop Sensation*. Franklin Watts, a division of Grolier Publishing, New York, 1999.

Guzman, Sandra. *The Latina's Bible*. Three Rivers Press, New York, 2002.

Hill, Anne E. *Galaxy of Stars: Jennifer Lopez*. Chelsea House Publishers, Philadelphia, 2001.

Hoobler, Dorothy and Thomas. *The Mexican American Family Album*. Oxford University Press, New York, 1994.

Keenan, Shiela. *Scholastic Encyclopedia of Women in the United States*. Scholastic, Inc., New York, 2002.

Leon, Vicky. *Uppity Women of the Renaissance*. Conari Press, Berkeley, California, 1999.

Machamer, Gene. *Hispanic American Profiles*. One World, Ballantine Press, New York, 1993, 1996.

Macksey, Joan and Kenneth Macksey. *The Book of Women's Achievements*. Stein and Day, New York, 1975.

Marvis, Barbara. *Real-Life Reader Biography, Selena.* Mitchell Lane Publishers, Inc., Childs, Maryland, 1998.

Menard, Valerie. *A Real-Life Reader Biography: Jennifer Lopez.* Mitchell Lanes Publishers, Inc., Delaware, 2001.

Meyer, Nicholas, E. *Biographical Dictionary of Hispanic Americans,* second edition. Checkmark Books, Facts on File, New York, 2001.

Mirandé, Alfredo and Evangelina Enriquez. *La Chicana: The Mexican-American Woman.* University of Chicago Press, Chicago, Illinois, 1979.

Nava, Yolanda. *It's All in the Frijoles.* Fireside, New York, 2000.

Nelson, Pam, ed. *Cool Women.* Writers: Dawn Chipman, Mari Florence, Naomi Wax. Girl Press, Chicago, Illinois, 1998.

Nomura Morey, Janet and Wendy Dunn. *Famous Hispanic Americans.* Cobblehill Books, New York, 1996.

Novas, Himilce. *Everything You Need to Know About Latino History.* PLUME/Penguin Group, New York, 2003.

Ochoa, George. *Amazing Hispanic American History.* A Stonesong Press Book, John Wiley & Sons, Inc., New York, 1998.

Reyes, Luis and Peter Rubie. *Hispanics in Hollywood: A Celebration of 100 Years in Film and Television.* Lone Eagle Publishing Company, Hollywood, California, 2000.

St. John, Jetty. *Hispanic Scientists.* Capstone Press, Mankato, Minnesota, 1996.

Stefoff, Rebecca. *Hispanics of Achievement: Gloria Estefan.* Chelsea House Publishers, Philadelphia, 1991.

Suntree, Susan. *Hispanics of Achievement: Rita Moreno.* Chelsea House Publishers, New York, 1993.

Telgen, Diane and Jim Kamp, eds. *Latinas! Women of Achievement.* Detroit, Michigan: Visible Ink Press, a division of Gale Research, 1996.

Thompson, Kathleen. *Sor Juana Inés de la Cruz.* Raintree Publishers, Milwaukee, Wisconsin, 1990.

Ventura, Varla. *Sheroes.* Conari Press, Berkeley, California, 1998.

Wheeler, Jill C. *Reaching for the Stars: Selena, The Queen of Tejano.* Abdo & Daughters, Edina, Minnesota, 1996.

Extended Bibliography

Writers

Isabel Allende
Previous Hispanic Heritage Awards Honorees, Isabel Allende, 1996,
www.hispanicheritageawards.org
Isabel Allende, *www.isabelallende.com*

Julia Alvarez
2002 HHA Honorees: Julia Alvarez, *www.hispanicheritageawards.org/hispanic*
Las Mujeres, Julia Alvarez, *www.lasmujeres.com*
Julia Alvarez, biography of the Latin American Author; Julia Alvarez, About Me,
www.alvarezjulia.com/about

Sandra Cisneros
"Being Sandra Cisneros: The Award-Winning Author Shares a Glimpse of Her
'Ideal' Life," by Michelle Reale, *Catalina Magazine*

Yasmin Davidds-Garrido
"Empowering Latinas: Yasmin Davidds' Life Story Inspires Others to Succeed,"
by Katherine A. Diaz, *Hispanic Magazine*, June 2002
Yasmin Davidds-Garrido, *www.empoweringlatinas.com*
Yasmin Davidds-Garrido Empowers and Enlightens, *www.elclick.com/entertainment*
Latino Role Models: Yasmin Davidds-Garrido, *www.lsac.net/emagazine*

Julia de Burgos
Julia de Burgos, *www.elboricua.com*
Quien es Julia Burgos?, *www.literatura.us/julia*
Julia de Burgos, *www.galegroup.com/free_resources*

Nancy de los Santos
Producer of New Documentary on Latino Contribution to Movies to Lecture and
Present Work, Nov. 29–30 (November 14, 2003), *www.spanix.com*, *www.wga.org*,
www.chicana.com
University of Notre Dame News, *www.ned.edu*

The Bronze Screen Debuts on Cinemax, Hollywood (September 25, 2002), *www.latinola.com*

Laura Esquivel

Laura Esquivel, Author of *The Law of Love*, *www.randomhouse.com/features*
The Sacred Fire by Laura Esquivel, Ethos Channel, *www.ethoschannel.com/personalgrowth*
Salon: Love and Other Illegal Acts, *www.salon.com/oct96*
Las Mujeres: Laura Esquivel, *www.lasmujeres.com/lauraesquivel*

Cristina Garcia

Cristina Garcia, Voices from the Gap, *http://voices.cla.umn.edu/newsite*
Las Mujeres: Cristina Garcia, *www.lasmujeres.com/cristinagarcia*
Cristina Garcia, "Monkey Hunting," *www.mostlyfiction.com*
New York State Writers Institute—Cristina Garcia, *www.albany.edu/writers-inst*
"Caught Between Two Cultures: A Fresh Generation of Latino Writers Is Creating a New and Distinctive Literary Landscape," by Susan Miller, *Newsweek*, April 1992, *http://victorvillasenor.com/nswek4_92.html*

Carolina Garcia-Aguilera

Voices from the Gaps: Women Writers of Color, Carolina Garcia-Aguilera, *http://voices.cla.umn.edu/newsite*
NEON First Person, "Author Carolina Garcia-Aguilera Worked as a Private Investigator Before Writing Detective Novels," by Ken White, *Las Vegas Review Journal*, *http://reviewjournal.com*
"Author Launches Hispanic Heritage Month: Carolina Garcia-Aguilera Speaks About Writing, Culture to Opening Ceremony Crowd," by Nin-Hai Tseng, *The Independent Florida Alligator Online*, *www.alligator.org/edit*

Liza Gross

"A Latina Lois Lane Who Made It Without Superman," by David Everett, *Latino Leaders Magazine*, 2001
International Women's Media Foundation, Live Chat, *www.iwmf.org/features/4478*

Sandra Guzmán

The Latina's Bible, Sandra Guzmán, *www.thelatinasbible.com*
Leading Authorities, Sandra Guzmán, *www.leadingauthorities.com*
Alumni Notes, Sandra Guzmán Lectures on Life, Love and Being Latina, *www.alumni.rutgers.edu/alumnews*

"Magazine Editor Discusses Latino Life," by April R. Smith, University of Delaware, *www.review.udel.edu/archives*

Angeles Mastretta

Angeles Mastretta Biography, *www.penguinputnam.com/Author,*
www.marcelalandres.com, *www.epdlp.com/mastretta.html,* *www.poesie.org/mastretta.htm*
Angeles Mastretta: Women of Will in Love and War, by Barbara Mujica,
www.lasmujeres.com/angelesmastretta/women.shtml

Gabriela Mistral

Gabriela Mistral Biography, Nobel e-Museum, *www.nobel.se/literature/laureates*
Distinguished Women of Past & Present: Gabriela Mistral,
www.distinguishedwomen.com/biographies

Nicholasa Mohr

Nicholasa Mohr, 1997 Hispanic Heritage Award Honoree,
www.hispanicheritageawards.org

Cherrie Moraga

University of Minnesota, Voices from the Gap, Women Writers of Color/Cherrie
Moraga, *www.cla.umn.edu/authors*
FemmeNoir Online, Leaders & Legends—Cherrie Moraga,
www.femmenoir.net/weblogonlinediary

Dolores Prida

Latino Artists Roundtable, Biography, *www.lartny.org/biografias*
"Even Some of the Reporters Couldn't Hide Their Emotions," by William R. Long,
The Miami Herald Latin America Staff (September 9, 1978), *www.rosehulman.edu*
The University of Arizona Press, *Puro Teatro,* A Latina Anthology,
www.uapress.arizona.edu
www.repertorio.org/education

Pam Muñoz Ryan

Pam Muñoz Ryan, Scholastic Press
Pam Muñoz Ryan Biography, *www.pammunozryan.com*

Esmeralda Santiago

Esmeralda Santiago, Random House Reading Group Center,
www.randomhouse.com/vintage

"Daughter of the Island of Enchantment," *Hispanic Magazine* online 2002,
www.hispaniconline.com/a&e

University of Minnesota, Voices from the Gaps, Women Writers of Color:
Esmeralda Santiago, *http://voices.cla.umn.edu/newsite*

Esmeralda Santiago Biography, *www.esmeraldasantiago.net/bio*

Activists

Elvia Alvarado

"Elvia Alvarado Speaks About Human Rights for Hondurans," by Sarah J. Kimmel,
www.colorado.edu/studentgroups

Honduran Activist to Speak on Fair Trade Coffee, *Colby College News*,
www.colby.edu

"Two Women, Two Fighters, Two Fronts," by Bob McCubbin, San Diego, Workers
World News Service (November 20, 1997), *www.blythe.org*

Speakers & Artists, Elvia Alvarado, Human Rights, Land Reform and
Globalization, *www.speakersandartists.org/People/ElviaAlvarado.html*

Lourdes J. Baird

Judges of the United States Courts, Lourdes G. Baird

"Bush Nominates District Judge," Associated Press, Monterey County, *The Herald*,
January 21, 2004, *www.montereyherald.com/mld*

Lourdes G. Baird, *http://politicalgraveyard.com/geo*

Minerva Bernaradino

Hispanic Heritage Awards Foundation 1995 Honorees,
www.hispanicheritageawards.org

Minerva Bernardino Foundation, Biography,
www.mbernardinofoundation.org/MBBIOGRAPHY.htm

Women's Human Rights: A Historical Countdown, *www.undp.org/rblac*

Violeta Chamorro

HERSTORY: Women Who Changed the World. Violeta Chamorro Profile, by S. Suzan
Jane

Newsmaker Profiles, Violeta Chamorro, *www.cnn.com/resources*

Encyclopedia: Violeta Chamorro, *www.nationmaster.com/encyclopedia*
Violeta Chamorro, *http://en.wikipedia.org/wiki*
1991 Democracy Award, *www.ned.org/events*

Linda Chavez-Thompson
Past Mujer Award Recipients, National Hispana Leadership Institute,
www.nhli.org/pastaward.htm
Fact Monster Almanac, People: Linda Chavez-Thompson, *www.factmonster.com*
Current DNC Leadership—Linda Chavez-Thompson is DNC Vice Chair,
Democratic National Committee, *www.democrats.org/about*
Linda Chavez-Thompson, 2003 Women's History Month Honoree, National
Women's History Project, *www.nwhp.org*
AFL-CIO Leaders, *www.aflcio.org/aboutaflcio/leaders*

Josefina Fierro de Bright
Chicanas!, *http://chicanas.com*
Everything You Need to Know About Latino History, by Himilce Novas
"The Legacy of Bert Corona," *The Progressive*, *www.findarticles.com/cf_dls*
"Left Turns in the Chicano Movement, 1965–1975," *www.findarticles.com/cf_dls*
El Congreso de Pueblos de Habla Española, *http://college.hmco.com/history*
Chicano Timeline, *www.geocities.com/minoritiesinamerica*

Maria de Lourdes-Pintasilgo
Council of Women World Leaders, Maria de Lourdes-Pintasilgo,
www.womenworldleaders.org/members
"New Organization Supports Female World Leaders," by Ken Gewertz, the *Harvard University Gazette*, September 25, 1997, *www.news.harvard.edu/gazette*
Greatness Through Power WIC Biography—Maria de Lourdes-Pintasilgo,
www.wic.org/bio
Women's World Keynote Speakers, *www.skk.uit.no/WW99/keynote.html*
Millennium Exhibition, *www.ica.ie/international*
Women Leaders: Past, Present & Emerging, *http://people.brandeis.edu/~dwilliam*

Juana Beatriz Gutierrez
"Northridge Honors Four 'Phenomenal Women'" California State University,
Northridge press release, *www.csun.edu/hfoao102*
The Good Housekeeping Award: "Women Heroes of Environmental Activism," by
Rose Marie Berger, *Sojourner Magazine*, *www.sojo.net*

National Hispana Leadership Institute, Past Mujer Award Recipients,
www.nhli.org/pastaward.htm
The New Environmentalists, by Irma S. Jarcho
The Teachers Clearinghouse for Science and Society Education,
http://freeinfo.org/tch, *www.fpm.wisc.edu/campusecology*
The Teacher's Lounge, *www.missmaggie.org/mission2_parts*

Antonia Hernandez
Hispanic Heritage Award Foundation, Antonia Hernandez,
www.hispanicheritageawards.org

Dolores Huerta
Hispanic Heritage Awards Foundation, Dolores Huerta, Leadership (2000)
Dolores Huerta, Fact Monster Almanac/People, *http://print.factmonster.com/ipka*
Dolores Huerta American Labor Leader and Social Activist, *www.theglassceiling.com/biographies*

La Pasionaria (Dolores Ibarruri)
The Columbia World of Quotations, *www.bartleby.com/66/74/30174.html*
La Pasionaria's Farewell Address, *www.english.uiuc.edu/maps*
Dolores Ibarruri, Spanish and Portuguese History, Biographies, *www.1upinfo.com/encyclopedia*
Ibarruri, Dolores, *www.factmonster.com/ce6*
Culture: Tracks of Women: Dolores Ibarruri, La Pasionaria, *www.solonosotras.com*
Dolores Ibarruri—Education on the Internet & Teaching History Online,
www.spartacus.schoolnet.co.uk/Spibarruri.htm
Spanish Cockpit: An Eyewitness Account of the Political and Social Conflicts of the Spanish Civil War, by Franz Borkenau, 1937

Jovita Idar de Juárez
Scholastic Women's History: Jovita Idar, *http://teacher.scholastic.com/researchtools*
Info Please Jovita Idar Biography, *www.infoplease.com/ipa*
Newswatch: Milestones in Journalism Diversity, *http://newswatch.sfsu.edu/milestones*
The Handbook of Texas Online, *www.tsha.utexas.edu/handbook*

Rigoberta Menchú
Biographies: Rigoberta Menchú Tum, *www.mujereslatinas.com/bios*
Rigoberta Menchú, Distinguished Women of Past and Present,
www.distinguishedwomen.com/biographies

HERSTORY: Women Who Changed the World, edited by Ruth Ashby and Deborah Gore Ohrn, profile by Deborah Gore Ohrn
Sheroes: Bold, Brash (and Absolutely Unabashed) Superwomen, by Varla Ventura

The Mirabal Sisters
Museo Mirabal, *www.semdom.50megs.com/mirabal_museo.htm*
Mujeres Latinas Bios, The Mirabal Sisters, *www.mujereslatinas.com/bios*
In the Time of the Butterflies, Book Review, *www.historyamericas.com/ In_the_Time_of_the_Butterflies_0452274427.html*
The Mirabals, *www.learntoquestion.com/seevak*
Julia Alvarez, Latinas Abriendo Camino, *www.hepm.org/juliaalvarez.htm*
History of the International Day for the Elimination of Violence Against Women, *www.womanaid.org/16days*

Luisa Moreno
The Reader's Companion to American History: Moreno, Luisa, *http://college.hmco.com/history*
The Journal of San Diego History, "Luisa Moreno: A Hispanic Civil Rights Leader in San Diego," by Carlos Larralde and Richard Griswold del Castillo, *www.sandiegohistory.org/journal*

Janet Murguia
NCLR Selects Janet Murguia as New Executive Director, National Council of La Raza La Raza, January 7, 2004, *http://nclr.policy.net/proactive*
University of Kansas, Office of University Relations, *www.ur.ku.edu/new?02N*
"Political Conventions Show Latino Coming of Age," by Ricardo Vazquez, Latino.com, *www.puertorico-herald.org/issues*
"NCLR Selects Janet Murguia as New Executive Director," *Hispanic Business*, January 8, 2004, *www.hispanicbusiness.com/new*

Dr. Antonia Pantoja
Past Mujer Award Recipients, National Hispana Leadership Institute, *www.nhli.org/pastaward.htm*
Hispanic Heritage Awards Previous Honorees, Dr. Antonia Pantoja, *www.hispanicheritageawards.org*
ASPIRA: Our Founder—Dr. Antonia Pantoja, 1922–2002, *www.aspira.org/pantoja.htm*

Eva Perón

Eva's Early Life, *www.jlhs.nhusd.k12.ca.us/classes*
Women Who Changed History—Extraordinary Women,
edited by Catherine M. Edmonson
Biography: To Be Evita, *www.evitaperon.org/part1.htm*

Felisa Rincón

"The Lives of Pioneras: Bibliographic and Research Sources on Puerto Rican Women in the United States," by Altagracia Ortiz, *www.centropr.org*
Felisa Rincón de Gautier, *www.hechoenpuertorico.org/rincon.htm*
Felisa Rincón de Gautier, *www.preb.com/biog/felisare.htm*
Empowered Latinas, *www.geocities.com/Athens*
Felisa Rincón de Gautier, *www.welcome.topuertorico.org/culture*
Felisa Rincón de Gautier, *www.puertoricans.com/famous.htm*

Ileana Ros-Lehtinen

Hispanic Heritage Biography: Ileana Ros-Lehtinen, *www.galegroup.com/free_resources*
Ileana Ros-Lehtinen, Member United States House of Representatives, *www.house.gov/ros-lehtinen*

La Pola (Policarpa Salavarrieta)

www.villadeguaduas.gov.co/lapola
www.museonacional.gov.co/body_poli

Emma Tenayuca

Everything You Need to Know About Latino History, by Himilce Novas
Profiles of Chicana Activists: Texas Labor History, *http://online.sfsu.edu/~jdrew*
"Left Turns in the Chicano Movement, 1965–1975," by Jorge Mariscal (July, 2002), *www.findarticles.com/cf_dls*
Interview with Emma Tenayuca, Oral History Program, University of Texas at San Antonio, *http://womhist.binghamton.edu/pecan*
Emma Tenayuca, Personal Life, *http://lonestar.utsa.edu/ldalby*

Athletes

Rosemary "Rosie" Casals
2012 Olympics: San Francisco, 2012 Summer Olympics Bid Board of Directors,
www.basoc2012.org/board_casals_r.html
Women's Sports Marketing, *www.wslegends.com*
Marin County Women's Hall of Fame, *www.marinwomen.org*
Rosie (Rosemary) Casals, 1996 Enshrinee: International Tennis Hall of Fame,
www.tennisfame.com/enshrinees

Conchita Cintron
The Modern PWD—*www.starkennel.com*, *www.bom-tempo.de/en/history3.htm*
Conchita Cintron, the Golden Goddess, *www.antontioburgos.com*

Donna de Varona
Donna de Varona, *http://radio.sportingnews.com/experts*
Sports Biographies, de Varona, Donna E., *www.hickocksports.com/biographies*
Donna de Varona Receives NCAA's Highest Honor: 2003 Theodore Roosevelt
Award, *www.ncaa.org/releases*
Gale Free Resources—Hispanic Heritage Biographies: Donna de Varona,
www.galegroup.com/free_resources
100 Greatest Female Athletes, *Sports Illustrated Women*,
http://sportsillustrated.cnn.com/siforwomen
All American Speakers, Donna de Varona, *www.allamericanspeakers.com/speakerbio*
Donna de Varona, Swinging Chicks of the 60s,
www.swinginchicks.com/donna_devarona.html

Milka Duno
"Duno and Wallace Win Grand Prix of Miami!" *Hispanic Business Magazine*,
March 2004
www.milkaduno.com
www.racerchicks.com
www.dickbarbourracing.com
www.mensfitness.com/life/23
www.racinglines.com

Pam Fernandes

Pam Fernandes, The Power of Ability, US Paralympics Athlete Biographies, *http://groupbenefits.thehartford.com/usp*

Pam Fernandes, Athlete/Motivational Speaker, *www.latinoempowerment.org*

U.S. Paralympics, *www.usparalympics.org/usparalympics.htm*

Pam Fernandes, *www.pamfernandes.com*

Lisa Fernandez

Lisa Fernandez Prepares for Glory, *www.galegroup.com/free_resources*

"In the Zone: The World's Best Female Softball Player," by Michelle Kort, *Los Angeles Weekly*

Lisa Fernandez Biography, *www.lisafernandez16.com/biography.htm*

Lisa Fernandez, Pitcher/Third Base, The Official Site of USA Softball, *www.usasoftball.com*

Ana Gabriela Guevara

Ana Gabriela Guevara, *www.anagabrielaguevara.com.mx*, *www.run-down.com*

Ana Guevara, lesionada, *www.esmas.com/deportes*

"Mexicana Ana Guevara se Resiente de Una Lesion de Tobillo" (January 30, 2004), *http://mx.news.yahoo.com/040130*

Rebecca Lobo

Rebecca Lobo Biography, *www.galegroup.com/free_resources*, *www.rebeccalobo.com*

2003 and Previous HHA Honorees, *www.hispanicheritageawards.org*

Spotlight on WNBA Player Rebecca Lobo, *www.soyunica.gov.guests*

Nancy Marie Lopez

www.hispanicheritageawards.org

Rachel Elizondo McLish

Rachel: A Tribute to Bodybuilding's Most Beautiful Woman, *www.musculardevelopment.com/june98*

Rachel McLish, The First Ms. Olympia, *http://legendaryfitness.com/rachel_mclish.htm*

www.ifbb.com/Olympia

www.hispaniconline.com

Mia "The Knockout" Rosales-St. John

"Mia and Christy Hit L.A. Before Hitting Each Other," by David A. Avila, *www.maxboxing.com*

Mia Rosales-St. John Biography, *www.miastjohn.com/bio.htm*

The Latina's Bible, by Sandra Guzmán

Women's Boxing Page: Mia St. John, *www.geocities.com/colosseum,*
www.womenboxing.com

Vanessa Torres

Spotlight on Skateboarder Vanessa Torres, *www.soyunica.gov/guests*

Torres Wins Back-to-Back All Girl Skate Jam (July 25, 2003), *www.expn.com*

Xgirlsport Profile: Vanessa Torres, *www.xgirlsport.com/profiles*

Scientists

Angeles Alvarino de Leira

Women in the Fisheries Profession, *www.womentechworld.org/bios*

Margarita H. Colmenares

Biographical Dictionary, Notable Women in Engineering, Margarita Colmenares,
www.tamu.edu/west

Archived Information: Margarita H. Colmenares, Director of the Office of
Corporate Liaison, *www.ed.gov/offices*

Dr. France Anne Cordova

Hispanic Heritage Biographies—France Anne Cordova, *www.galegroup.com/free_resources*

Cordova bio, *www.asci.org/artsci99*

Speakers, Women in Science Conference, *www.ehr.nsf.gov/conferences*

Breakthrough, The Changing Face of Science, *www.pbs.org/breakthrough*

Ana Sol Gutierrez

Ana Sol Gutierrez Biography, American Society of Civil Engineers, *www.asce.org/pdf*

House of Delegates, *www.mdarchives.state.md.us/msa*

La Honorable Ana Sol Gutierrez es un Orgullo Salvadoreño,
www.departamento15.com/orgullo_salvadoreno_ASGutierrez.htm

Antonia Maury

Fleming, Maury, Cannon and the Classification of Stars, *www.eps.org/aps*

Antonia Caetana de Paiva Pereira Maury (1866–1952),
http://astroinfo.port5.com/m/antonia_caetana_de_paiva_pereira_maury.html

"Women in Astronomy IV," by Carmen Rush, *http://ottawa.rasc.ca/observers*

Ynez Mexia
Ynez Mexia, *www.mvschools.org*
Ynez Mexia, *www.geocities.com/Athens*

Adriana Ocampo
Adriana Ocampo, *www.planetary.org*
Adriana C. Ocampo, Women of NASA, *http://quest.arc.nasa.gov/people*
Space Geologist Adriana Ocampo, *http://net.unl.edu/wonderwise*

Dr. Ellen R. Ochoa
NASA Quest / Women of NASA, *www.quest.ar.nasa.gov/people*
NASA Biographical Data Ellen Ochoa, *www.jsc.nasa.gov/bios*

Dr. Lydia Villa-Komaroff
Lydia Villa-Komaroff, PhD, Associate Vice President for Research Administration, Northwestern University/Women Advancing Technology, *www.witi.com/center*
Hispanic Heritage Biographies—Lydia Villa-Komaroff, *www.galegroup.com/free_resources*
2003 Influentials: Lydia Villa-Komaroff, *www.hispanicbusiness.com/influentials*

Entrepreneurs

Linda Alvarado
Latinas! Women of Achievement, Diane Telgen, profile by Carol Hopkins
Linda Alvarado: Constructing a Better America, *www.usdreams.com/Alvarado6869.html*

Elizabeth Farrow
"Command Celebrates Hispanic Heritage Month," by Jack L. Gillund, *Stripe* Staff Writer, October 4, 2002, *www.dcmilitary.com/army*
"Elizabeth Lisboa-Farrow Talks About Her Roots, Her Journey, and Her New Challenge at the Top of the Hispanic Chamber," by Mayra Rodriguez-Valladares, *Hispanic Magazine*, April 2001, *www.hispanicmagazine.com/2001*
National Women Business Owners Corporation Success Stories, *www.nwboc.org/suc-elf.html*
Women & Minority Entrepreneurs, *www.entrepreneur.com/Magazines*

Christy Haubegger

Biography, Christy Haubegger, *www.greatertalent.com/bio*

Christy Haubegger: A Fresh Face in Niche Publishing, *www.lasmujeres.com*

Comedian/Actor and Magazine Founder will Join Other Latino Business & Entertainment Leaders at Imagine 2002, *www.latinoempowerment.com*

Woman of the Day—Latinas on the Move, Christy Haubegger, Magazine Publisher, *www.cybergrrl.com*

Inspirational Woman of the Year, Christy Haubegger to Visit UMM, *www.mrs.umn.edu*

The Rise and Rise of Latino Power by Marshall Loeb, *www.cbs.marketwatch.com*

Folio Christy Haubegger (April 30, 1999), *http://foliomag.com*

Christy Haubegger: Founder and Publisher, *Latina Magazine, www.girlscando.com*

Mary Rodas

Hispanic American Profiles, Article Preview: "Toy Wonder," by Ines Pinto Alicea, December 31, 1994, *http://static.elibrary.com/h*

Innovation Focus Articles, "The Customer as Creator," by Christopher W. Miller, Ph.D., *www.innovationfocus.com/articles*

Child Stars—Political, *www.silkhouse.co.uk/tytv*

Hispanic-American Hall of Fame, *www.unbeatables.com/maryrodas.jpg*

"Mary Rodas, Mastering the Science of Having Fun," by Mona Maria de Crinis, *www.saludos.com/saludosmagazine*

"Babes in Toyland: Donald Spector's Investors Hoped for IPO," by Jeremy Quittner, *BusinessWeek Frontier, www.businessweek.com/smallbiz*

Rossana Rosado

Women Shaping the 21st Century, *www.womensenews.org/2001women_b.cfm*

"Women Working 2000 + Beyond, Turning Obstacles into Opportunities," by Rossana Rosado, *www.womenworking2000.com/feature*

Profiles: Rossana Rosado, Publisher of *El Diario/La Prensa, www.prdream.com/patria*

"Book Club Boom: The Spanish-Language Answer to Oprah, Katie, and Kelly," by Brianna Yamashita, *School Library Journal*, December 2002, *www.findarticles.com/cf_dls*

Aliza Sherman

www.imdiversity.com/villages

Aliza Sherman, Greater Talent Network Celebrity Speakers Bureau

About Aliza Sherman, *www.holman.com*

Aliza Sherman: Cybergrrl at the Wheel, *www.cnn.com*

Aliza Sherman, Author, Author Transcripts, *www.worldwithoutborders.com/archives*

Julie Stav

Latino Role Models: Julie Stav, Latino Scholastic Achievement Corporation, *www.lsac.net/magazine*

Julie's Bio, *http://juliestav.com/English*

"Julie Stav, Invest in Your Future," by Ruben Sosa Villegas, *http://hispanicjournal.com*

"Author Bullish on Latina Financial Power," by Felix Sanchez, *Long Beach Press Telegram* (March 18, 2002)

"Helping Latinos Take Stock of Their Financial Futures," by Dana Calvo, *Los Angeles Times* (June 19, 2000)

Educators

Amalia Betanzos

John J. Marchi, 24th Senate District: Staten Island Women Honored by State Senate, June 6, 2003, *www.senatormarchi.com/press_archive_story.asp?id=6708*

Hispanic Heritage Awards Foundation Honorees, *www.hispanicheritageawards.org*

Wildcat Service Corporation, Amalia V. Betanzos Biography, *www.wildcat-at-work.org/Letter_from_the_President/biography.html*

Education, *www.manhattaninstitute.org*

"An Office Where Students Learn From 9 to 5," by Elizabeth O'Brien, *Downtown Express, www.downtownexpress.com/de_new*

Evelina Lopez-Antonetty

Centro de Estudios Puertorriqueños at Hunter College City University of New York: The Records of United Bronx Parents, Inc., *www.centropr.org/lib-arc*

Mari Luci-Jaramillo

Latino Role Models, Mari-Luci Jaramillo, *www.lsac.net/emagazine*

Irene Martinez

Irene Martinez interview with Sylvia Mendoza, February 1, 2004, Fiesta Educativa, *www.fiestaeducativa.org*

Sara Martinez-Tucker

Sara Martinez Tucker: Success No Coincidence, *www.communication.utexas.edu/alumni*

2003 Mujer Leadership Training & Awards Gala, *www.nhli.org/mujer.htm*

About Hispanic Scholarship Fund, *www.hsf.net*

HSF President, Former Laredoan, Martinez Tucker Provides Summer Commencement

Address at A&M International, *www.tamiu.edu*

Cover story, Hispanic Scholarship Fund CEO Sara Martinez Tucker Is Changing Our Future, *www.hispanicmagazine.com*

Graciela Olivarez

Empowered Latinas, *www.geocities.com/Athens*

Vicky Ruiz

"The Latina Legacy," *Latina Style* magazine, *www.latinastyle.com/punto.html*

"Vicki Ruiz Integrates Storytelling, Conventional Research to Shed New Light on American History," by Karen Morris, University of California, Irvine, *http://today.uci.edu/profiles*

UCI Department of History: Faculty, Vicki Ruiz, *http://yoda.hnet.uci.edu/history*

Maxine Baca Zinn

"Sociologist at Murray Center to Study Changes in Family," *Harvard University Gazette*, *www.news.harvard.edugazette/1997*

Diversity in Families, Book Review, *www.findarticles.com/cf_dls*

www.chicana.com

The Arts

Alicia Alonso

Scholastic Encyclopedia of Women

"The Purest Form of Communication," by Jennifer de Poyen, Dance Critic, *San Diego Union-Tribune* (November 9, 2003)

UNESCO, Biography of Alicia Alonso, *http://portal.unesco.org/en*

National Ballet of Cuba and Alicia Alonso: "National Ballet of Cuba," by Patricia Boccadoro, *www.culturekiosque.com/dance*

Judith Baca

Fact Monster Almanac/People: Judy Baca, *www.print.factmonster.com*

Hispanic Heritage Awards Foundation Past Honorees, *www.hispanicheritageawards.org*

Marisol Escobar

Pop Art—Marisol, *www.fi.muni.cz/~toms/PopArt/Biographies/marisol.html*

Latina! Women of Achievement, by Diane Telgen and Jim Kemp

Art Museum of the Americas—Marisol Escobar, Pop Art Biography, *www.museum.oas.org/permanent/pop_art/marisol/bio.html*

Suzanna Guzmán

Latino USA, radio interview with Maria Hinojosa, *www.latinousa.org*
It's All in the Frijoles, Yolanda Nava, *www.classicalsinger.net*
Suzanna Guzman: Biography and Operatic Repertoire, *www.newcentury.nu/guzman_bio.html*

Viviana Guzmán

Viviana Guzmán, *www.inscenes.com/viviana.shtml?viviana*
Viviana Guzmán Biography, *www.festivaloffour.com/aboutus.htm*
Divas Latinas: A Trio of Jazzy Young Performers, *www.topentertainment.com/Divas_Latinas*
Viviana Guzmán's Personal Note, *www.viviana.org/personal.html*
"La Flauta Magica de Viviana Guzmán," *Cosmopolitan en Espanol*, July 2003

Amalia Hernández

Ballet Folklorico de Mexico de Amalia Hernández,
http://balletamalia.com/biography.html
"A Little Latin Flavor: Traditional Mexican Dance Is Epitome of Culture,"
by Erica Brown, *www.siue.edu/ALESTLE*
VIII Festival Internacional de Otoño, Homenaje Nacional: Amalia Hernández,
www.geocities.com/festival_otono/homenaje.htm
Ballet Folklorico de Mexico to Honor Late Founder October 3, University of Iowa,
(September 14, 2001), *www.uiowa.edu/~ournews*
"Ballet Folklorico," *Arts San Antonio View Newsletter, www.artssanantonio.com/newsletter*

Yasmin Hernández

Yasmin Hernández, *www.yasminhernandez.com*
"Meet the Artist . . . Yasmin Hernández," El Boricua.com, October 2002,
www.elboricua.com
Urban Latino Magazine, "Urban Legends Artist, Yasmin Hernandez" (Summer
2003), *www.urbanlatino.com*
"The Art of Womanhood, Exhibit by 18 Female Artists Focuses on Their Power—
and Plight," by Renee Lucas Wayne, *Philadelphia Daily News* (October 16, 1998),
www.yasminhernandez.com/PhilaDailyNews.html

Carolina Herrera

A Unique Style, *www.carolinaherrera.com*

Biography and Profiles of Fashion Designers—*Who's Who*: Carolina Herrera, *www.infomat.com/whoswho*

Hispanic Designers—Carolina Herrera, *http://americanhistory.si.edu/hispanicdesigners*

Frida Kahlo

Knowledge Cards, Pomegranate Publication

Frida: A Biography of Frida Kahlo, by Hayden Herrera

Frida Kahlo, *www.artchive.com/artchive/K/kahlo.html*

The Permanent Collection from the National Museum of Women in the Arts, *www.nmwa.org/collection*

Frida Kahlo, by Hedda Garza

Tania León

Tania León, 2003 Women's History Month Honoree, *www.nwhp.org/tlp*

Tania León, *www.galegroup.com/free_resources*

Lourdes Lopez

The George Balanchine Foundation News & Events: Lourdes Lopez Named Executive Director of the George Balanchine Foundation (September 2002), *www.balanchine.org/05*

The Off Festival of the International Festival of Havana, *www.pointemagazine.com/articles*

LBO Talk Archive—"On a Mission to Cuba, Bearing Balanchine," by Suki John, *www.nuance.dhs.org/lbotalk*

Zarela Martinez

Zarela Martinez, The James Beard Foundation, *www.jamesbear.org/events*

Zarela's Zesty Garlic Shrimp, Forbes.com, *www.forbes.com/2002*, *www.expo-comida-latina.com/nyc*

Chef Zarela Martinez, Travel Channel, *http://travel.discovery.com/fansites*

www.zarela.com

Maria Martinez-Cañas

Maria Martinez-Cañas, *www.edelmangallery.com/canas.htm*, *www.saulgallery.com/canas/bio.html*, *www.art.surfwax.com*

Definitive Guide to Art Photography, *www.photography-guide.com*

"Artistic Bohemians Are Turning Little Havana into Cultural Mecca,"

by Oscar Corral (October 28, 2003), *www.centredaily.com/mld*
Women in Photography International, *www.womeninphotography.org*

Tina Ramirez
Ballet Hispanico, Tina Ramirez, Artistic Director,
www.ballethispanico.org.general_information/about_tina.html
Everything You Need to Know About Latino History, by Himilce Novas
Tina Ramirez the Dancer, *www.cs.colorado.edu/VDC*

Luisa Roldán
Luisa Ignacia Roldán, Martin D'Arcy Museum of Art, *http://darcy.luc.edu/highlights*
Artists—Luisa Roldán, The Getty Museum Collectibles, *www.getty.edu/art*
Women Artists, Seventeenth-Eighteenth Centuries, *www.csupomona.edu/~plin*

Christy Turlington
Turlington: Une Belle Naturel, *www.the-eclectica.com/turlington~2.htm*
Christy Turlington Biography, *www.askmen.com/women*

Carmen Zapata,
www.hispanicheritageawards.org, www.bfatheatre.org

Doctors

Jane Arminda Delano
Jane Arminda Delano, *www.nursingworld.org/hof*
Jane Delano Society, American Red Cross, *www.redcross.org/services*
Jane Arminda Delano, Dir. of Army Nurse Corps, *www.arlingtoncemetery.net/jadelano.htm*
Women in American History, Jane Delano, *www.search.eb.com/women*
"Historical Perspective—Jane Delano: American Red Cross Nurses Continue to
Walk in Her Footsteps," by Kristin Rothwell, *NurseZone*, *www.nursezone.com/stories*

Dr. Jane Delgado
Jane L. Delgado, *www.pewenvirohealth.jhsph.edu/html*
National Alliance for Hispanic Health—FDA Commissioner Announces New
Effort to Empower Hispanic Health Consumer, *www.hispanichealth.org*
National Consumers League to Honor Jane Delgado with 2003 Florence Kelley
Consumer Leadership Award, *www.nclnet.org/delgadoadv.htm*
Latinas and Health, Interview with Dr. Jane L. Delgado, *www.print2webcorp.com/news*

Clarissa Pinkola Estés

The Rhythm of Compassion, Gail Straws
Dr. Estés, *www.mavenproductions.com/esteswindow.html*

Sor (Sister) Maria Isolina Ferre

www.puertorico-herald.org/issue
Sister Isolina Ferre, Medal of Freedom recipient, dies at 85, *www.cnn.com/2000*
Encyclopedia: Sor Isolina Ferre, *www.nationmaster.com/encyclopedia*,
www.hispanicheritageawards.org
Puerto Rico Profile: Sr. Isolina Ferre, *www.puertorico-herald.org/issues/vol4n02/ProfileFerr-en.shtml*
Sister M. Isolina Ferre, 1914–2000—Internet Obituary Network,
http://obits.com/ferresmi.htm

Dr. Ana Nogales

Doctor Ana Nogales, *www.drnogales.com*
"Cultural Differences," *Latina Magazine*, *www.latina.com*
Author Profile, Dr. Ana Nogales, *www.marcelalandres.com*
"Navigating Hispanic and Black Marital Relationships," by Marily Gardner,
The Christian Science Monitor, *http://search.csmonitor.com/durable*
*Latina Power: Using the 7 Strengths You Already Have to Create the Success You
Deserve*, by Dr. Ana Nogales with Laura Golden Bellotti

Antonia Novello

www.mujereslatinas.com/bios/anovello_bio.htm
Antonia Novello, M.D. Biography, *www.achievement.org/autodoc*
The Glass Ceiling Biographies—Antonia Novello, *www.theglassceiling.com/biographies*
Antonia C. Novello (1990–1993), *www.surgeongeneral.gov/library*

Dr. Helen Rodriguez-Trias

Presidential Citizens Medals to 28 Honorees (June 8, 2001), *http://clinton5.nara.gov/WH*
Helen Rodriguez-Trias, M.D., FAAP, UCLA Health Care Symposium Speaker
Biography, *www.medstudent.ucla.edu/msocal*
Helen Rodriguez-Trias, 72; "Health Care Advocate for Women, Youth," by Mary
McNamara (December 29, 2001), *Los Angeles Times* Obituaries
Helen Rodriguez-Trias, M.D., Teachers Scholastic,
http://teacher.scholastic.com/researchtools
Changing the Face of Medicine, Dr. Helen Rodriguez-Trias, *www.nlm.nih.gov/
changingthefaceofmedicine*

"The Face of Women's Health: Helen Rodriguez-Trias," by Joyce Wilcox, *American Journal of Public Health*

Dr. Nora Volkow

Unlocking the Mysteries of the Brain that Stand in the Way of Treatment and Prevention, *www.whitehousedrugpolicy.gov/ctac*

Imaging Reveals Secrets of Hidden Addiction: Brain Awareness Keynote Lecture, *www.mc.vanderbilt.edu/reporter/?ID=2583*

"Revolutionary Thinker," by Guy Gugliotta, *The Washington Post* (August 21, 2003), *www.washingtonpost.com/ac2*

A Scientist's Lifetime of Study into the Mysteries of Addiction. Spotlight on Dr. Nora Volkow, *www.soyunica.gov/guests*

National Institutes of Health, Dr. Nora Volkow Named New Director of NIH's National Institute on Drug Abuse, *www.nih.gov/news*

Society for Neuroscience, NIDA Director Discusses Successes and New Directions in Drug Addiction Research, *http://web.sfn.org/content*

Trailblazers

Benvenida Abravanel

Woman of Influence, *www.saudades.org/Woman_influence.htm*
A History of the Jewish People, by Max L. Margolis, 1958, *www.questia.com*
The Meaning of Names Among Mediterranean Jews, by Marc Eliany, *www.virtualpublications.ca/html*

Mercedes Cubria

Military Intelligence History, *http://usaic.hua.army.mil/history*

Saint Teresa de Avila

St. Teresa of Avila, Doctor of the Church, *www.catholic.org/saints*
Catholic Online—Saints—St. Teresa of Avila
Catholic Encyclopedia: St. Teresa of Jesus (Teresa of Avila), *www.newadvent.org/cathen*
St. Teresa of Avila, *www.karmel.at/eng*

Queen Isabella I de Castile

Isabella of Spain profile, *www.newadvent.org*
Isabella I of Spain, Women's History Profile, *http://womenshistory.about.com*

Sor Juana Inés de la Cruz

Raintree Hispanic Stories: Sor Juana Inés de la Cruz, by Kathleen Thompson
www.photoaspects.com/lilip/poets/cruz.html
www.oregonstate.edu/instruct
www.femrhet.cla.umn.edu

Maria de la Mercedes Barbudo

Women in San Juan, 1820–1868, Felix V. Matos Rodriguez
Women of Puerto Rico with Courage and Love, *www.angelfire.com/home*
"Latinas Get a Chance to Speak for Themselves," by Barbara Crossette, *The New York Times*, *www.puertorico-herald.org/issues/vol14n14/Latinas-en.shtml*

Sandra Ortiz del Valle

Las Vegas Review-Journal Sports Briefs, "Judge Reduces Award to Female Referee," *www.reviewjournal.com*
"Crying Foul: Ref Gives the NBA a Full-Court Press," by Barbara Campbell, *www.newyorkmetro.com/nymetro*
Female Referee's Award Reduced in Her Gender Discrimination Suit vs. NBA, *http://law.marquette.edu/cgi-bin*

Juana Briones de Miranda

"Juana Briones, A Feminist Pioneer in North Beach," by Sarah Coleman, *www.feminista.com*
"Enterprising Women, Juana Briones," *Harvard Magazine* (January 2003), *www.harvard-magazine.com/on-line*
Who's Juana?, *www.brioneshouse.org/juana.html*
Juana Briones de Miranda, *www.harcourtschool.com/activity*
Small Business Association, Women's Business Center/Women's History Month: Juana Briones, Rancher, Businesswoman, Innkeeper, Healer, *www.onlinewbc.gov/whm_mkgjb.html*

Sophia Hayden

Sophia Hayden, *www.search.eb.com/women*
Sophia Hayden Bennett, *http://web.mit.edu/museum*
Distinguished Women of Past and Present, Sophia Hayden, *www.distinguishedwomen.com/biographies*

Dolores Jiménez y Muro

www.u.arizona.edu/ic

La Malinche

Malintzin Tenepal, *www.mujereslatinas.com/bios*
U.S. Latina Perspectives on La Malinche, *www.gateway.library.uiuc.edu/mdx*
"Quien es La Malinche?" by Carol Brochin, *www.utexas.edu/students*
Cortés and La Malinche, *http://thedagger.com/archives*

Lola Rodriguez de Tio

Women of Puerto Rico With Courage and Love, *www.angelfire.com/home*
Lola Rodriguez de Tio Biography, *http://lcweb.loc.gov/rr*
Lola Rodriguez de Tio, *www.prboriken.com/lola.htm*

Loreta Janeta Velázquez

http://carlisle-www.army.mil/usamhi
www.womenandthecivilwar.org
www.confederatezone.50megs.com/custom2.html
www.scv.org/education
http://docsouth.unc.edu/velazquez
www.geocities.com/leonelcabrera
www.womenshistory.about.com/library
http://home.att.net/~mysmerelda
www.geocities.com/civilwarlady186
Machisma—Women & Daring, by Grace Lichenstein, 1981, Doubleday & Co., Inc.

Television

Giselle Fernandez-Farrand

"Giselle Fernandez is Fit, Fabulous and Flying," by Cathy Areu Jones, *Catalina Magazine*
www.sitv.com
www.giselle.com

Daisy Fuentes

Actress Daisy Fuentes: A Portrait of Compassion, *http://premium.si.cnn.com/caring*
Perfect People: Daisy Fuentes, *www.perfectpeople.net/biopage.php3*
Daisy Fuentes Biography, *www.sitv.com/daisybio*

Daisy Fuentes, *www.fulllatin.com/daisy_fuentes_bio.htm*
"Everything's Coming up Daisies," by Elisa Ast All, *Health & Fitness Magazine* (November 2003)

Nely Galán
www.nelygalan.com
Hispanic Heritage Month, Nely Galán, *www.cambios.org*

Lisa Guerrero
"A Candid Talk with Lisa Guerrero: The Most Popular Female Sports Reporter Gives Us the Little-Known Female Perspective of the Industry," by Cathy Areu Jones, *Catalina Magazine* (May 2003)
Lisa Guerrero Profile, *Latina Style Magazine*
"Lisa Guerrero," by Erin Harvego, Women's Sports Foundation
Lisa Guerrero, *www.karmaproductions.net/lisaguerrero*

Maria Hinojosa
Latina Leaders Magazine, 2001
Telephone Interview: Maria Hinojosa CNN Urban Affairs correspondent
Latinas! Women of Achievement, by Diane Telgen and Jim Kamp
www.cnn.com
www.npr.org/about
www.rothtalent.com/speakers
www.hyperage.com/search
www.latinousa.org/pressrelease

Sonia Manzano
Latinas! Women of Achievement, Sonia Manzano profile, by Luis Vasquez-Ajmac
Sonia Manzano, *www.soniamanzano.com*
AEI Speakers Bureau, Sonia Manzano, *www.aeispeakers.com/Manzano-Sonia.htm*
Sonia Manzano Conference Keynote Speaker, *www.ca-headstart.org*

Maria Elena Salinas
www.mariaesalinas.com/biography.htm
www.newsday.com
www.kingfeatures.com/pressroom
www.univision.net
Maria Elena Salinas' Column to Appear Weekly in *Hoy*, *www.newsday.com*

Maria Elena Salinas, *www.kingfeatures.com/features*
Maria Elena Salinas biography, *http://t3.preservice.org*

Cristina Saralegui

www.roadandtravel.com/celebrities
Celebrities Pets—A One on One with Cristina Saralegui, *www.pettribune.com*
Human Rights Campaign National Dinner, *www.hrc.org/newsreleases*
www.roadandtravel.com
www.thirteen.org

Entertainment

Lola Beltran

"Remembering Lola Beltran," by Shana Hugh, *www.pacificpearl.com/archive*
Lola Beltran, Stories, *http://stories.lamusica.com/LolaBeltran.shtml*
Lola Beltran, "La Reina de La Musica Ranchera,"
by Raymundo Eli Rojas, *www.geocities.com/Broadway*

Vikki Carr

Vikki Carr Biography, *www.elmariachi.com/artists*
www.vikkicarr.net

Iris Chacon

Encyclopedia: Iris Chacon, *www.nationmaster.com/encyclopedia/Iris-Chacon*
The Resume: Iris Chacon, *www.amiannoying.com/2001*
"Desde Borinquen—Puerto Rico," by Elmer Gonzalez, *Latin Beat Magazine,*
www.findarticles.com
Junno Faria & Iris Chacon, Profiles of Success, *www.powervision.net/ebusiness*

Charo

Latins in the Spotlight, *www.azodnem.com/Lounge/Latins.htm*
Charo, Wikipedia, the Free Encyclopedia, *www.en2.wikipedia.org/wiki*

Imogene Coca

Imogene Coca Biography, *www.movies.yahoo.com*
Actress Imogene Coca Dead at 92 (June 2, 2001), *www.cnn.com/entertainment*
320   Dance History Archives by Streetswing—Imogene Coca, *www.streetswing.com*

Celia Cruz
"Latin Music Icon Celia Cruz Dies," by Rose Arce, *www.cnn.entertainment*
Celia Cruz, Hispanic Heritage Awards, *www.hispanicheritageawards.org*

Gloria Estefan
Gloria Estefan, Pop Sensation, by Leslie Gourse
"Gloria's Gift," by Liz Balmaseda, *Hispanic Magazine* (February 2004)

Astrud Gilberto
Astrud Gilberto Biobraphy, *http://alexander.nu/astrud*
Astrud Gilberto Biography, *www.astrudgilberto.com/biography.htm*

Salma Hayek
Salma Hayek Biography, *www.factmonster.com*
More About Salma Hayek, *www.celebritywonder.com*
Salma Hayek, *Frida*, *www.oscar.com*
"Salma Hayek Talks About *Frida*," by Rebecca Murray and Fred Topel,
www.romanticmovies.about.com/library

Rita Hayworth
www.ritahayworth.com

La India
"India Burning Again/Salsa Singer Rebounds From Series of Setbacks," by Jonathan
Curiel, *www.puertorico-herald.org*
"India Wows the Crowd at the Puerto Rican Day Parade," August 2000 spotlight,
www.latina.com

Jennifer Lopez
"I Know My True Love Is Destiny," by Dotson Rader, *Parade Magazine*
People/Jennifer Lopez, *www.factmonster.com/ipka*

Lydia Mendoza
Worship Guitars, Lydia Mendoza, *www.worshipguitars.org/lydiamendoza*
Review, *Lydia Mendoza, A Family Autobiography*, *www.arhoolie.com/titles*
American Roots Music, The Songs & The Artists: Lydia Mendoza,
www.pbs.org/americanrootsmusic

Review, "Lydia Mendoza's Life in Music," by Yolanda Broyles-Gonzalez, Aardbargain Books, *www.aardbargain.com/lydmenlifinm.html*

Carmen Miranda

Carmen Miranda: Bananas Is My Business, by Gary Morris, *www.brightlightsfilm.com*
Brazilian Music & Folklore—Carmen Miranda, *www.maria-brazil.org/carmen.htm*

Rita Moreno

Rita Moreno (Hispanics of Achievement), by Susan Suntree
www.factmonster.com/ipka
www.hispanicheritageawards.org

Violeta Parra

Center for Latin American Studies, a Conversation with Horacio Salinas, *http://ist-socrates.berkeley.edu:7001*
Violeta Parra, Cantos de Chile, *www.delcanton.com/cds*
"Between Dreams and Reality, Folk Musician Violeta Parra Also Left a Rich Visual Legacy," by Roger Hamilton, *www.iadb.org/idbamerica*
Parra, Violeta, *www.biography.com*
Violeta Parra, *http://setiathome.berkeley.edu/davea*

Flora Purim

www.melt2000.com/artists
Critic's Choice, Flora Purim, *Baltimore Weekly Online*, *www.citypaper.com/2001-07-25*
Flora Purim Biography, *www.vh1.com/artists*
Flora Purim Bio, *www.berkeleyagency.com*
Flora Purim's Biography, *www.florapurim.com/flora-bio.html*

Chita Rivera

www.chitarivera.com

Linda Ronstadt

www.latinousa.com
"The Singing Ronstadts and Canciones de Mi Padre: a Musical Family," by Jim Griffith, *www.library.arizona.edu/images*

Luisa Espinel Ronstadt

"The Singing Ronstadts and Canciones de Mi Padre, a Musical Family," by Jim Griffith, *www.library.arizona.edu/images*

Arizona Historical Society, *www.ahs.dreamteamtech.com*

"Luisa Espinel, Another Ronstadt Family Superstar," by Ana B. Gutierrez (October 12, 1985), *The Tucson Citizen*

"Spanish Songs Bring Plaudits," by Bernice Cosulich, *The Tucson Citizen* (December 6, 1933)

"Louisa Ronstadt (Luisa Espinel) Will Publish Volume of Rare Old Spanish Songs of the Southwest," *The Tucson Citizen* (April 23, 1929)

Selena (Selena Quintanilla Perez)

Selena, The Queen of Tejano, by Jill C. Wheeler
Selena, Real-Life Reader Biography, by Barbara Marvis
"Selena, the Making of the Queen of Tejano," by Rick Mitchell, *Houston Chronicle*, 1995
Selena, *www.selenaetc.com*

Liz Torres

Liz Torres, Board of Advisors, *www.writeactrep.org/liz_torres.htm*
www.filmbug.com/db
Liz Torres, Biography, *www.thewb.com*

Raquel Welch

"Becoming Raquel," by Sandra Marquez, *Hispanic Magazine* (April 2003)
"All in La Familia," by Don Braunagel, *San Diego Magazine* (February 2002)
"In Step with Raquel Welch," by James Brady, *Parade Magazine* (March 17, 2002)
Raquel Welch Biography, *www.starpulse.com/actresses*
Raquel Welch Biography, *http://us.imdb.com/bio?Welch*
Leonard Maltin's Movie Encyclopedia, by Leonard Maltin

Index